ADVANCE PRAISE FOR "RIPE FROM AROUND HERE":

"jae steele blows away our idea of all things vegan being bland and boring. *Ripe from Around Here* exudes passion and enthusiasm, the recipes could put a gentle smile on the most hardcore carnivore, and the ideas help us return food to where it belongs; close to home, back to the center, and into the hearts of our families and communities."

—Michael Ableman, farmer and author of *From the Good Earth, on Good Land* and *Fields of Plenty*

"jae steele's new book, *Ripe from Around Here*, brings a bright sense of joy and compassion for people and animals, and a knack for sharing fun tips and making new information accessible. As a dedicated 'vegan foodie,' this book literally jumped off the page and into the kitchen! jae's holistic approach encompasses more than the food we eat—it's about the entirety of our day to day lives—the choices we make as we navigate ways to feel connected to community and accept our important role as protectors of the planet. Making the transition to vegan, local foods can change your life and the world. jae's book gives readers the gentle support they need, wonderful recipes, and a sense of camaraderie as they begin a journey to live more simply and sustainably."

—Joy Pierson, Nutritional Consultant, Candle Cafe/Candle 79 (New York)

"Combine fresh and whole foods with organic, home-cooked, locally and sustainably grown all-vegan dishes, mix it up with zest and what do you have? Someone's politically correct wishlist for a healthy future? No! It's jae steele's scrumptious and fun-raising cookbook. She helps you live up to the potential of food to transform lives and communities."

—Wayne Roberts, author of *The No Nonsense Guide to World Food* and manager of the Toronto Food Policy Council

RIPE FROM AROUND HERE

A Vegan Guide to Local and Sustainable Eating
(No Matter Where You Live)

jae steele

Foreword by
Paul DeCampo, Slow Food Toronto

ARSENAL
PULP PRESS

RIPE FROM AROUND HERE: A VEGAN GUIDE TO LOCAL AND SUSTAINABLE EATING
(NO MATTER WHERE YOU LIVE)
Copyright © 2010 by jae steele

ARSENAL PULP PRESS
#102, 211 East Georgia Street
Vancouver, B.C.
Canada V6A 1Z6
arsenalpulp.com

The publisher gratefully acknowledges the support the Government of Canada through the Book Publishing Industry Development Program and the Government of British Columbia through the Book Publishing Tax Credit Program for its publishing activities.

The author and publisher assert that the information contained in this book is true and complete to the best of their knowledge. All recommendations are made without guarantee on the part of the author and Arsenal Pulp Press. The author and publisher disclaim any liability in connection with the use of this information. For more information, contact the publisher.

Book design by Electra Design Group
Cover photograph by Laura Berman, www.greenfusephotos.com
Color food photography by John Cullen, www.johncullenphotographer.com
Copyright for photographs used in this book resides with their owners

Printed and bound in Canada

Library and Archives Canada Cataloguing in Publication:

Steele, Jae, 1980-
    Ripe from around here : a vegan guide to local & sustainable eating no matter where you live / Jae Steele.

Includes index.
ISBN 978-1-55152-254-8
    1. Vegan cookery. 2. Cookery (Natural foods). 3. Natural foods. 4. Local foods. 5. Food supply.
I. Title.

TX837.S8254 2010   641.5′636   C2010-900742-5

Dedication

To organic family farmers—hardworking and heroic growers of green things.

To my ever-loving mum, Nancy, with her openness to relearning food systems.

To my dad, Gerald, who started taking me to markets when I was just wee, in search of the best quality ingredients.

And to Ryan, who shares my love for alternative farming as a means of social change, and for good food.

TABLE OF CONTENTS

FOREWORD

As part of the Karma Food Co-op community in Toronto, I was delighted to get to know jae and to track her process through the gestation, birth, and growth of her first book, *Get It Ripe*, published in 2008. When our shopping trips to the co-op coincided, we'd cycle through the small, rustic space buried in a West-end back alley, share recipes, our excitement for seasonal treats, thoughts on new products, and laughter.

I bought jae's book partly out of a sense of community support, but I quickly fell in love with its tone, warmth, depth, and flavors. I was introduced to unfamiliar ingredients and astounded by the rich, varied, and satisfying array of foods we were guided to produce with only plant-based ingredients. Although we are not a vegan household, we appreciate the personal and global health benefits of the animal-free dishes and are proud to share them with our friends. More than once, I've had to take *Get It Ripe* from the shelf to prove to guests that the delicious dip or soup or cookie we were serving was indeed vegan!

In that first book, jae clearly demonstrated the connection between food and individual health. Now, in *Ripe from Around Here*, she sharpens our focus on food from farm to plate and shows us how the health of our communities depends in many ways on the health of our food systems. This understanding is fundamental to Slow Food, the international volunteer organization that defends biodiversity, traditional food-producing communities, the environment, and our right to choose food that is healthy and delicious. Among the many concerned voices that oppose the injustices of the industrial food system, Slow Food asserts that food production, distribution, and consumption must respect traditions, protect the environment, and fairly reward farmers in order to maintain a truly sustainable society.

I value jae's commitment to research and analysis from which she develops clear criteria to judge the quality of ingredients. This book gives us the tools we need to enhance the resilience and self-reliance of our local food networks. By directly supporting these networks, we become allies in defending biodiversity and all its many benefits. Making time to cook and share food is not easy, but perhaps we can give up a little face-time with our computer screens and redirect that energy into connecting with loved ones around food.

In *Ripe from Around Here*, jae encourages us to create handmade, personal food. She even equips apartment dwellers with the information they need to turn their food scraps into compost—with the help of some red wriggler worms. The inclusive, non-doctrinaire tone of *Ripe from Around Here* provides a positive model for those of us who work to develop local, sustainable food systems. All communities need to rebuild the traditional networks that have eroded in a world of anonymous, globalized food. jae illustrates the many rewards that accrue when farmers and consumers rely on each other as neighbors. However, in order to scale up these systems to sustainable volumes, we need to engage the broader population to make incremental changes, not set rigid, idealized standards that are unattainable. We must also be mindful of distant farming communities whose economies have developed to serve our needs. It is not enough to tend to one's own perfected and protected garden if one's neighbors are suffering. We need to recreate a transparent, cohesive food system that nourishes our bodies, sustains our rural communities, and invites all the world's eaters to the table.

A good start will be to make food a priority, connect with local growers, make time to cook from scratch, and share a table with those we care for. jae's philosophy and delicious recipes draw a vivid map for the journey we must take together to create a sustainable society.

Paul DeCampo, Slow Food Toronto
www.slowfood.to

PREFACE

This book is not the 100-Mile Diet. You might be disappointed (or relieved) to hear that, but I thought I'd share this information with you from the get-go so you don't read all the way to Chapter 3 before discovering that I'm not going to tell you to eat exclusively what you can find within an hour's drive from home.

But I am indeed an advocate for local foods. If you read my first book, *Get It Ripe*, you might recall that my love for whole foods began on a small organic farm in eastern Canada. So, of course, I needed to write a second book that helps people become more aware about what it means to come back to a culture that supports local family farms. When I pass a parked car on my street with a bumper sticker that reads "Farmers Feed Cities!" it warms my heart because I know it's true. And I know that more city folks know it too, more than they have in decades, thanks to the current locavore movement. It reminds me that I'm grateful for all the tireless work, commitment, creativity, and risks taken in all kinds of weather conditions by farmers in order to get fresh, nourishing foods to my kitchen table in my big-city home.

I knew I wanted to do a sequel to *Get It Ripe*, sharing the approach and values I'd presented in my first cookbook, but this time with a substantially greater focus on locally grown and produced foods. As I began my research, though, grey areas seemed to emerge, and it was hard to juggle all my priorities. How could I maintain my core purpose of creating health-supporting and great-tasting recipes when it seemed that there was a clash between veganism and local-foodism? Beyond produce, many local foods, no matter where you live, are animal or animal-derived. Cured meats, artisanal cheeses, farm-fresh eggs, and unpasteurized honey are no-go's by vegan standards. I decided that despite the local focus, this book had to be **vegan first** (which ruled out local whole foods like honey and butter), **nutrition-oriented second** (which meant using spices from afar for both their flavor and health benefits, and olive and coconut oils from afar instead of non-vegan local butter or local but often genetically modified canola oil), and **local third** (which still allows us access to lots of produce, as well as seeds, grains, and legumes, and less common crops when they're at their best, such as fiddleheads, new garlic, and wild leeks in the spring, and root crops, that might otherwise only be prepared for traditional celebrations, all winter long).

I've made a concerted effort to ensure that the recipes include more ingredients that can be sourced locally, though not everything here is grown within a tight radius of my home. I've endeavored to keep everything simple and create recipes that are basically accessible to those who aren't necessarily living in a bioregion similar to mine, or aren't able to make it out to the farmers' market each week.

I'd like to encourage more talk in the vegan community about a variety of food issues without neglecting the animal rights cause: issues such as organics, the working conditions of farm laborers, capitalism, environmentalism, consumerism, and health. These are topics of public conversation and personal thought that challenge me daily and spur me into action, whether by supporting a community screening of a documentary that reveals the realities of dealing with big agribusiness, or laying down a few extra dollars for fresh, healthful produce that has been grown on a small scale by caring individuals who are able to make a living wage doing something they love, like helping to feed others.

I want to promote sustainability when it comes to what we put in our mouths, so that while we prepare our meals, we also consider and value our communities, the environment, and our health. I love bananas, mangos, chocolate, coconuts, and olive oil as much as the next gal. But my local sensibility tells me that these far-traveling foods simply can't be major staples in my diet without some negative environmental consequences. I buy organic and fairly traded versions of these products from my food co-op, but I savor them as the treats they are. And what I want to do with *Ripe from Around Here* is to encourage people to get a better sense of just how far some of their food has been traveling, and how we can all take steps, one at a time, toward keepin' it local—no matter where you live.

ACKNOWLEDGMENTS

My mum, Nancy Steele, is such a super-duper woman and is my greatest supporter. If she hadn't helped with all sorts of odds and ends during my season of writing, this book sure would have come together at a much slower pace.

Lisa Pitman (petite powerhouse that she is) lovingly encouraged me through this project week after week. She was my regular companion at farmers' markets. She came over for more cook-dates during the recipe creation and testing phase than I can count, and even convinced her brother Dan to help me out with some web stuff (thanks, Dan!).

David Powell and Ann Powell's line drawings again freckle the pages of my book.

Susan Safyan, my editor, is the most perfect blend of skill, kind patience, and enthusiasm. Continued warm thanks also to Brian Lam, Shyla Seller, Janice Beley, and Robert Ballantyne at Arsenal Pulp Press for all their work in getting these books together and out into the world.

John Cullen, dashing, creative, and easy-going young man that he is, did such a wonderful job with the food photographs—don't you agree?

Elise Moser, a continuous support and Canning Queen!

Marika Collins, Ms Madcap Cupcake, who started off as recipe tester and wound up being my food stylist!

Now let's take an extra special moment to talk about the lovely and enthusiactic Kathryn Wehrle, who tested a whopping 134 recipes for this book! I always enjoyed her cute anecdotes on the recipe forum. When she told me I was the Julia to her Julie, I was almost beside myself.

And the rest of my sweet and committed testing team who helped fine-tune the recipes to ensure their usability: Shannon Harrison, Carrie Williams, Chantal Clement, Marcella Idsinga, Kristin Fields, Jenny Howard, Anne-Kristin Thordin, Brianne Hunsley, Jennifer Prescott, Kim and Fred Lahn, Denise Muller, Blaine Tacker, Ashley Gibson, Wendie Moore, Michelle Cavigliano, Aimee Kluiber, Liz Carter, Robyn Wade, Michelle Lee, Joan Farkas, David Porter, Sarah Liechti, Erin Cullen, Teressa Jackson, Ana Cruz, Elise Desaulniers, Bea Fetzer, Ali Berkok, Shamima Mahamad, Matthew Gruman, Kimberly Roy, Nicole Aube, Andrea Bertoli, Becky Ellis, and Maev Beaty.

Paul DeCampo, more hip than hippie in his steadfast commitment to local and the Slow Food Movement, so kindly wrote the foreword to this book.

Wayne Roberts, tireless crusader for much-improved food systems, offered wisdom and support.

Mary-Margaret Jones, supportively enthusiastic about my pursuits, made herself available last-minute to help make sure my lip gloss was on and bra wasn't showing at the cover photo shoot.

Emily Van Halem, who certainly has her fingers on the pulse of Toronto's progress in food-activism, generously helped with local food research.

Dan Evans at The Bookshelf in Guelph, Ontario, makes me feel like an author princess every time I come into town.

Michael Armstrong, co-op produce manager extraordinaire, was always willing (when cornered) to answer the question "Where is this fruit/vegetable coming from, and when?!"

Skillful and generous recipe sharers: Julie Daniluk, Emilie Hardman, Dan Olsen, Mahalia Freed, and Renee Loux.

Everyone who publicity wrote or said nice, encouraging things about *Get It Ripe*, including: Damian Rogers at *Eye Weekly*, Jennifer Bain at *The Toronto Star*, Karen Gordon at CBC Radio, Michael LaPointe at *The Tyee*, Katie Drummond at *CanadianLiving. com*, Michelle Kehm at *Bust* magazine, and Roseanne Harvey at *Ascent* magazine.

Rebecca Nixon of Girl Friday Clothing (*girlfridayclothing.com*) for generally keeping me well dressed, and particularly for the lovely dress I'm wearing on the cover.

Cathy's Crawly Composters (*cathyscomposters.com*), kindly gifted a pound of worms and a home for them to live in.

Manitoba Hemp helped me get going on some hemp-y recipe creation and testing.

Everyone who contributed photographs of scenes from farmers' markets, urban backyard gardens, and local farms, helping to enhance the meaning in this book.

And a final thanks to all of you—too many to be named—whom I've gotten to interact with through my blog (*domesticaffair.ca*) or on Facebook or Twitter. What a crazy time we live in where we can converse with people we've never met about the mundane (like what smoothie I'm drinking at a given moment, or what it means if you fart mostly in the evening) to the paramount (how to get kids to eat real food, or how to donate to Doctors Without Borders during a crisis), and receive a sense of satisfaction and belonging.

PART I

Before You Hit the Kitchen

Me, on a mountain of hay mulch

Aron, Jae & Graham bring hay
to the field for mulching

Chapter 1: Happiness is Healthiness: An Important Place to Start

ENJOY!

In my constant quest to figure things out (and I mean that in the broadest possible sense), I am coming to understand more and more that what we need out of life is joy. We ought to do anything we can to get a greater feeling of joy, for ourselves and for others. His Holiness the Dalai Lama, has said repeatedly that we sentient beings are all just trying to be happy. He suggests that we keep this in mind when we look at each other, and it will help us have empathy for one another. Empathy, as I see it, is one of the key components of true joy.

How can we maximize our happiness? First, we can recognize what generates happiness within ourselves and nourish whatever that is. The next step is to identify what is keeping us from being happy, and try to address that in our lives: approaching it directly, possibly getting rid of it, or finding a way to accept it, so that we come to a place that brings us joy.

So is the primacy of joy something you're willing to get behind? I'll expand a bit further: When you are in a relationship and it's going smoothly, doesn't it nourish you and inspire generosity in you? Alternately, when you're having a rough time with someone, and you've had the feeling for a while that there's more bad than good, isn't it time to call it quits and seek out something more enjoyable? Or, on a more day-to-day level, let's look at taking out the trash. Sure, maybe it doesn't feel like the most joyful thing to do while you're doing it, but you know you and others in your home

feel better when it smells fresh, not stinky. It's seeing that balance that helps us take out the trash with joy.

But how does this relate to food and the way we choose to eat? How can food help us be joyful? There are lots of ways. Let's look first at food choices.

FOOD CHOICES

"To eat with a fuller consciousness of all that is at stake might sound like a burden, but in practice few things in life can afford quite as much satisfaction."

—Michael Pollan, *The Omnivore's Dilemma*

If you're reading this, I'm willing to bet you are someone who wants to and likely already does make ethical and informed choices about what you eat. When we deviate from the ever-pervasive standard North American diet and make more educated and balanced choices, we need to stay grounded in our beliefs and reasoning. Perhaps you've taken animal products out of your diet because you have respect for them as sentient beings and don't believe they should be used for food (or fashion, etc.). Let's say that you also know that the empty calories in refined sugar are causing painful chronic inflammation in your body, and you have consciously decided to cut sugar out of your diet to rid yourself of this health problem. Keeping those reasoned choices—the "whys"—in mind will make it easier for you to enjoy a family meal even when the rest of the family is gobbling down turkey and apple pie á la mode while you eat bean soup and roasted vegetables.

Recently we have become aware of the environmental advantages of choosing to eat foods grown locally. The joy of consuming a juicy sweet pineapple on a cold winter day in Toronto is now tempered by our new awareness that we can help care for the earth and protect it for ourselves and future generations by eating a (locally grown) warm baked apple instead. Finding new ways to eat can be daunting, but we shouldn't let ourselves become overwhelmed, especially if we are contending with other issues. It doesn't benefit us to focus on the negative and scare ourselves and others into making changes. It's more beneficial to learn about a situation, take an approach that feels right for us, and then feel good about it. I'm not suggesting that we stagnate in our old patterns of eating because they are comfortable in the short term. Instead, I hope you'll feel inspired by the challenge to make wise and healthy choices. It's not enjoyable if you're feeling shamed or guilted into it, so let's focus on doing the best we can—and doing it joyfully.

ENDING NUTRITIONAL STRESS

In *The Thrive Diet*, Brendan Brazier agrees that the unproductive stresses in our lives are a major obstacle to achieving happiness. The stress of working in an unsatisfying job, having to deal with people who are unpleasant, having to make decisions that may feel like the wrong ones—all these situations make us unhappy and challenge our bodies' health.

Research is clear that stress of this sort messes with our immune response and often leads to illness. Brazier goes on to explain that unhealthy food choices lead to nutritional stress. This stress comes when we fill our bodies with food that not only doesn't nourish us, but that actually hurts us. Eating foods that are unhealthy causes digestive difficulties *and* deprives us of the nutrients our bodies need to repair themselves. It also causes a buildup of toxins that damage our organs. While our bodies are dealing with this hidden stress, we are much less able to handle the more obvious stresses that can weave their way into our daily lives. The impact of nutritional stress, says Brazier, can be completely removed by eating a plant-based, whole foods diet. A body that doesn't have to deal with nutritional stress is much more able to resiliently handle life's many other stresses.

EATING TO NOURISH

The message here is to choose the foods that are going to provide the fuel our bodies need to run and the nutrients that are needed to keep our organs in good repair. How can we do this in the most joyful way? My answer would be: "Slowly and holistically," meaning that we do it in a way that supports the well-being of the whole person—body, mind, and spirit. Although some people are naturally drawn to holistic health, others only come to it when they have a health crisis and have been unsatisfied with the offerings of the conventional medical community. As a holistic health practitioner, I often see these people in crisis, but I believe that if they had previously received the support to change to more healthy eating practices, slowly and holistically, they would probably not have reached a crisis state. As it is, they may have to make dramatic changes that feel really difficult at a time when they are feeling quite vulnerable and in need of comfort. Sure enough, there is wisdom in the old adage, "An ounce of prevention is worth a pound of cure."

EATING WITH JOY

I never ask my clients to eat foods that they decidedly dislike, because I can only imagine that when they put those foods in their mouths, all their digestive organs tense up and they are unable to break down and assimilate the nutrients in those foods. I say, eat foods you like. Take pleasure in both the preparation and the eating of your food. Ours is a culture where the focus is on quick, low-maintenance meals. I'd like to suggest you find joy in the process of preparing your food: revel in the textures, the smells, and the development of your culinary skills! Invite a friend or two to cook with you. Make it a party. I'm not saying you should eat your favorite foods every single day—you may develop an intolerance to them with overexposure—but there is no reason to sit down to a meal that is nutritious but doesn't satisfy you. Find tasty ways to prepare unfamiliar ingredients. Make sure each meal is tasty and fulfilling.

EATING MINDFULLY

Our relationship with food is rarely simple. Like all other animals, we have evolved to recognize when we need to eat or drink so that we don't dehydrate or starve to death. Our brains send us needy signals that say "hungry" or "thirsty." And when we meet those needs, our bodies send us back happy, pleasurable sensations.

The problems arise when this process gets out of whack. We may find that we want those pleasurable sensations to compensate for stress or sadness in our lives, so we eat when we aren't really hungry just to get those lovely dopamine hits. We develop habits that we probably aren't even aware of that have us eating food that tastes good but is either not good for us or not good in the amounts that we are consuming it.

How many of us inhale our meals in five to ten minutes flat? If that is your habit, it will take a real effort to change it, but it's one that I think is well worth making. I'm going to suggest that you try to change that habit, not by either ignoring or denying yourself food, but rather by focusing intensely and "mindfully" on the food you eat. First, you need to understand what you actually do when you eat mindfully. Here's an exercise that will get you started. You don't need to do it with every bite of food you eat, but doing this exercise every now and again will help you change your eating habits (if that is what you want to do).

Let's start with an apple. Typically you probably give your apple a quick rinse and chomp right in. This time, start with the rinse, but then dry it off, and as you dry your apple take a really good look at it. Notice the colors and how they change over the surface of the skin. Consider your apple starting its life as a flower on a tree somewhere and slowly growing with all the other apples into the firm, juicy fruit you are holding in your hand. Sometimes you can see, by the difference in skin color, where your apple was shaded by a leaf. Imagine your apple (let's hope it's organic) sucking sweet rainwater from the ground and ripening with all those others in the sun. Before you take a bite, put the apple right up to your face and breathe in deeply. Can you smell that lovely apple fragrance? Now you're ready for the first bite. Feel the texture of the apple skin against your lips. Notice the pressure of your teeth against the skin as you bite, hear the sound that your teeth make as they bite off a piece. Taste the juice on your tongue. Chew this bite slowly, noticing the different texture of the skin of the apple and its flesh as you chew. Notice how your mouth fills with the juice and how you swallow it even before you swallow the pulp of the apple. Eat your apple slowly, tasting and feeling the texture of each mouthful and hearing the satisfying crisp sound of each bite. Take a break. Are you still hungry or could you save the rest of this apple for later? By eating slowly you are giving your stomach a chance to catch up and tell you if you have had enough for now.

You may find that you can do this exercise for the first few bites and then want to go back to eating as you normally do. Go right ahead. Your goal is to try to increase the length of time you can eat mindfully each day. As more and more of your eating becomes mindful, you will begin to change those mindless eating habits.

> *To make smart, healthy eating choices, your body and mind work together to send you essential clues about what you need and want to eat. These clues give you information about "how much" and "what" to eat. The sensations and emotions that signal when you're full, famished, or just wanting to eat something rich and delicious are a complex combination of bodily and emotional feelings. If you are attentive and responsive to these cues, your eating will be healthy, in control, and well regulated.*
>
> —*Susan Albers,* Eating Mindfully

MEDITATION

I encourage all my clients to get into a routine of meditating. This helps us all stay (or get) balanced mentally and emotionally, which in turn helps us maintain balance in our bodies too. Over time, meditation is a reliable way to increase your joy. There are some very specific ways to practice meditation, but it needn't be complicated to be beneficial. Even if you have never done it before, you can pretty much take a go at it whenever and wherever you like. Meditation can be as simple as sitting or lying still and watching the movement of your breath through your body. *In ... out ... in ... out ...* Inevitably, thoughts will come into your head, but you don't need to latch on to them. Simply acknowledge them and then bring your focus back to your breath. You may intuitively know when you're done, but it's often helpful to set a timer for anywhere from five to sixty minutes (it's good to start with a short length of time and work yourself up to a longer period, if you like).

In order to get the most out of meditation, establish a regular practice. Ideally, do it at the same time of day, such as first thing in the morning and/or the same time each evening (as long as you're not too sleepy then). Just as with an exercise regimen, it's better to do ten minutes each and every day than an hour on the days you remember to get around to it, like a few times a month.

CHANGE YOUR MOOD, FEEL BETTER

When I think of it, I play something that I call the "Isn't It Nice" game (inspired by the work of Abraham-Hicks). I play it when I'm cranky, frustrated, disappointed, or downright negative. Say it is winter; I'm in the car, and I'm late for my food co-op board of directors' meeting. While my initial inclination might be to have less patience in traffic, resent the obligation to attend these meetings, or begrudge the cold weather, instead I'll say: "Isn't it nice that I was able to enjoy a warming meal before I left the house?" and "Isn't it nice that my dad gave me this '97 Ford Villager Minivan so that I can bring groceries home this evening? And isn't it nice that this twelve-year-old car is still running? Isn't it nice that there's a good chance that people will understand if I'm a few minutes late for this meeting?" At some point during this exercise, my mood will change from grumpiness to gratitude, and I feel like it's all going to be all right. I like to play this with someone else, but it works just fine on your own, too.

MORE JOY IN VEGAN LAND

Here's a topic I specifically want to discuss before ending this chapter. The vegan movement is big on "compassion" and "cruelty-free," but how far does that go for you? You are compassionate toward animals, stepping out of the equation that ends their lives at a slaughterhouse, but shouldn't these ideals apply to your fellow humans, too?

Maybe take a moment to consider your thoughts, actions, and interactions in everyday life. This starts with your relationship with yourself. Are you the first person to put yourself down in any given situation? Are there things you feel you can't do, or that you don't deserve? (The possibilities for you to thrive are really only as endless as your beliefs let them be.) When you get compliments do you roll your eyes, or allow for the possibility that the words are sincere and gratefully let them sink in and nourish you?

How about your money and the ways in which you consume? Do you choose fair trade or horizontally traded products when they're available to help protect laborers who produce your food and treats? ("Horizontally traded" means that the groups involved in the trade are really rooted in the communities that produce what's being traded.)

When it comes to those around you, do you support local businesses financially, or do you find yourself haggling and looking for deals, then paying full price for industrially created items at the big box stores?

Do you show up for your friends and family and support them emotionally, or are you inclined to trash-talk others? Do you get fired up by gossip? There is strength in your words and actions, so choose wisely.

I wonder if we all tried coming to terms with ourselves on this subject (I know that I sure am trying), and seeing what habits we can adjust, we'd generate even more compassion in our individual lives, and as a movement. And what I think we'll find is that more compassion leads to more joy.

RESOURCES:

Albers, Susan. *Eating Mindfully: How to End Mindless Eating & Enjoy a Balanced Relationship with Food.* Oakland, CA: New Harbinger Publications, 2003.

Haskvitz, Sylvia E. *Eat by Choice, Not by Habit: Practical Skills for Creating a Healthy Relationship with Your Body and Food.* Encinitas, CA: Puddledancer Press, 2005.

Hay, Louise. *You Can Heal Your Life.* Santa Monica, CA: Hay House, 1987.

Kabat-Zinn, Jon. *Full Catastrophe Living.* New York: Delacorte Press, 1990.

——. *Wherever You Go, There You Are.* New York: Hyperion, 1994.

Liebler, Nancy and Sandra Moss. *Healing Depression the Mind-Body Way.* Hoboken, N.J: Wiley, 2009.

Myss, Caroline M. *Why People Don't Heal and How They Can.* New York: Harmony Books, 1997.

Tiwari, Bri Maya. *The Path of Practice: A Woman's Book of Ayurvedic Healing.* New York: Ballantine Books, 2001.

Caroline Dupont's meditation CDs are available from *carolinedupont.com*.

(For more information, see the Resources list, pp. 255–257.)

Chapter 2: Closer to Home: Reaching for Local

"Shipping is a terrible thing to do to vegetables. They probably get jet-lagged, just like people."
  —Elizabeth Berry

"Local" and "seasonal" are two of the biggest buzz words among foodies these days. Farmers' markets are more popular than ever, and I'd like to think that people are more adventurous now about cooking from scratch using fresh, whole ingredients than they have been in a few decades. I created the recipes in this book to help you use local foods in season; here are some of the reasons I think it's important to do so.

WHY GO LOCAL?

The benefits of eating locally grown foods are many. Taste, food security, nutrition supporting local businesses, a healthy planet, and a healthy economy—these are all reasons to think about finding more of our food close to home. Let's explore some of them in greater depth.

1. Locally grown food simply tastes better.

"Vine-" or "tree-ripened" are advertising claims that sound good, but I often find that I have a different definition of "ripe" than big-box stores. Although I prefer to patronize my food co-op or the local farmers' markets, I sometimes find myself shopping at supermarkets. Attracted to their advertisements, I'll reach for a "tree-ripened" peach or nectarine and discover that it's rock hard. Most foods that come from far away are picked before they are ripe, then prevented from ripening too soon by refrigeration, and finally encouraged to ripen (often using gases) just before they arrive at your supermarket. Food that is going to be sold locally, however, can be given more time to ripen slowly on the plant, vine, or tree. It can be picked perfectly ripe (and with a more impressive nutrient profile) and arrive the same day at the market. Yum.

2. It's safer to have a short food chain.

These days, not too many people know and trust the folks who have grown their food. Michael Pollan, in his book *In Defense of Food*, points out that there are huge benefits in trying to shorten our dangerously long food chain. I think of this when I see a conventional garlic bulb at my big-box supermarket and the label informs me it was grown in a country half a planet away. There are lots of these garlic bulbs in this store, and the store is just one of many in a chain across the country, so I suspect that these bulbs come from a big farm that is probably devoted to growing only garlic. I wonder about the farmers who grew them. What are the conditions in which they live and work? Are they paid a fair wage? What fertilizers and pesticides are they allowed to use in their country? (We have regulations banning certain pesticides from use in Canada, but I know some are still being used in other countries.) Do they have food-safety regulations? If they do, can I be sure those regulations have been followed?

And then there is the travel. Has this garlic been irradiated to keep from spoiling on its long journey? Once it has crossed the border, have inspectors made sure that our own food safety requirements have been met? Even though we are told our food is regularly inspected, we still have our own food-safety problems and food recalls.

Generally, the food we buy in supermarkets does not make us sick, but when it does in an obvious and immediate way, we hear about it and that food is recalled. But what about the long-term effects of pesticides and additives? These days, the path most food takes to travel from farmers' fields to us is long and convoluted, and there are many points along the way where we have to trust people we have never met to ensure that nothing has happened that will make us ill. There are those who warn that our long food chain makes us vulnerable to bio-terrorists, but that is a whole other pot of potatoes. Pollan argues, and I agree, that a short food chain, in which we eat what is grown close to our homes, gives us a much better chance of ensuring food security.

So what can we do to shorten our own food chain? We can start by trying to support and get to know local farmers by buying at co-ops, farmers' markets or Community Supported Agriculture groups (CSAs), and to encourage our supermarkets to be local-farmer friendly. When we make personal connections with local farmers, we can ask them about how they grow our food. They are more likely to choose to take good care of their customers if they know them personally. Here in Toronto, you can contact Field Trip (*fieldtriptoronto.ca*) to get in on one of their visits to local farms. Perhaps

there is an organization near you doing the same thing. If not, maybe you can start one!

3. Eating locally supports small farmers in your community.

This is a good thing, not only because it shortens the food chain, but because small-scale farmers are more likely to plant a variety of crops and are often the only ones growing diverse species of common edible plants. Plant diversity is important. It provides variety in our diets, which makes eating more exciting and, in many cases, more tasty. (Heirloom or heritage tomatoes are a case in point.) It also protects from massive plant die-offs from disease. If we only have one variety of potato, and it can't resist a fungus we can't control, we'll soon be potato-less. This caused major problems when it happened in Ireland in the 1840s. The potato famines there took the lives of a million people, and we aren't entirely immune to such a crisis today. If we can keep these farmers on their farms, we can preserve a bit of the country close to the city, encouraging more responsible land development and helping us city dwellers know what it is to be close to nature. (There's more of an exploration of farmers and community in Chapter 4.)

4. Eating locally protects the environment.

The reason for going local that we hear most often is to protect the environment from the carbon emissions of the planes, trucks, and ships that bring food to us from far away. Although this seems, at first, to make a lot of sense (clearly, flying strawberries from California to Toronto must produce more

CO_2 than trucking them from a local farm), when we look more deeply, the relationship between local foods and carbon emissions is not simple at all. The effect that food production has on the environment has to be examined in its entirety before we can see the real impact that particular production decisions make. Wayne Roberts, head of the Toronto Food Policy Council and co-author of *Real Food for a Change*, told attendees at the Guelph Organic Conference in 2009 that we really need to look at our food system from "farm to fart" instead of package to plate; in other words, we need to think about what happens to our food from its origins on the farm to its impact on us when we eat it.

Those who are concerned about this issue (including governments trying to be responsible and businesses hoping to label their products "eco-friendly") talk about the concept of life cycle assessment. This idea seems to have started in the 1980s, mostly in Europe, but it's now becoming popular in North America, Australia, and other places where food is plentiful. A life cycle assessment (LCA) examines the impact of every aspect of a particular food item's production, from the preparation of the soil, the making of the fertilizers and pesticides and the machines that are used to apply them, and the watering, weeding, and harvesting of the plants to the shipping to grocery stores and eventual home storage, in coolers, refrigerators, or freezers, until the moment of consumption. What LCAs are revealing is that the environmental impact is much greater at the beginning and the end of the production cycle than it is in the middle, or shipment, section of the process. In some instances the fuel required to heat a greenhouse in the winter in Canada to grow strawberries may produce more CO_2 than that produced by burning the fuel used to fly strawberries to Canada from warm and sunny southern California.

What we environmentally concerned consumers need is labeling that indicates the total energy consumption involved in producing the foods we see on the shelves. This labeling may be on its way (fingers crossed!). The Swedish food-consumer organization KRAV announced the creation of a new label for "climate-friendly" foods in 2007. In Canada, France, Switzerland, the UK, and the US, standards for carbon labeling have been developed and implemented. As with organic and fair-trade labeling, consistent standards will need to be developed and regulated by governments if we are to know whom to trust.

But until this happens, how can we make good choices in the grocery store? In terms of carbon emissions, we can be fairly certain that locally grown in-season food is going to be the best choice for those who want to protect the environment. Fuel burned during shipping is minimal and little energy is used to store the food, which tends to be picked when it is ripe and sold quickly. Of course, this means you need to know what foods are in season and resist the huge temptation to buy out-of-season produce that is available and affordable in most grocery stores.

A generation ago, foods that were out of season were far too expensive for most folks to buy regularly. As recently as the 1980s, only the fairly well-to-do in Canada would consider buying kiwis flown in from New Zealand, for example. Perhaps in order to protect the planet, we will need to price foods to reflect the environmental costs that their production incurs. But if this happens, fewer of us will be able to afford to eat in the way to which we have grown accustomed in the last thirty years. In the meantime, if you live in Canada or the US, you need to eat your strawberries in late June. Waiting for them and reveling in them when they arrive is a joy in itself!

5. Buying locally makes money sense.
Buying locally not only supports the local economy, but it also saves your country money in environmental cleanup. Brian Halwell, a senior researcher at the Worldwatch Institute, has written a book called *Eat Here: Reclaiming Homegrown Pleasures in a Global Supermarket*, in which he points out that:

> *A study by the New Economics Foundation in London found that every £10 spent at a local food business is worth £25 for the local area, compared with just £14 when the same amount is spent in a supermarket. That is, a pound (or dollar, peso, or rupee) spent locally generates twice as much income for the local economy. The farmer buys a drink at the local pub; the pub owner gets a car tune-up at the local mechanic; the mechanic brings a shirt to the local tailor; the tailor buys some bread at the local bakery; the baker buys wheat for bread and fruit for muffins from the local farmer. When these businesses are not owned locally, money leaves the community at every transaction.*

Another study, done by researchers at the University of Essex and at City University in the UK, concluded that eating food grown really close to home (12.5 miles/20 km) would save a huge amount of environmental clean-up. They claim that Britain would save £2.1 billion (about $3.4 billion US) annually in environmental costs. They also estimated that if all the farms in the UK were to turn organic, it would save the country over a billion pounds in environmental cleanup annually. Another £100 million would be saved each year if people walked, bicycled, or took the bus to the shops instead of driving. These facts must also be considered in the light of our global responsibility to make sure that all countries, especially those that were exploited by European colonialism, are able to feed themselves. The transition to eating locally cannot be made so rapidly that countries dependent on exports to wealthy nations to feed themselves are left to go hungry.

WHAT'S GROWING WHERE AND WHEN?
Because I live in southern Ontario, I know that I can get apples and carrots and maple syrup from nearby farms, but what about ginger root or sesame seeds or walnuts? When in doubt, a little research is in order. I am lucky to have several farmers' markets and my food co-op close by; I can talk to the farmers and the co-op's produce manager about what they know. But what about someone who only has the Internet as a resource? I tested it out myself, narrowing my search to foods I knew something about: peaches, tomatoes, and

pecans, and set to work. One of the things I discovered was that the websites available are works-in-progress, and should improve as more time is spent collecting and inputting available information. Given that limitation, however, I was amazed by the amount of information I found. Here are the results of my search:

The website of the Natural Resources Defense Council (*nrdc.org/health/foodmiles*), with 1.2 million members dedicated to stopping global warming, is a great resource for folks in the US (and includes a scattering of farms in Canada as well). You can click on any state and find out what foods are seasonal for any particular month, as well as what foods are available in any bordering states. The site also offers the option of clicking on a particular state and finding what is growing throughout the whole year.

Some websites require a little patience while they work out the glitches. On the United States Department of Agriculture site, for example (*www.ams.usda.gov/AMSv1.0/FarmersMarkets*), you can find farmers' markets all over the US. When, in the summer of 2009, I typed in my aunt's town in New Jersey, nothing came up, but when I searched the whole county it gave me ten nearby markets, and for the state of New Jersey, there were 123 listings. (Sadly, there doesn't seem to be a similar service offered by either the federal or provincial governments of Canada.)

A really useful site for Canadians, however, is the 100 Mile Challenge website (*100mile.foodtv.ca/providers/foods/on/4*). Not only can you find out what's being grown when and where in Canada, but you can also view some interesting videos. One features a couple who buys and cans truckloads of produce in their tiny apartment. Another has interviews with people who grow fruits and vegetables on their urban balconies. I decided to see how thorough the site was for where I live, so I searched for "peaches" within 100 miles of Toronto. It resulted in a map that included several farms and farmers' markets in the Niagara Peninsula, not too far from my home. (This is the closest peach-growing area to me.) The disappointing thing was that my favorite farm for peaches, Two Century Farm near Grimsby, Ontario, did not get a mention. (I know of this farm because they supply my food co-op with peaches that are very nearly pesticide-free.) Also missing from the site were many of the farms that sell at my local farmers' markets whose produce is Local Food Plus certified (see sidebar).

Local Food Plus (LFP) is a Toronto-based nonprofit organization. According to their website (www.localfoodplus.ca), "LFP certified farmers and processors work to:

- *Employ sustainable production systems that reduce or eliminate synthetic pesticides and fertilizers; avoid the use of hormones, antibiotics, and genetic engineering; and conserve soil and water.*

- *Provide safe and fair working conditions for on-farm labor.*

- *Provide healthy and humane care for livestock.*

- *Protect and enhance wildlife habitat and biodiversity on working farm landscapes.*

- *Reduce on-farm energy consumption and greenhouse gas emissions."*

Another site that folks in the US will find useful is that of Local Harvest (*localharvest.org*). When I again typed in my aunt's New Jersey address, it listed two farms that had all sorts of their own produce for sale as well as peaches brought in from farms close by.

Some websites I tried were a bit disappointing, but perhaps they will improve with time. The Rodale Institute website's Farm Locator (*www.newfarm.org*) is a great idea, but their search engine was unable to find any farms growing tomatoes within 100 miles of my aunt's place (I know they are there) or any farms that had pecans within 100 miles of Atlanta, Georgia (which also seems unlikely).

Chefs Collaborative (*chefscollaborative.org*) has a database where those who live in Canada or the US can discover what farms in their area are supplying sustainably grown produce to restaurants, information you could pass along to your favorite eatery.

Although these websites were useful for common or garden produce, they couldn't provide me with any insight into local sources for ginger root, sesame seeds, or walnuts. Ginger root grows in tropical climates, mostly in India, China, and Indonesia. The only ginger locally grown in North America is wild ginger, and only in temperate zones. It is not really related to ginger, but its rhizomes have a similar taste. (A warning, however: it is a powerful diuretic, so use it with caution.) And you should know that conventionally grown spices, including ginger, may be irradiated, so buying organic is a good idea. The closest sesame seeds available for North Americans are grown in Mexico. Ninety-nine percent of the walnuts available in North America come from California, but some are grown in southeastern Canada and the northeastern United States, so if you live in that region, you could hunt out local walnuts if you were keen.

AN AT-A-GLANCE GUIDE TO WHAT'S RIPE AND AVAILABLE WHEN

Imported foods are a luxury that leaves us a little disconnected from understanding what locally-grown produce is available when. Here's a guide that generally applies to my North American bioregion (southern Ontario)—it may be mostly in line with, or vastly different from yours, depending on where you're situated (maybe you have a different variety of crops available to you). A cooler spring will delay crop harvesting, an unusually warm summer may see maturation a week or two early. Check with your nearby farmers (or farmers' market coordinators) if you can.

▬▬ Harvest Period
▬▬ Availability Period

VEGETABLES	JAN	FEB	MAR	APRIL	MAY	JUNE	JULY	AUG	SEPT	OCT	NOV	DEC
Asparagus					●	●						
Beans, Dry	●	●	●	●	●	●	●	●	●	●	●	●
Beans, Lima									●	●		
Beans, Snap							●	●	●	●		
Beets	●	●	●				●	●	●	●	●	●
Beet Greens					●	●	●	●	●			
Broccoli						●	●	●	●	●	●	
Brussel Sprouts									●	●	●	●
Cabbage	●	●	●	●		●	●	●	●	●	●	
Carrots	●	●	●	●			●	●	●	●	●	●
Cauliflower								●	●	●	●	
Celery								●	●	●	●	
Collard Greens							●	●	●	●	●	●
Corn								●	●	●	●	
Cucumbers								●	●	●	●	
Eggplant								●	●	●	●	
Garlic						●	●	●				
Herbs	●	●	●	●	●	●	●	●	●	●		
Kale									●	●	●	●
Leeks								●	●	●		
Lettuce					●	●	●	●	●	●		
Mustard Greens						●	●	●	●	●	●	
Onions	●	●	●	●	●	●	●	●	●	●	●	●
Parsnips	●	●	●	●	●	●				●	●	●
Peas						●	●	●	●	●	●	
Peppers							●	●	●	●		
Potatoes	●	●	●	●	●	●	●	●	●	●		
Pumpkins									●	●		
Radishes					●	●	●	●	●			
Rhubarb					●	●	●					
Spinach					●	●	●	●	●	●		
Squash, Summer						●	●	●	●	●		
Squash, Winter	●	●	●					●	●	●	●	●

	JAN	FEB	MAR	APRIL	MAY	JUNE	JULY	AUG	SEPT	OCT	NOV	DEC
Swiss Chard								●	●	●	●	
Tomatoes						●	●	●	●	●		
Turnips	●	●	●	●						●	●	●
Turnip Greens					●	●	●	●	●			
Zucchini								●	●	●	●	

FRUITS	JAN	FEB	MAR	APRIL	MAY	JUNE	JULY	AUG	SEPT	OCT	NOV	DEC
Apples	●	●	●	●	●	●	●	●	●	●	●	●
Blackberries							●	●				
Blueberries							●	●	●			
Cantalopes							●	●	●			
Cherries, Sweet						●	●					
Cherries, Tart							●					
Currants							●	●				
Grapes								●	●	●		
Peaches							●	●	●			
Pears	●	●	●					●	●	●	●	●
Plums							●	●	●			
Prunes								●	●	●		
Raspberries						●	●		●	●	●	
Strawberries					●	●	●					
Watermelon								●	●	●		

How can you decide whether to buy local but conventionally grown produce or organic produce from elsewhere? This is not an easy question to answer. Local organic produce is your best option. Local sustainably grown is the second best. If you can't find the fruit and veg that you want that is both local and organic or sustainably grown, there are a few things you can do. Check out some of the websites listed on pp. 256–257 to see if you can find an association of organic farmers, or farmers who are using sustainable practices, near you, in order to find more eco-friendly produce.

If this doesn't work and you are left to choose, you might want to consider what criteria you are using to make your decision.

Base your decision on caring for your own health.

Some studies indicate that there are significantly higher amounts of some nutrients in organically grown food; one study published in the *Journal of Alternative and Complementary Medicine*, for instance, showed that there was 25 percent more vitamin C in organically grown tomatoes.

Other studies claim that the nutrient content is basically the same for organic and conventional food—although, if our food is only as healthy as the soil it's grown in, and organic farmers enrich their soil with cover crops, manure, and sea-vegetable solutions, I can only assume their produce would be more mineral-rich. Some foods lose their nutritional value the longer the delay between harvesting and consumption. This loss may detract from the possible nutritional benefits of long-distance organics. So, the jury is really still out on that one.

The harmful effects of pesticides on human health have been well documented, and some pesticides (like DDT) have been banned in Canada and the US as a result. Pesticide residues have been found in human breast milk. Despite this sad fact, breast milk is still considered the best food for babies. While you are pregnant or nursing, you might choose to eat non-local organic but still advocate for local organic options.

Base your decision on the health of the planet.

Research conducted by the British journal *Food Policy* in 2005 concluded that buying local food is better for the environment than buying organic. The study also claims that canning or freezing locally grown food is an environmentally friendly thing to do. It doesn't mention the effects of conventional farming on topsoil depletion, however, which is becoming a huge problem worldwide. We can look forward to more research being done in this area that includes not only CO_2 emissions, but also the effects of conventional farming

on soils. Typically such studies are funded by businesses that have a vested interest in the outcome of the research. As agribusiness is not likely to find this research useful, we really need our governments to step up to the plate and fund this work.

WHERE TO SHOP FOR LOCAL FOODS
Farmers' markets.

Since I wrote *Get It Ripe* in 2007, the number of farmers' markets in Canada, the US, and Europe seems to have grown exponentially. Use the Internet to find one close to where you live. You might also want to check out the folks who run the market; some insist that farmers sell only their own produce, while others allow farmers to sell produce from nearby farms. You might want to ask if farmers who state that their produce is organic or sustainably grown have had their certification checked. What you want to avoid are markets filled with vendors—not farmers—who have had nothing to do with the farming of the produce themselves.

Food co-ops.

Some people are put off by the idea of shopping at a co-op because they think that it requires something other than their custom. Granted, some co-ops do require a time commitment from their members. My local co-op, Karma (and others like it), offer customers a discount if they put in two hours of work each month. (Working members at Karma pay eighteen percent less than nonworking members.) Other co-ops are worker-owned, and typically require that their employees support the philosophy of the co-op and be committed to providing their customers with good information as well as good service. Over time, employees of this type of co-op become shareholders in the company, but generally, anyone can shop there.

Community supported agriculture.
Farming—especially small-scale, high-quality operations —is a costly business. Farmers need to have money to buy seeds and run their farms for the season before they actually begin to make money selling the produce they've grown. The idea for CSAs arose because small local farmers were having difficulty finding capital. What if people who wanted to buy the produce paid for some of it in advance? The farmers could use these investments to plant and tend their crops, and the results of the farmers' labor would be shared among the people who had contributed. When each crop became ready for harvesting, the members of the program would receive their share. Many CSA members want to be actively involved and join in to weed or harvest crops and experience a bit of "farm life" themselves. If this sounds like fun, find out if there are any CSAs in your neighborhood.

I sometimes wonder what *can* be grown closer to home but isn't? Adventurous farmers are likely to experiment with this kind of thing. Foods we typically get from afar could come from somewhere closer, given the right conditions (temperature and other weather variables, type of soil, etc.). Although they typically grow in Tibet, for example, I managed to sprout gogi berry seeds last spring.

CHANGING OUR RELATIONSHIP WITH THE KITCHEN
For some, eating with a greater emphasis on local implies more cooking from scratch. But marketers in the food industry know that what's most appealing to busy people is time efficiency and, for people who lack comfort in the kitchen, simplicity. I'm not sure quick and easy is a good basis for most meals. (And I've got a whole movement backing me up on this belief—you might have heard of it?—Slow Food.) I know that when my meals are consistently put together in a rush, it's a sign that my life is out of balance. And there are times when that makes sense: when I'm moving house, during a school-exam period, when something very emotionally involving has come up, when I'm working to meet a tight deadline. But that can't be my everyday state. I hope that books like this and *Get It Ripe*, and maybe some informal cooking lessons or more formal culinary classes, will get you to a place where you can take a few enjoyable hours each week to cook something tasty and wholesome. Nourishing your body shouldn't be an afterthought, and when it is, I'm sure your body knows it on some level and will protest (with some sort of digestive upset or food intolerance or allergy, reduced energy, etc.).

GIVING UP FOODS FROM FAR AWAY
When people decide to "go local," the product many miss most is coffee. Now, I have lived with dear souls hooked on the stuff who found it a challenge to function smoothly without it, so I get it. Sorta. It smells great, it's a drug you can legally consume, it keeps

you alert at work (heck, your job may even provide it for you!), and its consumption is a celebrated ritual for many of us. But it also takes minerals out of your bones, can make you anxious and jumpy, and for most of us, it's not locally produced. If you are trying to wean yourself off coffee, drink more water and caffeine-free teas that you find satisfying (like red rooibos tea or chai), and take deep breaths through your nose whenever you feel your energy dwindling. But if you insist on the stuff, do buy organic and fair-trade (it's getting easier to find all the time—even at rest stops off the Vermont freeways!).

For kids (and some of us adults), a major non-local food product is often sugar. With my nutritionist's hat on, I'd say you'd be better off to avoid feeding and hooking your kids on sugar in the first place. But for those of you with kids past infancy, it's not too late to change their eating habits. It's possible, and worthwhile, to prepare satisfying meals for your kids that don't include sugar. These can include more natural, and hopefully more local, sweeteners such as maple syrup or agave nectar or stevia or even licorice root. If you get your kids involved in the cooking and baking, they'll likely be more inclined to eat what you serve them. But don't make a big deal about the switch to healthier foods; their palates may change without them even noticing.

And the same goes for you, no matter how old you are. Your palate will change over time if you're open to it, whether you decide to put a greater emphasis on whole foods, cut out products like coffee or sugar, or go vegan or locavore. If I'm in the habit of having baked goods every day, that's what I look for and crave; a big bowl of steamed broccoli just won't excite me the way a slice of toast with buttery spread will. But that also means that if I'm in the habit of enjoying a large fresh salad every day at lunch and a pile of braised kale or beet greens on my plate at dinner, I will also notice and miss them on days when I don't. Once you've made the switch to less processed foods, you may find that the foods you used to love aren't as amazing as you remembered (or at least, best enjoyed in smaller quantities).

MY NEAR PANTRY (NON-PRODUCE ITEMS FROM MY BIOREGION OF SOUTHERN ONTARIO):

- canned goods and condiments, including applesauce, apple butter, apple cider vinegar, fruit jams, salsas and chutneys, ketchup, tomatoes, and other tomato products
- grains, such as amaranth, buckwheat, cornmeal, oats, spelt (flour), and wild rice
- dried herbs—so many of them!—such as rosemary, basil, oregano, thyme and mint
- legumes like black beans, chickpeas, lentils, soybeans
- maple syrup
- seeds, including flax, pumpkin, and sunflower
- sunflower oil

FORAGING

Free food for anyone around to enjoy? How exciting! Finding edible foods in the wild may connect you with a more animalistic side of your being or some feeling from a very past life, in a time before agriculture. Be very cautious about what you pick; some poisonous mushrooms, for example, are difficult to distinguish from edible ones. Educate yourself before setting out to forage, and/or gather together a group of people and invite along an expert forager. Just don't harvest too much from a given area to ensure that it will be available for years to come.

EIGHTEEN EASY WAYS ANYONE CAN GO (MORE) LOCAL:

1 | Prepare your foods at home. With packaged prepared foods, the food chain could be as complicated as farmer to distributor to processing plant to packaging plant to another distributor to grocery store to you (six steps). If you make your meals from scratch, however, the chain could be as short as farmer to market to you, or even less if you grow your own. Even if the chain is farmer-distributor-store-you, it's still an improvement, which also likely means a reduction in carbon emissions.

2 | Forget about bottled water. I can see Lake Ontario from my bedroom window, so why would I need water packaged and trucked from rural Québec or worse— Evian, France? When we acknowledge that air quality is compromised by shipping this "cleaner" water, and too many single-use plastic bottles are chucked in the recycling, we see it's not that clean after all.

3 | Make your own non-dairy milk. Even if the almonds or rice are sourced from afar, the water didn't travel from California (or wherever the packaged milk you buy is made).

4 | Buy dried beans instead of canned. Bulk dried beans, even if, again, they weren't grown locally, are lighter to transport than foods canned in water and shipped from wherever they were prepared, and there's less packaging, too.

5 | Assuming you live in a climate with four unique seasons, preserve the local summer bounty by canning (pp. 57–61), dehydrating, and freezing.

6 | Know where everything in your kitchen came from. You might keep a running inventory and set goals for yourself to make your purchases as local as possible.

7 | Make a habit of shopping at your farmers' market every week. (Just be sure you're buying from the farmers and not distributors, who are permitted at some markets.)

8 | If one doesn't already exist, produce a local food directory that lists all the local food sources in your area, including CSA arrangements, farmers' markets, food co-ops, restaurants emphasizing seasonal cuisine and local produce, and farmers willing to sell direct to consumers year-round.

9 | If you buy bread, find delicious artisanal loaves from local small-scale bakers instead of buying the factory-made stuff or frozen specialty breads that come from afar.

10 | Seek out local vineyards, especially organic ones. Wines, ciders, beers … It's likely that grapes and hops are growing close to you.

11 | Quit your coffee and/or chocolate addiction. When fresh herbs are ready to harvest, make some healing tea blends (pp. 86–88).

12 | Ask your local grocers to stock more locally grown foods. Be sure to talk to someone who is knowledgeable and open to answering your questions, not just a random stock clerk.

13 | Encourage your favorite local restaurants to follow the lead of innovative vegan restaurant Candle 79 in Manhattan and other eateries that highlight local produce on their menus.

14 | Host local potlucks, harvest parties, or all-local celebrations (like summer picnics and barbecues, Thanksgiving, etc.) featuring in-season foods.

15 | If you eat non-local foods, make sure they're in season, and from the closest possible place. So, for example, if I'm joncsing for a mango, it's best that I get an organic one from Mexico in the spring as opposed to a mango from India at another time of the year.

16 | Enjoy non-local foods as treats rather than as daily staples. As inexpensive as it may be to buy a banana at your local grocers, there are a whole lot of hidden costs (see pp. 42–43).

17 | Also consider (and try to reduce) the distance traveled by the clothes, toiletries, and home furnishings you buy.

18 | Do your best to burn energy from your own reserve, rather than the planet's. To start, do your shopping on foot or bike.

LOCAVORE'S ALPHABET

Here's an at-a-glance way to enforce some of the information offered to you in this chapter, as well as a peek at what lies ahead.

Antioxidants promote health by maintaining the balance of free radicals in your body. Free radicals are to your body like rust is to your bike or car and can lead to heart disease, other degenerative diseases and some cancers. Fresh fruit and vegetables, especially blueberries, pomegranates, broccoli, tomatoes, spinach, and carrots (the more color, the better!) will get you the anti-ox action you need, as they're rich in antioxidant vitamins A, C, and E. Antioxidant-rich foods may not be as effective after months of storage, so enjoy your produce in season!

Breathe in all that air that's cleaner because you chose to buy foods that didn't need hundreds of gallons of fuel to get to you. Deep breathing oxygenates the blood to energize and ground you. The high quality of the air is essential for whole-body health.

Canning the bounty from summer harvests is a super way to enjoy local produce all year round (and doesn't require the on-going energy needed to freeze foods). See p. 58–61 for details.

Drink water from your nearest fresh water source. There's no need for far away spring-water sources to be taxed to the extent they are, not to mention that crazy plastic packaging. Instead, invest in an effective water filter that screens out chlorine and other gunk.

Educate yourself about your food options, and take steps to understand the issues around the food choices your already make on a daily basis.

Farmers' markets are probably the best places to buy locally grown foods. The produce from small-scale local farms does not usually appear on supermarket shelves because chain stores tend to buy from producers who can supply their entire chain. While prices may be higher at farmers' markets, remember that you are not only paying for variety and freshness, but you are also, helping to support the local economy and protecting the planet while you do so. And as stated earlier, at farmers' markets you have the added bonus of meeting and talking to the people who have grown your food.

Garlic is undoubtedly a superfood. Enjoy it in salad dressings, sauces, soups, stews, and more. It stimulates metabolism and has antibacterial, anti-carcinogenic, antifungal, antiparasitic, and antiviral properties. Yeah! You can pretty much stick garlic in any orifice of your body, and it'll ... something good for you.

Hemp seeds offer us a balanced range of essential fatty acids. They are about twenty percent highly digestible protein. Much of the hemp supplied to North America comes from Manitoba, Canada. This hearty quick-growing plant can be farmed without the use of herbicides (and few to no pesticides). Hemp plant fiber is also a sustainable source for paper, fabric, and more.

Irradiation exposes food to a controlled amount of radiation that kills micro-organisms without raising the temperature of the food significantly. The health organizations acting on behalf of the Canadian and US governments consider it safe, but given it's a practice that hasn't been around for too long, I'm skeptical. In Canada, onions, potatoes, wheat, flour, spices, and dehydrated seasonings are currently approved for irradiation and sale. If the idea of radiation irks you even the slightest, go organic instead, and buy from small-scale producers for foods with more naturally vibrant energy.

Jerusalem artichokes, when roasted, make my favorite kind of oven fries. Funnily enough, they're related to the sunflower and aren't actually part of the artichoke family at all. It seems that the "Jerusalem" part of the name was also a miscommunication (around the 1600s), as they seem to have originated along the east coast of North America. These tubers are also known as sunroots or sunchokes. They are a great natural source of the fructose inulin, which is beneficial for those with diabetes. Jerusalem artichokes are good for supporting the lungs and can alleviate constipation (sometimes too effectively, so enjoy them in moderation until you know how your body responds to them). They will happily replace chestnuts or water chestnuts in stir-fries, and be enjoyed raw, sliced, or grated in salads.

Kitchens are more than just rooms with appliances or places to store food with counters to lean against while you quickly shovel something pre-made into your mouth. Or at least they should be. The kitchen is where all the action is in my house. There's often something simmering on the stovetop, roasting in the oven, or drying in the

dehydrator; if nothing else, the kettle is likely boiling. It's also a space that's esthetically enjoyable with a functional setup; my table has been the setting for many a good conversation. If you create a kitchen space you love, you're more likely to have fun with food preparation and the process of nourishing yourself and the ones you love.

Labeling food items is a complicated process, and the requirements that must be met to have an "organic" label are mandated by governments. Remember that on produce labels, PLU codes that start with 9 are organic (yay!), and 8 means they're genetically modified (boo!). Let's advocate for more labeling that will give us a better idea how eco-friendly our foods truly are and take into account their carbon footprints.

Minerals are needed in the soil to produce foods with the quantities of micronutrients you need for optimal health. Conventional farming methods often deplete the micronutrients in soil. Organic farmers, on the other hand, are required by regulation to protect and nourish the soil.

Nightshades include tomatoes, potatoes, eggplants, and peppers (both bell and hot). These are found in abundance in most farmers' markets and at other local food vendors (especially in the warmest months). They're all delicious when roasted (try the Ratatouille on p. 197). Unfortunately, some people are intolerant to nightshades, which are said to be a source of grief for those with arthritis and other inflammatory conditions. If you're not sure if that applies to you, take them out of your diet for a month and then reintroduce them one at a time and see how it goes.

Oats are one of my favorite grains. They nourish the nervous system, which makes them comfort food—especially for a girl like me with a Scottish heritage. Oats processed in gluten-free facilities are becoming more available for those who need 'em.

A well-stocked **pantry** is essential for ensuring delicious, wholesome meals and snacks. I know when my blood-sugar level gets low, and I can't find anything good to eat, I'm more likely to go for junkier items—sugary things, refined-flour things, deep-fried things. Get into the habit of always having whole grains and legumes, spices, oils, vinegars, and other favorite seasonings in your pantry. Maybe you'll can fresh produce in the summer (see p. 57), lining your shelves with local ingredients to enjoy all winter long.

Quick foods—like an apple to chomp into or a stalk of celery to gnaw on—I'm into that. But fast foods that seem to save me time but have had to go through numerous processes before I eat them? No thanks. Do what you can (being honest with yourself) to allow time throughout your week to cook healthy meals.

When I talk about "getting it **ripe**," I mean nourishing your body with high-quality, fresh, and whole foods. Fruit allowed to ripen on the tree and eaten within a short time of picking will be richer in the vitamins, antioxidants, and other nutrients you need to stay healthy, and it's also easier to digest.

Share the goodness. When you're invited to someone's house for dinner and you're

not sure how much of the meal you'll be able to partake in, bring a dish that will make the meal satisfying for you and be plentiful enough to pass around the table to your dinner companions. Who knows? You may get some converts.

Teas can be made with nourishing and medicinal herbs growing right in your neighborhood (and possibly as close as your own backyard or window box). See p. 86–88 for some suggestions. If you're going to buy non-local black, green, or red (rooibos) teas, be sure they're fairly traded (and ideally organic, too).

Unite with other food-excited people! No need to reinvent the wheel; get and stay inspired by community action.

Vote with your dollars! Propel the local and sustainable food movements by purchasing from nearby producers, shops, restaurants, and other companies that are taking steps to be environmentally sensitive. When you know pears are in season, make a point of tracking down local ones instead of grabbing the ones shipped from Argentina (unless you live in Argentina, of course).

Wash your produce in fresh water before eating it; root vegetables and other hearty produce should get a good scrub. This may not fit with your romantic image of buying a bunch of fresh carrots at a farmer's stall and munching on one as you meander around the rest of the market, but parasites do live in the soil that produce is grown in, and you don't always know if someone sneezed into their palm and handled the produce before you bought it.

Xenoestrogens can be released from plastic packaging, and these synthetic hormone compounds can mess with your endocrine (hormonal) system. Buying items with less disposable packaging and more stable, recyclable materials (like glass or stainless steel containers and unbleached cotton bags) is a better choice for personal and planetary health.

The **yummiest** and most satisfying foods are homemade foods. You can experience a whole new level of enjoyment from preserves that you've canned yourself, and pickier kids are more likely to try unfamiliar foods if they had a hand in preparing them.

Zucchinis (courgettes) are a member of the summer squash family and grow happily in backyards and farm fields in the summer throughout North America. For the best texture and flavor, choose zucs that are up to eight inches (twenty centimeters) long. Larger ones (sometimes called marrows) can be grated into baked goods (see the Zucchini Spice Cake on p. 214) or stuffed and baked (p. 201).

Chapter 3: A Conscious Balance: Finding Sustainability in the Vegan and Local Food Movements

Our eating identities are more complicated, but I would also say more informed, than ever before. A couple of years after I became a vegetarian but before I became vegan, I no longer drank cow's milk, but I still ate cheese, yogurt, and butter. My reasons for this weren't complicated; I'd simply decided that I wanted to add soy milk into the mix of foods I consumed daily. My eventual veganism came about because of a big, fat crush on a vegan (as *Get It Ripe* readers, or anyone who's ever heard me speak, are likely to know). As the intricacies of the diet became challenging, I began to ground myself in what had drawn me to it in the first place, which made me feel that changing my diet was a worthwhile challenge.

Everyone is different. Some people only consume non-cow milks (from goats, sheep, and buffalo) because they can digest them better and because these products often come from smaller-scale farms. Some people feel strongly about avoiding honey, as it is the product of the bees' labor. I recently heard it suggested that people who identify as vegan but choose to eat honey might call themselves "beegans." Our eating identities are so often in a state of flux that I suspect there are as many types of vegetarians as there are people who call themselves vegetarians. As you probably know by now, rather than judge, I'm going to support any decision you make to be a more conscientious, healthy, and mindful eater.

EATING IDENTITIES

Let's define a few eating-identity terms:

It is generally accepted that a **vegetarian** does not eat animals but may eat animal products, such as dairy, eggs, and honey—thus the **lacto-ovo vegetarian.**

Some people who don't eat meat but eat fish and vegetables consider themselves **pescetarians** (which is a clearer and more accurate way to say "I'm vegetarian, but I eat fish").

A **vegan** eats no animals and no animal byproducts either—but you knew that one already.

Those who prefer to eat locally grown or produced food sometimes call themselves **locavores** or **localvores**. What is considered local can vary between your own backyard and as many as a hundred miles from the eater.

Bioregionalists will try to eat the food found in their bioregion. Bioregions are defined by their physical features, which include watershed boundaries and their particular terrains, such as British Columbia's Okanagan Valley, with its lush fruit trees.

You may be a combination of these identities, depending on your values or your personal health. Wherever you place yourself on the spectrum—**flexitarian** (occasional meat-eater) to **vegan raw-foodist** to **meat-eating locavore** to **vegetarian bioregionalist**—I hope you will do your best to find out the implications of your choices, not only for your own health, but for the health of the planet.

THE GREAT HONEY DEBATE: LOCAVORES VS. VEGANS

Technically speaking, honey is not vegan. The more I understand that many vegans' choices come from the belief that no other beings—especially ones who can't stand up for themselves—should be expected to provide anything for them, the clearer that is to me. But the question remains vague to some, I think, because different things draw people to this diet. If animal rights are at the top of your list, then it is more likely that you will adamantly avoid honey. If health is your reason for being vegan, you might feel differently. You have to decide for yourself and avoid bullies (and resist bullying others 'cause y'all know it doesn't really work).

I met beekeeper Mark McAlpine at a *Get It Ripe* dinner in Guelph, Ontario, and we've been in touch about foodie things a few times since. When I posted my thoughts about the possible conflicts between vegan and local eating on my blog, he left me this comment:

I'm now in my twentieth year as a vegan, and originally became vegan because of animal rights and ethical concerns, and have been very active in the animal rights/liberation community over those twenty years. And I now keep bees (for two years now). To some, this may seem like a contradiction, but I'm serious when I say I think it may be time for ethical vegans to re-consider their position on local and backyard beekeeping and honey use. We are very close to a tipping point with honey bees—wild bee populations are next to nonexistent. Colony Collapse Disorder, as well as mite infestations and other diseases, are destroying bee populations, and so we're left with eighty or ninety percent of the honey bees pollinating the foods we vegans love coming from "kept" hives. Without beekeepers, we'd basically have no honey bees, and without the honey bees, some estimates say we'll have no fruit or veggies within four years. What saddens me is that the vegan position on boycotting local honey produced by ethical beekeepers actually does the bees more harm than good. Without sounding too dramatic, beekeepers are keeping honey bee populations alive, and they need to be supported. Anyway, that's what drew me to beekeeping, and every time I visit the hives in my yard, it's a decision I'm glad to have made.

PAYING THE PRICE

I've noticed that the word "local" seems to get people who aren't even necessarily on the "organic" train excited. There can be a negative vibe toward people who feel strongly about wanting to eat organic, a feeling that they are being too picky, too purist. And you can sort of understand the impression of elitism that it might convey. Organic food is almost always pricier than its conventional counterparts. People who have barely enough money to feed their families are denied the opportunity to purchase organic apples that are twice the price of conventional ones. This is a huge social injustice, but there are people working to address this problem; organizations like FoodShare and the Stop Community Food Centre in Toronto are working to supply local organic food to people in less privileged neighborhoods.

But what about middle-class people who can afford to buy organics but complain about the price? What they don't consider is the hidden cost to their health of eating conventionally grown foods. The pesticides and herbicides used in their cultivation can lead to illness and disease. As well, such foods are often irradiated, resulting in fewer of the vitamins, minerals, and antioxidants available in organically grown foods. What you save at the grocery store today you may end up spending in health-care costs tomorrow. So eating organically may be much cheaper in the long run. And, of course, there is the benefit to the environment of organic farming methods. The devastation caused by conventional farming has been exhaustively documented. There are lots of reasons to pay the extra cost of organically grown foods.

Recently, local foods have become almost as sought-after as organics. Across North America, people are rallying to help the environment by buying local. Restaurants are noting their local food sources on their menus; stores are identifying local produce. Since most of the food North Americans eat is not locally produced, this new interest in local and seasonal eating needs to be nurtured and promoted until many of our environmental problems can begin to be turned around. I think the way to do this is through education and re-education.

Now, more than ever, people in the western world are eating for taste. Anything and everything we crave is available to us—at the twenty-four-hour supermarket, the drive-through fast food outlet, the corner store, the chichi food boutique, the local food co-op, or the farmers' market. North Americans have been spoiled with choice, and giving up our foods from far away will seem like real deprivation to those of us who like the taste of fresh strawberries when there is snow on the ground. But I believe that if most people really understood the impact that carbon emissions from transport trucks or from huge industrial greenhouses are having on our world they would willingly save the delights of strawberries for a time when they are available locally. I hope our schools and the media will partake in the job of educating people about why eating locally grown food is so important.

The other major change in the last fifty years has happened to our taste buds. Companies that produce processed foods, which have become a major component of most people's diets, have recognized the addictive nature of foods that contain additives and fats that are tasty but not healthy. If your taste buds are used to a diet with lots of fat, salt, and other additives, you will need to re-educate them before they will say yum to a big bowl of steamed greens with nutritional yeast. But re-educate them you can. The pay-off comes in the knowledge that you are not clogging your arteries, but instead giving your body what it needs to repair itself and become healthy. You can see the effects of the typical North American diet when you look at images of the general public that are shown on TV. Celebrities may be keeping their weight under control, but the rest of us are not. Nearly one-third of Americans over the age of twenty are obese and will probably suffer from concomitant health problems (type 2 diabetes, hypertension, heart disease, and increased risk for breast, colon, prostate, and endometrial cancers). A change in the way we approach food would be good for all of us. I hope the informational chapters in this book will help you understand the importance of moving toward local eating, and that the recipes will help you re-educate your taste buds.

Now that you are more knowledgeable about the effects of your eating choices, how will you make your own decisions about what to eat? Will you eat local food whenever you can, even if it is produced by conventional farming methods? Or will you always opt for organics no matter where they are grown? These are decisions you must make for yourself. I can only suggest that you aim for a balance in this and all the other decisions you need to make in life. First Nations people, whose teachings around food are ethically based, tell us that we should always be asking: "What will be my gift to the universe?" Where the gift of your eating choices is best bestowed is up to you. Remember to keep in mind the balance between care for yourself, for other beings (including those in the future), and for the environment.

MY NON-LOCAL PANTRY (OF COURSE, YOUR LIST WILL BE RELATIVE TO WHERE YOU LIVE)

- Agave nectar *is a neutral-tasting and sometimes raw sweetener. Raw local honey would be a local alternative for some recipes, but it's not vegan.*

- Almonds *are a great source of calcium and the only nut that mildly alkalinizes the system (that's a good thing).*

- Cacao and chocolate products *(fair trade) we love for their taste and try to rationalize our eating of them by exclaiming what a great source of antioxidants and magnesium they are. Carob might be a more local substitute for chocolate, but I'm not in the camp that believes they're all that interchangeable when it comes to flavor.*

- Chia seeds *are great source of omega-3 fatty acids and fiber, and though they're exponentially more expensive than flax seeds, they're also more easily digested. I use sprouted chia (I buy it that way) on cereal or in a smoothie, or whole seeds in a pudding or porridge.*

- Coconut oil, *as long as it's non-hydrogenated, may be more heart-healthy than other saturated fats and is good for frying, as it has a higher smoking point than olive or sunflower oils. It's gorgeously rich and makes flaky pie crusts and biscuits. You can use it on the outside of your body, too, for smoother skin and hair. Organic butter would be a local cooking alternative for many recipes, but it's not vegan (or acceptable for people with dairy allergies).*

- Dates *make a great source of fruit sugar, and are very popular in raw treats. They're a good "build-up" food, beneficial for people suffering from weakness. Organic raisins would be a local alternative for some recipes, but their flavor and texture aren't all that similar to dates.*

- Gogi berries, *which typically come from Tibet, taste fruity and a little smoky to me. They have eighteen kinds of amino acids, including all eight essential amino acids (like isoleucine and tryptophan), as well as about twenty essential and trace minerals (the main ones being zinc, iron, copper, calcium, selenium, and phosphorus). I soak the berries before blending them into smoothies or snack on them with equal parts cacao nibs and pumpkin seeds. Raisins or dried cranberries could be a more local replacement, but they don't match the gogi berries' flavor or nutritional value.*

- Olive oil, *the really good, cold pressed, extra-virgin, single-estate stuff in particular, is delicious. It's also a versatile culinary oil for salad oils and for cooking. Oleic acid, which is the main fat in olive oil, contains vitamin E and carotenoids, which are antioxidants, and olive oil can displace omega-6 fats without affecting omega-3 fats, which leads to a healthier balance of those fats in the body. You can use olive oil (a mild-tasting, late-harvest olive oil is best) for baking and pastry recipes because the olive essence disappears in the cooking. Organic butter would be a local alternative for some recipes, but it's not vegan (or acceptable for people with dairy allergies). Local flax seed oil makes a nice omega-rich alternative in many salad dressings (and other recipes where the oil is not heated), but should not be used in cooking.*

- Quinoa—*there's no other grain like this one, in my opinion. It provides calcium, protein, and fiber, and has a fun look and texture. I use it as a side dish or as a base ingredient in a grain salad.*

- Rice (brown) *is a great source of gluten-free fiber. The long-grain variety is a nice addition to a plate of Indian food, and the short grains are great in sushi.*

- Sea salt *helps make other flavors in food pop. If you live near an ocean you could boil down some water to make your own salt, but I'm not sure just how many salt-eaters would be willing to do that.*

- Sea vegetables *have a nutritionally impressive selection of minerals and contain lignans and vitamin K. They are often a more absorbable option than a mineral supplement and have been used to help balance the endocrine system.*

- Spices *offer a fantastic array of flavors that not only make meals exciting but are also very healing for the digestive system and generally have anti-inflammatory effects on the body. Cinnamon (½ to 2 tsp daily), for example, helps to balance blood-sugar levels and inhibits the growth of bad bacteria in the gut. Other spices that get regular use in my kitchen include black pepper, cardamom, cayenne, chipotle pepper, cloves, cumin, ginger, nutmeg, and turmeric.*

- Sugar (organic, fair trade)—*sometimes you just want the crunch that sugar gives a cookie or the top crust of a loaf, muffin, or pie. Maple sugar would be a local (in my part of the world) and more nutritionally beneficial but also very expensive substitute (which I would be happy to make when I either get rich or marry a maple farmer).*

THE SLIPPERY SIDE OF BANANAS

I am a great enjoyer of bananas—always have been. They make an impressive egg-replacer, adding moisture, sweetness, and an improved texture to baked goods. Contributing a thick creaminess, they're practically essential for a satisfying smoothie. On their own, they're also a satisfying, quick snack when you're looking for something denser than an apple or pear but less heavy than some sort of bread product. Nutritionally, they're a good source of vitamin B_6 and a good source of vitamin C, potassium, dietary fiber, and manganese. Organic bananas give you quite a bang for your buck (compared to other produce), and are available all year round.

And it's all that that makes it hard for me to tell you this. First, here in North America bananas do not grow near most of us, since they need a tropical climate. Second, we need to consider the history and politics of banana production.

Bananas started out in Southeast Asia and were domesticated (bred to produce tastier fruit with tiny seeds) long ago. Foods travel with traders or armies, and so they spread to Africa and across the north of Africa to Spain. When Europeans began to colonize tropical countries they found that they could make money by buying (or taking) land that had been used for subsistence farming and turning it into "plantations" that produced a single product, often a tropical fruit, for export. Plantation owners found that they could protect their investments by getting involved in the local politics and making sure that the governments gave them what they needed (tax breaks, few annoying labor laws that protect workers, etc.), hence the description of some of these countries as "banana republics."

The big companies became bigger and were able to outsell the smaller farmers because of economies of scale. These big companies also found they could make more money if they used pesticides and even more if they didn't provide protective clothing to the workers who were spraying the toxic chemicals. Dole and Chiquita are the major banana producers for the North American and European markets. There is currently a lawsuit against Dole by the heirs of seventy-three workers who claim that the company provided protection money to a paramilitary organization (known as the AUC) that the US government has designated a terrorist group. Dole is now accused of contributing, through this payout, to the murder of trade unionists, banana workers, and organizers who were targeted and killed by the AUC. It's sad to think that the cheap bananas in our grocery stores have made the people who grew them sick and, in some cases, led to their deaths.

Fair-trade bananas have been grown so as to take care of the needs of the workers as well as the needs of the owners. Buy fair-trade bananas if you can, and if your store does not carry them, request that they do. Say you will pay more for them. Many stores think of bananas as "loss leaders," cheap foods that bring people into the store. You can use your consumer power to help protect banana plantation workers.

Third, there's the issue of extinction. Originally, there were lots of different types of bananas (and there still are in the countries where they are grown). It is more lucrative, however, for large plantations to cultivate just one type of banana. The bananas that most North Americans and Europeans know and love, those grown and sold by Dole and Chiquita, are called the Cavendish cultivar. When you grow only one type of any food, you make yourself vulnerable to any pest or disease that that particular crop cannot fight. The Cavendish is now under attack by such a disease, which may mean that it may not be able to be grown on a large scale ten to twenty years from now. Tests are being done to see if a genetically modified version of the Cavendish can be created that will resist the disease. (See *Get It Ripe* for concerns about genetically modified organisms or GMOs.) Hybrids are also being developed.

Fourth, there's the banana's carbon footprint. As with most foods, determining carbon footprint is complex. You have to consider the footprint of the fertilizers, pesticides, and machinery that have been used to grow and harvest the fruit. Bananas are picked green, and their transportation requires refrigeration to keep them in this state until they arrive at their destination. They are usually shipped via ocean freighter and then trucked to depots in refrigerated

containers. When they arrive at their retail destinations, they are stored at a slightly higher temperature, often in the presence of ethylene gas to promote ripening. If they have been packaged in any way, the footprint of that process must also be included. Chiquita Brands International is working with the Massachusetts Institute of Technology's Energy Initiative Research team to try to identify ways they can determine and reduce their banana-production carbon footprint.

So enjoy fair-trade bananas in moderation, but if you can wean yourself off them entirely, even better.

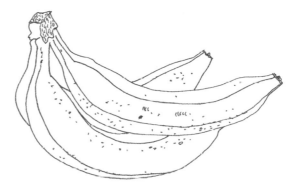

Chapter 4: Friends and Neighbors: Seeing Your Community through Food Goggles

"Local eating isn't just switching the foods you used to buy at the supermarket for local foods that are the same, it's about changing the way you live, and the relationship you have with the people who produce your food, and the place that you live in. If you only go halfway there you miss the deepest parts of the experience."
—James (J.B.) MacKinnon, *The 100 Mile Challenge* (Food Network Canada)

BACK TO THE LAND

We humans haven't always farmed. For millions of years our ancestors hunted and gathered their food. But with the end of the most recent Ice Age, about 12,000 years ago, we began to understand how saving seeds to plant each year would enable us to grow more food than we were previously able to find. We figured out how to use tools to plough and how to enrich the soil with natural fertilizers (manure), and we were in business. In places that were really suitable for farming, great civilizations arose, built on the surplus food provided by the farmers. You'd think that farmers would be celebrated and treated well in this system. After all, they made it possible. But no. The folks who were able to take power did not really give credit where it was due and proceeded to tax farmers into poverty and often near starvation. Farm owners were sometimes rich—but agricultural workers? Those who tilled the fields and harvested the crops? Never.

Enter the industrial revolution. The nineteenth century saw another big change in the way we humans in "civilized" countries lived. Wealth now began to move from those who owned and controlled land to those who owned and controlled industries. In Europe, poverty-stricken farmworkers left farms in droves to try to find work in the new factories that were springing up in the cities. (This same phenomenon is occurring in China today.) Those who were left working the farms continued to eke out a living.

This brings us to farming in the twentieth and twenty-first centuries. With the development of advanced farm machinery, petroleum-based fertilizers, and chemical pesticides, farming changed again. The horse and plow disappeared and, in developed countries, agribusiness began to replace the family farm. Small-scale farmers who grew most of their own food and who were able, with the help of neighboring farmers, to meet the nutritional needs of all the families in their communities began to disappear, supplanted by huge agribusinesses growing food for export to whoever would pay the best price. Small farmers were seldom able to compete. Now, in the twenty-first century, family farms continue to scrape by if they are lucky and the weather holds.

You might imagine that if you were able to examine the total output of all North American farms, you would see great amounts of affordable food that would represent a balanced diet for all. Sadly, this is not the case.

If we look at what farmers are growing here in Canada, for instance, we see that like most business folks, they try to grow what they know they can sell at a good price. Most of Canada's farmland is devoted to field crops like wheat, barley, and corn. Between the years 2000 and 2005, prices overall fell, and Canadian farmers were not doing very well. However, when corn prices rose in 2006 (mainly to supply those who make ethanol for fuel), farmers planted more of it. This drove up the price of the displaced crops, like oats and barley. Seed oils like canola have also become very popular, and they too went up in price in 2006. Farmers who had these crops in long-term storage sold them and managed to push up the total cash receipts of all farms in Canada by ten percent over the year before. Much of the food grown by Canadian agribusiness farms is grown for export. This is where the money is. Consequently, we are forced to import much of the food we need to eat well.

There is some good news, however. According to Statistics Canada, organic farming is growing by leaps and bounds. The number of farmers growing organic crops increased by nearly sixty percent from 2001 to 2006. This sounds great, but organic farms make up only 1.5 percent of Canada's 229,373 (or so) agricultural operations. As in conventional farming, the major organic crops grown in Canada are hay and field ones like wheat and barley—most of which is exported. (You need organic food for those organic cows.) Oil seeds, chick peas, and lentils are also grown. Some of these are

processed for humans to eat, and some fed to livestock. In 2006 less than one-third of Canada's certified organic farmers reported growing fruits and vegetables (instead they grow the aforementioned field crops). The problem Canadian small organic fruit and vegetable farmers have is that they are in competition with the larger organic farms in the US (like Earthbound Farms in California). These big operations can undercut the prices of the small farmers because of economies of scale. What the small farmers are hoping is that the demand for local will intersect with the demand for organics. At that point, their produce will be seen as preferable, even though they must charge more than the larger organic farms that now supply major Canadian supermarkets with most of their organic produce.

While the shift to organic farming is strong among farmers, the job of farming itself seems to be threatened. In 2008 an Ontario organic farmer told a Toronto newspaper that "[i]n the last five years we've lost more than 20,000 farms in Canada. We're seeing generations of farm equity lost." The problem is that farmers can no longer make a living just from farming. Many are moving from growing fruits and vegetables to cash crops and livestock. When land developers offer them money for a farm that has been providing an income of only $5,000 a year (and sometimes less), they are often tempted to jump at it. If you look closely at this situation, you will see that the economic philosophy of capitalism underlies the food industry in much the same way that it underlies the auto industry or the world of computer technology. Maybe it's time for a change.

But the picture painted above is clearly not one that promotes food security. The Food and Agriculture Organization of the United Nations declared at the World Food Summit in 1996: "Food security exists when all people, at all times, have equal access to a safe, personally acceptable, nutritious diet through a sustainable food system that maximizes healthy choices and community self-reliance." We need to change the way we look at food production if we want to provide not only Canadians but all citizens of the world with food security. A person who is doing just that is Carlo Petrini, the founder of Slow Food International. Petrini claims that capitalism has led us to believe that development is a process that will go on forever. This philosophy portrays nature as an infinite resource. He says we have treated the earth that provides our food as if there were no need to reinvest in it, no need to help rebuild the soils we deplete or clean the water we poison. What has recently become apparent to anyone who reads the news is that this is not true. We are looking at a global environmental crisis, and we need to do something about it. Luckily for us, Slow Food International and the Slow Money movement, led by Woody Tasch, have answers that will address the problems we now face, and you and I can be part of the solution.

I won't dwell on the statistics about what our present consumer societies have done to the planet. If you need convincing, you can read Tasch's book, *Inquiries into the Nature of Slow Money: Investing As If Food, Farms, and Fertility Mattered*. For now, I'll offer just one statistic that I think you might want to remember and tell others about. An inch of topsoil can take anywhere from 100 to 1,000 years to be replaced, depending on where it is on the planet. According to a World Resources Institute report, topsoil is disappearing at a rate of sixteen to 300 times faster than it can be replaced. No topsoil = no food. But we can all do something to help. Organic farmers commit to reinvesting in the soil. Support organic farmers by buying organic produce whenever possible. Ask your supermarket if they can source local organic produce instead of, or as well as, that from the mega-sized organic farms.

SLOW MONEY

In order to enhance food safety and food security; promote cultural and ecological health and diversity; and accelerate the transition from an economy based on extraction and consumption to an economy based on preservation and restoration, we do hereby affirm the following Principles:

- *We must bring money back down to earth.*

- *There is such a thing as money that is too fast, companies that are too big, finance that is too complex. Therefore, we must slow our money down—not all of it, of course, but enough to matter.*

- *The 20th Century economy was an economy of Buy Low/Sell High and Wealth Now/ Philanthropy Later—what one venture capitalist called "the largest legal accumulation of wealth in history." The 21st Century economy will usher in the era of nurture capital, built around principles of carrying capacity, care of the commons, sense of place and non-violence.*

- *We must learn to invest as if food, farms and fertility mattered. We must steer major new sources of capital to small food enterprises.*

- *Let us celebrate the new generation of entrepreneurs, consumers and investors who are showing the way from Making A Killing to Making a Living.*

- *Paul Newman said, "I just happen to think that in life we need to be a little like the farmer who puts back into the soil what he takes out." Recognizing the wisdom of these words, let us begin rebuilding our economy from the ground up, asking:*

  i. *What would the world be like if we invested 50 percent of our assets within 50 miles of where we live?*

  ii. *What if there were a new generation of companies that gave away 50 percent of their profits?*

  iii. *What if there were 50 percent more organic matter in our soil 50 years from now?*

Not Far from the Tree: Community food-security action

My good friend Lisa best describes this relatively new organization enjoying much popularity in Toronto:

When I moved to Toronto, I never envisioned that I would find myself harvesting fruit from high atop a backyard tree as the sun set over the city skyline. I never saw Toronto as a fruit-bearing place before I got involved with Not Far from the Tree; now I can't wander through the streets without being overwhelmed by how many trees are bursting with apples, pears, cherries, apricots, mulberries, etc. It has completely changed the way I see the city.

Not Far from the Tree (NFFTT) is an organization that has helped many others to make this critical connection. They provide the opportunity for fruit-tree owners to register to have their tree harvested by volunteers. The bounty is then divided up: with one third staying with the tree-owner, one third delivered to a direct-service organization (food banks, shelters, etc.), and one third shared among the volunteer pickers. In NFFTT's first year, we picked over 3,000 pounds of fruit from backyards, and by the end of the 2009 Season, NFFTT had harvested 8,135 pounds of fruit!

A pick is an incredible collaboration because it involves so many different players in the process of bringing fresh fruit to people. The fruit tree owners are often grateful to have help accessing the fruit and managing the amount of produce that ripens all at once. I have picked for a lot of older individuals, women with young babies to tend to, and couples who just can't keep up with a fruitful tree. The volunteers are often young professionals living in rental properties, apartment buildings, and condos. For many of them, this is an opportunity to be an active part of creating a food system that makes fresh produce accessible. They often find themselves engaged throughout the neighborhood during a pick: meeting people while trying to obtain the perfect-sized ladder, searching for another cloth bag, or explaining how others can get involved by registering their trees. Neighborhoods seem to come alive during a pick, creating the opportunity for people to meet after living next door for years. The volunteers are often surprised by what Toronto trees produce; many never imagined they would find themselves toting home bags of cherries from a neighbor's backyard.

cont'd...

By volunteering with NFFTT, you learn a lot about seasonality, as the window of time for each fruit seems so short and so bountiful. I find myself unable to ponder eating one more apricot just as we move on to harvesting plums. We are learning to maximize the potential of this fruit by creating canning workshops and regular preserving events. Last year volunteers learned about preserving pears and apples using the acidic properties of crab apples and sumac. We learned to dry fruit, create sweet fruit leathers, and freeze purées for future baking projects. The direct-service agencies received jars and bags full of preserved products that help them provide nutrient-rich treats well into the winter. One of the hubs this year is hosting a weekly community preserving collective.

My involvement with NFFTT has allowed me to see my own role in the food system. It has reminded me of the potential that lies in our soil and in the hands of our communities. I have learned about the history of this city and the heritage varieties of fruit that thrived here. I have been inspired by the families that share their fruit, the volunteers who contribute their passion, and the organizations that distribute the bounty to those who need it most. Plus, there is no better way to enjoy dusk than from the branches of an apple tree in Toronto.

There are similar projects going on in various cities, such as Urban Harvest in Houston TX (*urbanharvest.org*) or KW Urban Harvest in Kitchener-Waterloo ON (*kwurbanharvest.org*). If you can't find something near you, maybe it's a gap you'd like to fill! Visit the NFFTT website for more information and inspiration: *www.notfarfromthetree.org*.

Chapter 5: Health in All Seasons

If you are even the slightest bit of a health nut, you know that all you have to do is go to a couple of workshops or lectures or find a few books or websites that resonate with you, and you can quickly make a list of a thousand habits you can change and foods you need to put in or take out of your diet—immediately. Of course, I always feel the need to remind readers (and clients and even people who want to talk health at parties) that most of us can't change everything overnight and have it stick for any decent amount of time. Even as a health practitioner, I get can get overwhelmed at times—I'm not always certain exactly where I should focus my efforts in moving toward greater health and well-being. I often let the principles of traditional Chinese medicine (TCM), which highlight various elements in particular seasons, be my guide. What a relief to know that in TCM each season is connected to two vital organs and a specific emotion, sensory organ, element, and color.

I encourage you to read the following section on whatever season you're in now and identify one to five things you might try before the seasons change again as a way of developing connection with yourself and the world around you.

RESOURCES:

Haas, Elson M. *Staying Healthy with the Seasons*. Berkeley: Celestial Arts, 2003.

Kaur, Sat Daurum, Mary Danylak-Arhanic, and Carolyn Dean. *The Complete Natural Medicine Guide to Women's Health*. Toronto: Robert Rose, 2005.

Reichstein, Gail. *Wood Becomes Water: Chinese Medicine in Everyday Life*. New York: Kodansha International, 1998.

(For more information, see pp. 255–257.)

SPRING

I know that spring in the northern hemisphere technically begins at the end of March, but here in Ontario things are slow to start. There's nothing like those first precious warm days to help thaw out my winter hibernation tendencies. I'm thrilled when magnolia trees around the city gorgeously burst into bloom. It's a time for new beginnings. On nearby farms, farmers are sprouting seedlings indoors, waiting for the weather to warm up and the ground to thaw before they can begin planting in the fields. The abundance of summer produce can still seem a long way away, but I notice that even on the grey wet days of spring, things are green and budding. If you're looking to get involved in a Community Supported Agriculture (CSA) food-box program, now's the time to act fast, as farmers' lists are likely filling up.

According to TCM, spring is the season to care for your liver, eat sour foods, and address your anger. Your liver, situated under your ribcage on the right side of your body, does an impressive 400-plus things for you each day, including the filtration of toxins (like alcohol, drugs, and germs). There's a lot you can do to show it some love and help it to function effectively.

Come spring, fresh produce becomes available in a big way, and we can start to enjoy local asparagus, baby greens, dandelion greens, radishes, and spinach to get some important minerals and fiber into our bods. Steam or grill the asparagus, put the dandelion greens in a salad or through your juicer, dip radishes into your favorite hummus, and pour hot soup over organic baby spinach or blend those tender spinach leaves into a berry smoothie. Just be sure that at least half your plate is covered in vegetables at every meal! The liver is especially fond of the phytonutrients of vegetables found in the Brassica family (not necessarily all of these are in season in spring) such as bok choy, broccoli, Brussels sprouts, cabbage, cauliflower, collards, and kale.

Enjoy foods that are said to nourish the Wood element (ideally, if in season locally for you): barley, oats, rye; green lentils, mung beans, black-eyed peas, split peas, peanuts; globe artichokes, green peppers, broccoli, raw carrots, lettuce, parsley, green beans, rhubarb, summer squash (zucchini, patty pan); sour apples, sour cherries, avocado, sour currants, coconut, grapefruit, kiwi, lemon, lime, sour oranges, pineapple, plum, pomegranate, quince; alfalfa; bay leaf, caraway, cumin, dill, marjoram, nutmeg, tarragon, cloves; Brazil nuts, cashews.

The mention of sour brings citrus to mind, of course, so start spiking your water with fresh lemon juice. This is especially beneficial and refreshing to do first thing in the morning (I'm talking pre-coffee, if that's part of your established wake-up routine). Limes are just fine too.

If you're often feeling angry, now may be the time to take a look at it. Five minutes of conscious breathing—first thing in the morning, last thing at night, or whenever you need it—make a real difference when you make it a daily habit. If something really gets on your nerves, instead of wallowing in feeling pissy, make a deliberate effort to conjure up the most pleasant feeling you can think of. It could be something or someone in your life you feel good about, or simply the smell of spring in the air.

GROW YOUR OWN: CONTAINER GARDENING WITH URBAN ACRE

Most of my friends are renters, not homeowners, which means that they can't always be sure that their outdoor space will be in the same place from one year to the next—heck, they may not even have  access to a garden. They may be lucky enough to have a porch, balcony, or back deck, though, where they can do some container gardening. Other folks may have a driveway but don't own a car, and would like to come up with an alternative use for it. All of these people appreciate the juicy goodness of a tomato fresh from the vine or the delicate crispness of recently picked salad greens. They, like me, may not have been born with the greenest of thumbs, but would like to try their hand at producing food as local as it comes—just a few feet away from the kitchen door.

With bucket planters, growing veggies and herbs is cheap, effective, and fun—even for lazy gardeners. My good friend Ryan Johnston, who studied permaculture and market gardening on Cortes Island in BC and now has his own company, Urban Acre, in Toronto, is keen on finding urban spaces to grow good clean food and encouraging others to do so in whatever city space they have, no matter how small. For Ryan, it's a joyful action in response to conventional food systems.

Bucket planters, a.k.a. sub-irrigation planter (SIP) systems, are his thing. He was introduced to them by the Montreal-based community organization Santropol Roulant and adapted their design. These planters are similar in design to a common self-watering pot or container. The principle behind the effectiveness of this design relies on capillary irrigation.

"Capillary irrigation" sounds high-tech, but in this context, it's very simple. It refers to the ability of soil to move water from wet areas to dry ones. Think of the wicking action that happens when you put a drop of water on a piece of paper towel. The water rapidly wicks away from the place where it was dropped. In a bucket planter, water from beneath the planting bucket is wicked up into the soil through a porous tube. In conventional farming or gardening, the water is applied to the surface of the soil. The SIP system allows plants to be self-regulating; moisture and nutrients are taken up into the growing mixture and the roots of the plants from the water beneath, as needed.

The advantages of this type of container for gardening are many. First of all, the buckets are light. If you've ever used a big terracotta planter you know that, especially when filled with wet, dense soil, it can be super heavy. Bucket planters, especially before their water reservoirs are filled, are really lightweight and easy to move. You can put them wherever you have enough sun to grow vegetables; this may be your sunny balcony, an accessible rooftop, or even an area covered in concrete. Five to six hours of daily direct sunlight will be enough to grow most things. Also, if you need to move your planter around once it is filled and planted (perhaps to take advantage of the sun each day), it can easily be placed on wheels to transport. In cold climates, where roofs are often constructed to support a heavy weight of snow, these planters are perfect for rooftop gardening. In the summer, the only added weight is that of the water in the reservoir and the light potting mix; in the winter, the planters can be turned upside down to be stored, adding almost nothing to the weight on the roof.

The lazy or busy gardener can relax, as plants in these containers mostly water themselves. When plants in conventional pots are in full sun they often need watering on a daily basis or even twice daily. But with this system, you can go away for days at a time knowing that your lettuce will not shrivel up and die. Also, conventional planters are watered from the top. However, most of the water will evaporate before it gets to where the plants need it most—at the roots. You don't need to worry about overwatering, either. Most plant roots need oxygen; having them sit in water is not a good thing. In this system, you don't need to worry about root rot.

Your veggies are only as healthy as the soil in which they're grown. Your backyard soil, or the soil of your neighborhood garden plot, may contain traces of harmful chemicals such as weed killers or lead from old paints or gas fumes. To find out about the quality of your soil, you can send a sample away for testing.

(If you search "soil testing" online, you should find a number of websites that will help you find what you need.) With buckets, you can determine the quality of soil in which your plants grow.

A nice light soil works best for your bucket planter; the planter soils sold at many grocery stores and garden shops are good to use. They are usually a mixture of peat, vermiculite, and composted soil. This makes them light but able to hold moisture. If you want to improve the quality of the nutrients feeding your plants, you can make compost tea from the lovely soil that your vermi-composter is producing (see p. 68). You can also make a nutritious watering liquid from kelp meal (1 tbsp meal to 1 qt/L hot water. Allow to steep and cool before use.).

Another advantage of bucket planters is that they can be made from plastic buckets that would otherwise be thrown away. Reclaiming plastic containers in order to grow organic greens and heirloom tomatoes is a great act of resistance! You can reuse something that has been made without any care for the earth to help green the planet. Visit local restaurants or their recycling bins to find the buckets that you need. Use food-grade buckets and definitely avoid chemical cleaner containers. If you aren't the DIY type, you can now find a model similar to Ryan's design (described below) called the EarthBox, available at Whole Foods, although it costs over fifty dollars, which is more than the annual fee for most community garden plots that have 100 times the growing space.

HERE'S WHAT YOU NEED TO BUILD YOUR OWN CAPILLARY IRRIGATION BUCKET PLANTER:

16-qt/L plastic bucket(s), one for each planter

10.5 qt/L bucket(s), one for each planter (a little trickier to find free; try a hardware store)

a 1.5-in/3.8 cm (diameter) PVC pipe—each bucket requires a piece 16-in/41 cm long

a 4-in/10-cm (diameter) PVC pipe, 5-in/12.7 cm long, 1 for each bucket

caps for the 4-in PVC pipe, one for each planter

hacksaw (for cutting pipes)

drill with:

> 1/8–1/4-in drill bit (for perforating pipe)
>
> 1/2-in hole saw
>
> 4-in hole saw (cutting diameter 4 1/4 in)

a 3–4-in/7.6–10 cm diameter funnel

coir fiber (from coconut husks)

soil for container planting

seeds or seedlings

To assemble:

1 | You'll likely want to make more than one planter and/or have a planter-building party with some similarly interested friends. An assembly-line setup can be more time- and labor-efficient (to limit the amount of time needed to change the drill bit, for example) than putting each one together from start to finish one by one.

2 | You may be inspired to first pull out your safety glasses. Start by cutting the longer pieces of PVC into proper lengths with the hacksaw. Cutting the PVC is easier if you set up a miter box on a work table or work horse. This will ensure a nice straight cut.

3 | For the 16-qt/L bucket design (the one Ryan prefers), the refilling tube should be made with 1.5-in PVC pipe that's 16-in long, just long enough for the pipe to extend above the surface of the soil. Cut the bottom on a bit of an angle.

4 | Now you are going to make the wick section. Again, put on those safety glasses. Using the hacksaw and miter box, cut a 5-in/13-cm length of 4-in/10-cm (inside measure) PVC pipe. Five inches is the distance from the inside of the 10.5-qt/L bucket to the bottom of the 16-qt/L bucket underneath. Keeping the pipe in the miter box, use a 1/8- to 1/4-in drill bit to perforate the pipe by drilling about twenty holes around the surface from top to bottom. The holes allow the water to penetrate the soil mixture inside. Put on the separate PVC caps for the bottoms of these pieces.

5 | Next comes the fun bit. You will need to invest in a couple of hole saws, one 1.5-in/4-cm in diameter and the other 4-in/10-cm. (Get together with some other bucket gardeners to share the cost.) In the 10.5-qt/L bucket, first drill the hole for the 4-in/10-cm pipe. Drill the hole right through the center of the bottom of the bucket. To do this you might want to anchor the bottom with your feet or have a pal hold the bucket tight. *Important*: Start drilling at a high speed and drill with light downward pressure. This will get you started right. Once the cut has been started, slow the speed and gently add more downward pressure. (If you have a drill with an adjustable clutch, set it to 10/15.) The clutch reacts to resistance, which can occur if you are applying too much downward pressure, and the hole saw will snag. Please use caution.

6 | Next, drill the hole for the refilling pipe. This is done the same way as the first hole except you will use the smaller hole saw and position the drill bit closer to the edge of the bucket. If you're too close to the other hole, you run the risk of tearing the plastic between the two holes.

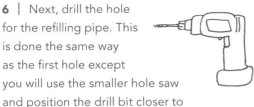

7 | Once all the pipes are cut to length, the 4-in one is perforated, and the 10.5-qt/L bucket has its two holes, you're ready to assemble the planter. Keeping the 16-qt/L bucket aside, push your PVC pipes through the smaller bucket you've prepared. The fit should be snug, so this will take some effort. Work the pipes through by pushing them with a firm downward pressure from all angles to stretch the plastic a little. You'll eventually get it.

8 | Once you have both tubes in, go ahead and insert the smaller bucket into the larger one to fit it all together. The last part of construction involves drilling an overflow hole in the 16-qt/L bucket using an 1/8-in bit. Drill just below the level/height of the bucket on the inside. Now you're ready to add the soil.

9 | Fill the inside bucket with potting soil. Fill the reservoir (the space between the two buckets) with water through the filler tube until the water starts leaking out the just-drilled overflow hole.

10 | When you decide to plant your seeds or seedlings will depend on what you want to grow and where you live. You'll want to consult a good gardening manual or online sources (both listed below) to get a sense of how to show the particular plants you're growing the special love they need.

11 | At the end of the growing season, empty the buckets and wash them out so they're ready for the following year. They can be stored outdoors or indoors, under your porch, or in the garage—wherever you have space for them. (Good thing they stack well!)

Ryan is always asked if bucket planters can be used to grow vegetables indoors. He doesn't recommend it, as indoor plants don't need the amount of moisture that vegetable plants exposed to the elements do and which a capillary irrigation system offers.

RESOURCES:
Books:

Coleman, Eliot. *Four Season Harvest: How to Harvest Fresh Organic Vegetables from Your Home Gardens All Year Long.* White River Junction, VT: Chelsea Green Pub., 1999.
Newcomb, Duane G. and Karen. *The Postage Stamp Kitchen Garden Book.* Cincinnati, OH, 1998.
Olson, Michael. *MetroFarm: The Guide to Growing for Big Profit on a Small Parcel of Land.* Santa Cruz, CA: TS Books, 1994.

Websites:
The Rooftop Garden Project: *rooftopgardens.ca*
You Grow Girl: *yougrowgirl.com*

SUMMER

I am one of those people who *loves* summer. Yep, I'm a summer lover. I'm never the first one to ask for air conditioning because the heat just feels so good, and I fantasize about summer throughout the rest of the year. It's a wonder I haven't yet moved to somewhere more tropical than Canada. Summer in the city can be smelly (the year there was a garbage-collector strike in Toronto in July is particularly memorable for my friend Liz, who was pregnant then), but it also feels very alive to me during this time. On farms, summer is a busy time, what with everything green and growing and needing to be maintained with watering and weeding; more veg and fruit in brighter colors are ready to be harvested.

Traditional Chinese medicine (TCM) tells us that summer is the season to be good to your heart (which pumps blood around your body, nourishing your cells, organs, and so on) and your small intestine (which is responsible for absorbing nutrients from the food you eat). It's the time to explore joy and sorrow, the time to sweat (how appropriate), the time to care for your blood and blood vessels, and it's the time to have some really good laughs.

Use summer as a reason to:

- Add liquid chlorophyll to your water: it is said to cleanse the blood and is considered an internal deodorizer, helping your breath, your sweat, and even your farts smell sweeter.
- Set up constant reminders for yourself that the purpose of life is joy. If you're not a believer yet, just make time to consider it.

- Surround yourself with people who make you laugh, rent comedies on DVD, and foster the ability to laugh at yourself.
- Work up a good sweat at least twice a week.
- Switch over from a conventional antiperspirant (like most of the kinds you get at the drug or grocery store with hard-to-pronounce ingredients) to a natural deodorant. You may need to try a few before finding one that works for you. If you're a smelly or profuse perspirer, a more detoxifying diet (more water, more veggies, more fruits, more organics) and lifestyle (avoid situations and habits that are not health-supporting) will help reduce the strong smell (although it may get worse before it gets better—that's the nature of detoxification).
- In the early summer, enjoy foods that are said to nourish the Fire element (ideally if in season locally for you): amaranth, yellow corn; red lentils; asparagus, arugula, red bell peppers, bok choy, Brussels sprouts, chives, collard greens, dandelion (both root and greens), kale, mustard greens, okra, snow peas, scallions, Swiss chard, turnip greens, tomatoes; apricot, guava, raspberries, strawberries; sesame and sunflower seeds, pistachios.
- In TCM, the late summer is about the spleen and the stomach. It's when you might look to give and receive sympathy. And the focus is more on the flesh and muscles during this period.

This is the time to:

- Work on being adaptable.
- Explore your access to deep relaxation. Perhaps take up meditation, or find some guided visualizations that work for you. Breathe deeply to nourish all the cells in your body, from your brain right down to your toes.
- Work on a balanced intake of everything in your life.
- Figure out what the word "faith" means to you and whether you want it and don't have it, have it, don't have enough, or aren't sure what it is.
- Explore any resistance you have to change. Try challenging yourself with something different, new, unexpected, "unlike you" each week. When change falls in your path, see what you can do to embrace it, accept it, or simply not fight against it.
- If you are hooked on some sort of drug—street drugs, pain meds, coffee, whatever—consider getting off them in some sort of holistic way. I typically subscribe to the idea that "slow and steady wins the race," but something else ("cold turkey"?) may be more effective for you.
- Look out for shallow breathing, nervous eating, and feelings of apprehension. Explore these things (can you relate them to a particular moment in your day? What purpose do they serve for you?), and let go of them.
- In the late summer, enjoy foods that are said to nourish the Earth element (ideally if in season locally for you): millet; chickpeas; corn on the cob, eggplant, Jerusalem artichoke, parsnip, sweet potato, winter squash; sweet apples, banana, cantaloupe, honeydew and muskmelon, sweet currants, dates, figs, grapes, mango, mulberries, sweet oranges, papaya, prunes, raisins, sweet cherries, tangerines; pumpkin seeds; allspice, anise, cardamom, cinnamon, licorice, turmeric, vanilla; almonds, hazelnuts, pecans, pine nuts, macadamia nuts.

CAN DO! PRESERVING THE BOUNTY

Truth be told, I've only canned twice in my life. I don't know why it hasn't become more of a summer ritual for me, but maybe this chapter will help make it a bigger part of my culinary life (and yours). The first time I tried it, it was strawberry jam with my friend Adrienne. We went to a berry u-pick just outside the city, and then we brought all those sweet and plump red jewels home and got to work. Wow, was it delicious! (I really do think putting our own hands in food projects improves taste.) The second time was with my dear friend Elise Moser (who is herself vegan and an author), when I first moved to Montreal. She was one of my favorite cooking companions while I lived there. I obtained a whole lot of local apples and brought them over to her kitchen, which had large pots, special tongs, and jars with lids that sealed. We cooked ourselves up a pretty pink mash (keeping apple skins on gives you pink applesauce), and sealed it up in jars to enjoy for months.

I asked Elise, creative home canner that she is, if she'd join us for this tutorial on preserving (also known as "putting up"), and she kindly obliged.

One of the most exciting parts about canning is that it allows you to have more control over your food supply. You can eat locally and seasonally available foods throughout the year. There's nothing like opening a jar of fragrant, fresh-tasting Ontario peaches in December—it's like sweet sunshine in a jar. It allows you to eat foods you can't find out of season or can't rationalize dishing out the dough for in the supermarket. I first started to can because my roommate's sister sent him a jar of dilled green beans and they were so delicious, I wanted more. It's a common enough recipe in canning books, but I've never seen a jar of dilled beans in the store. Similarly, I often slip a sage leaf into my peaches. It is a surprisingly lovely taste, but I've never seen that for sale anywhere either. I can my fruit with little or no sugar, and my salsa with extra chilies.

Canning allows you to buy food in quantity (small or large) when it's cheap. I have two jars of roasted red peppers put away for winter that I would never splurge on if I had to buy them in January. Putting up applesauce when the organic Macintoshes are ripe here, rather than buying apples shipped from another hemisphere later, is much more environmentally sensitive (much less airplane and truck exhaust) and supports farmers who practice sustainable agriculture that preserves our land and water and the insects, birds, and other creatures that live here with us. If you get a CSA basket, sometimes you end up with a giant bag of something you know you'll never eat before it goes bad. You can use it to can a small batch of something and eat it when you're ready. Almost anything can be made into a chutney, and having a few jars of homemade chutney in the cupboard encourages me to eat more of those simple, easy-to-cook grain-and-veg meals, with a spoonful of something sweet and spicy on the side. Canning offers a great opportunity to cook communally; buy in bulk, and then spend an afternoon cultivating relationships with your friends and neighbors. Homemade salsa, jam, or pickles make wonderful, inexpensive gifts. And it's really fun and creative. In a time when mass production has separated us from the fulfillment of most of our basic needs, canning puts us back in touch with the satisfaction of providing our own sustenance— especially if you have a garden. Never again allow a tomato or a zucchini to go to waste!

- You will need a big canning pot, probably one of those blue speckled enamel ones (with a rack that fits inside).
- Get some jars with two-piece metal lids. Jars typically come in half-pint, pint, and quart (or 125mL, 250mL, 500mL and 1 L) sizes. For jam, salsa, and delicacies, the smaller sizes are useful. If you know that in your house you go through a lot of salsa, then by all means, put it in a larger jar.
- Remember that you can reuse your jars almost eternally. Between harvest seasons your jars may end up, as mine do, in the cupboard, filled with dried beans or lentils, or in the fridge filled with leftover soup. (Do not use old jam jars sealed with paraffin, which is no longer considered safe.)
- Get yourself a wide-mouthed canning funnel and a pair of tongs to lift your jars out of the boiling water.
- A generous supply of clean tea towels is helpful, too.
- Canning jar makers (Ball, Mason, Kerr, Bernardin, etc.) offer inexpensive guides to canning, and I recommend getting one of these. It will not only give you some good basic recipes, but will help you troubleshoot.
- Apart from these items, you'll use your basic kitchen stuff: a large, non-reactive soup pot, a wooden spoon, a couple of sizes of silicone spatulas, and a ladle.

The method is very much the same, whatever you're putting up. The routine of canning is designed to preserve food *safely*. Follow *all* the instructions. It's important to get the acid balance right to inhibit growth of dangerous bacteria and mold. Fruits, pickles, salsas, and chutneys are high-acid foods and very safe. Tomatoes, although we think of them as high-acid foods, require added acid (e.g., lemon juice). It's always important to follow a recipe when canning, but especially for tomato products (stewed tomatoes, sauce, etc.) it is extra important to follow the recipe exactly, and not to change the proportions of the ingredients. For foods like prepared stews, soups, and tomatoes without added acid, use a pressure canner rather than the boiling-water bath method detailed here.

Always choose food that is fresh and ready to eat and in good condition. If you put up a jar of under-ripe pears, they will still be hard when you open them at Christmas. Canning is fundamentally cooking, and the food should taste good when you put it in the jar. As with any other kind of cooking, recipes can be helpful to give you ideas, get proportions right, and master the technique. Keep your hands, your tools, and your work surfaces clean. Wash your pots and jars and funnel with very hot soapy water before and after using.

Now that you know all that, here we go, step by step:

1 | Fill your big canning pot with water, cover it with the lid, and put it on the stove to heat. It will take a long time to come to a boil. While it's heating on a back burner, you can prepare the food.

2 | When the pot is boiling, put your still-hot (from the hot dishwashing water) jars into the boiling water and boil to sterilize them. Ten minutes is the most common amount of time, but follow your recipe. I recommend laying out a clean dishtowel on the counter or table nearest the stove, so that when the jars are sterilized they can be transferred onto the clean cloth. I put them neck down so they stay steamy, and only turn each one as I am about to fill it. Keep the water boiling, and set your lids in a small pot to boil for five minutes, so the sealing compound will soften.

3 | If you are making jam, you will have tested it to make sure it has reached the gel stage—not too runny, not too stiff—according to your recipe, and at this point you can ladle the jam in, leaving the required amount of space at the top. If you are making pickles, you'll have turned up all your jars and filled them with your green beans, dill heads, garlic, and peppercorns (or whatever) and then you will ladle your hot brine through the funnel.

4 | When the jars are full, take a clean spatula, preferably narrow, and gently run it around the inside walls of the jar. This will break up any air bubbles that are trapped in the hot food and that could, if allowed to remain, be breeding places for bacteria. A skewer or chopstick might work well for pickles. This might cause some extra air space at the top to form, so you can add a bit more jam or brine to bring it up to the amount of space called for in your recipe.

5 | When the air bubbles are gone, dip a clean dishtowel in boiling water, and use it to wipe the top rim of each jar. This ensures that the lid seals properly, and, like the air-bubble step, is very important for your food's safety.

6 | Using a fork or a special magnetized wand you can buy for this purpose, fish the lids out of their boiled water and press them gently onto the mouth of each jar. Then, holding the lid gently in place with a finger, screw a screwband top onto each jar, just "fingertip tight." (That is, you should be able to unscrew it using just your fingertips.) This leaves a little space for hot air to escape while the jar is being processed in the big boiling water pot, which means that when you lift it out and it hits the cooler air of your kitchen, the vacuum created sucks the lid down hard, sealing your jar. (Then it will make that cute little pop that is music to the ears of every happy canner.)

7 | Put the jars in the rack and then into the big pot, and boil for the amount of time called for in your recipe. Different foods need different processing times, and different-sized jars sometimes do too. Pay attention to these details.

8 | When the jars are processed, lift them out (I suggest tongs in one hand and, in the other, a dishtowel for the boiling water that drips down the sides of the jars). Set each jar on a clean dishtowel that is laid out in a spot where it can sit undisturbed for twenty-four hours. Leave a little space between jars. When the twenty-four hours are up, you can tap the lids. If any of them flexes up and down, it has not sealed. You can still eat the food, but you have to keep this jar in the fridge and eat it soon.

9 | Label each jar with the contents and date. The date is essential. This is a safety issue: you should not eat home-canned foods that are over a year old. It's also practical, because you or the person who receives this jar as a gift may not remember what's in there (my apple-raspberry-vanilla jam, for example, looks just like my strawberry-cherry jam). This also gives you a chance to note any ingredients that might be allergens for people who eat what you make. The label is also a nice place to exercise your creativity. My friend Ingrid often gives herbed vinegars or other homemade food treats for Christmas, and her labels are always simple but beautiful, hand-lettered, and painted with one or two elegant brushstrokes evoking plants or flowers.

10 | Store your booty in a cool, dark place. Enjoy all year. If a jar is not completely sealed when you bring it out of the closet, do not eat the food. ("When in doubt, throw it out" is the rule of thumb here.)

Many canning recipes, especially those sponsored in some way by the makers of canning-related products, will call for their brand of pectin, in liquid or powder form. Pectin is what makes jam or jelly gel, and it is present in many fruits, especially citrus fruit and apples. If you are making jam or jelly out of something that doesn't naturally contain pectin, you'll have to add it. You can make your own pectin out of apples or crabapples, which adds a delicate depth of flavor to your jam, but requires a whole extra series of steps. You can also choose a recipe for, say, strawberry jam made with apples in it, which produces a jam with a slightly less intense strawberry flavor, but requires less sugar and gives a greater yield for less money. If you choose to use packaged pectin, be forewarned that many of them contain lactic acid from animal sources, so you'll have to do some extra research.

FALL

As much as I resist letting go of the warmer, brighter (and sometimes more carefree) days of summer, I do admit that specific signs of autumn are like no other, and I love 'em. That back-to-school feeling, even when you're not going back to school. A crisper smell in the air. Cooler mornings and evenings that require cozy sweaters and close-toed shoes. The birthday presents … wait, don't you get birthday presents in the fall? I do, along with so many other Libras that seem to be ever-present in my life. My mum has always said that my birthday weekend is really the last weekend of the year to have an outdoor party.

When they lived in Montreal, my friends Melina and Carl always had an Apple Party in October. They'd go to an organic u-pick orchard just outside of town with the most incredible tasting fruit. After bringing home a few bushelfuls, they'd invite all their friends (BYOKCB—bring your own knife and cutting board), and we'd all sit on the living room floor, prepping apples as crumbles and pies and sauce were being made in the kitchen. We'd work for what we were fed fresh from the oven that night, and Melina and Carl would have a nice stash of stuff to freeze and can and enjoy for months to come.

Traditional Chinese medicine says that this is the season to heal the lungs and large intestine. Fall also relates to worry or grief; it is time to breathe deep and let go. We can also use this season as a time to pay extra-special attention to our skin and hair.

Enjoy foods that are said to nourish the Metal element (ideally, if in season locally for you): rice; Cannellini, Great Northern, navy, lima, and soy beans, tofu and tempeh; bok choy, cabbage, capers, cauliflower, celery (stalks and roots), cucumber, daikon, garlic, ginger, kohlrabi, leeks, onions, potato, radish, shallots, spinach, turnips, watercress; peach, pears; basil, cayenne, coriander, fennel, fenugreek, mint, pepper, thyme, sage; walnuts.

It's also a good time to:

- quit smoking
- address any bowel issues such as constipation (less than 1–2 poops per day), candida, or parasites. (A good cleanse would be an important starting point for this.)
- do arm massage to improve breathing— from front of shoulders down to your thumbs
- do abdominal massage to improve colon movement
- create a ritual to express or release grief

VERMICOMPOSTING

When I was in school for holistic nutrition, my conversational repertoire was so health-focused that when I called my mum one day and said excitedly, "I've got worms!" she thought I meant pinworms or something.

I was talking about red wrigglers.

Come on, you may be thinking—worms? What do worms have to do with good health or my culinary ventures? Well, I know you'll agree with me that we are only as healthy as the environment in which we live. So, if a key component of a healthy environment is appropriate waste management, it doesn't take any stretch of the imagination to see that composting—especially being able to do it right in your own home—is part of maintaining good health. Not to mention the fact that all those vegetable scraps you'll be accumulating as you prepare delicious plant-based meal after delicious plant-based meal ought to go to a more productive use than just being thrown in the trash.

I have been a devoted composter my whole life—my parents have had a couple of bins at the back of the yard for as long as I can remember. When I moved into my first apartment in university and discovered that tenants were expected to put all their food waste out by the curb to go to a landfill with the rest of the garbage, I looked for an alternative. I started freezing my food waste (so it wouldn't smell), and once I had a full bucket I would bike it over to a friend's place where there was a compost bin in their backyard. As a result, I only had to take out my "real" garbage maybe once every two weeks—and that's a far smaller environmental impact than most people on our continent can boast. Still, the system was less than ideal.

These days, some cities run green-bin programs that handle organic trash (food waste like coffee grounds or fruit and vegetable scraps as well as paper towels) separately from other garbage. It's a good program because it's user-friendly enough for people who don't have backyards or an interest in composting themselves, and reduces by about one-third the waste normally put out at the curb and sent to the dump. Forgive me if this sounds simplistic, but I can't see why it's not being done everywhere—it's

been successful in Toronto since 2004 and in Halifax since 1998!

What got me started on this whole worm thing was watching the environmental documentary *Go Further* with Woody Harrelson. I was reminded of how effectively worms consume food and plant waste and turn it into worm castings—which makes great fertilizer for plants. *I have lots of plants*, I thought. *They could do with some nice, rich fertilizer.* So I did some online research and visited my local environmental products store where they hooked me up with some worms, and I was on my way.

"But does it smell bad?" my pal Jamie asked when he was over for dinner one night. "Well, can you smell it now?" I asked him back, pointing to the vermi-bin that was only a few feet away from him in my kitchen. He hadn't smelled a thing.

TO GET STARTED VERMICOMPOSTING, YOU WILL NEED:

½–1 lb (225–450 g) red wriggler worms (see Step 3, below)

a 10-g (38-L) box with 2 lids

a drill with a ¼-in bit

about 1 sq. yd/m window screening and some duct tape (optional)

a permanent marker

worm "bedding" (see p. 64)

food scraps (see pp. 66–67)

Step 1: The box

You can get a pre-made vermicomposting box, or even a whole kit, that will provide you with everything you need to get started (just do an Internet search for a supplier in your area), but if you're handy enough with a drill and some scissors, you can DIY for cheap.

One option is a wooden box, but wooden boxes aren't always easy to come by, so plastic might be your best bet. It needs to be opaque, because worms are creatures of the dark. Go to your local hardware store and pick up a storage bin. The first time I tried this, I got one that was sort of shoebox-sized (3-gal/11-L), but I soon realized that wasn't big enough for even one person's food waste. A Rubbermaid Roughneck 10-gal/38-L bin (about 24 x 16 x 8.5 in/61 x 41 x 22 cm) is what I have now. And you'll want to get an extra lid (more on that in a moment).

Grab your drill and make some ¼-in/½-cm holes all around the box so those worms and their little friends (living organisms like microscopic fungi and bacteria that all help in the decomposition) can breathe. I'd space the holes out every inch or so—they don't have to be *all* over, but you'll want a few rows in the bottom, and a couple rows around the sides (at the top) and a few rows on the lid and all around the edge of the lid. Over time you'll be able to notice what the humidity is like in the box. If it gets too moist in there you may want to drill more holes, or even fit in some 1- or 2-in/2.5- or 5-cm soffit vents (plugs with air holes that you can get at the hardware store).

If you are at all like me when I started vermicomposting, the holes might get your mind wandering onto the idea of little wormies squiggling through them. They don't really do that, but there's something to be said for peace of mind, so you might want some screen to cover up the holes—you'll only need a yard/meter of it, at the most. You can just lay it down in a sheet across the bottom and up the sides, or cut little squares and duct-tape them on the inside of the bin.

The aforementioned second lid is needed to catch any vermi-juice that may leak out of the holes in the bottom (this juice is great for nourishing your plants, by the way). For maximum air circulation, you'll want to prop up the vermi-box by placing a few blocks underneath them on the tray (second lid). If you couldn't score a second lid, you might use a plastic boot tray.

Find a place in your house for the bin where it will get good air circulation around it and will be between 60 and 77° F (15 and 25° C). Worms work best at that temperature; below or above that, their activity may slow down and their population may decline. The box can live outdoors in the summer just as long as it stays out of the sun (so they don't bake) and rain (so they don't drown).

Step 2: The bedding

Just as you'd be uncomfortable living in an unfurnished apartment, your worms need a cozy environment in which to live and eat. We call this bedding. It needs to be made of materials that can retain moisture and are light enough to allow for good aeration. What we're talking about here is shredded newspaper, coir (coconut) fiber, and straw. These compostable materials are carbon-rich, which helps to create balance alongside all the high-nitrogen fresh food scraps. Bedding makes for a comfortable wormy home and is also a source of food.

Newspaper is easy to find and inexpensive (if not free!). The more finely shredded you can get it, the better. You don't need to worry about the inks—they're generally made from soy oil and carbon these days (even colored inks are fine—they used to contain lead, but that's illegal now). Just avoid heavily printed advertising flyers and any glossy paper. You can also shred up some brown paper bags.

I get coconut fiber, also called coir, from environmental-products stores in gardening season (it's typically used to make potting soil blends, so I'm sure you could find it at any old garden store). It comes in a dry block, so I soak it in water (which I then water my plants with). Once it's expanded like crazy, I squeeze it out thoroughly, breaking up any chunks, and toss it in the vermi-box. If you want to throw in some straw, you could use the litter pellets they sell in pet stores. A handful of sand or some potting soil that contains sand could be good to add, as it's just abrasive enough to help break down the food in a worm's gut.

The bedding should be moist but not soaking wet. Think of what you might like if you had a slippery worm body. Go for the feeling of a wrung-out sponge. While you need to achieve this level of moisture from the beginning, over time the food waste added to the bin should give it the moisture it needs (especially if you're putting in fruit and watery vegetables).

In total, you'll want about 4–8 in/10–20 cm of bedding to start. It's important to add more bedding, bit by bit, on a regular basis to keep

things in balance. The bedding can be added moist or dry, depending on what the environment is like in the bin at that time.

Step 3: The worms

Red wrigglers, or *Eisenia foetida*, if you want to get technical, are the vermicomposting worms. You can likely order these from your local environmental organization or store, online, or, if you're lucky, have a friend with red wrigglers to spare.

After you've set up your bin with the bedding, it's ready for worms. Local stores or online retailers will likely sell ½ lb/250 g for about twenty dollars. You'll want at least that many, if not twice that much. Over time, your worm family will grow on its own—the population should double every three to four months. Be sure to watch your gender pronouns when addressing these wrigglers: they're hermaphrodites (meaning they have both male and female parts)—though it still takes two worms to make babies.

They will likely arrive in a bit of soil or bedding or wrapped in newspaper. But they don't want to be there for long, so be ready to release them into their new home. If you're squeamish, you may realize, sadly, that this is where the good clean fun has to end. If you're tough enough for creepy-crawly, though, this is when it finally gets exciting! (As you might have guessed, I am somewhere between the two.) It's fine to pour the worms on top of the moist bedding; they'll slither down to where they want to be. If you get them from a friend and they come with a bit of food, you'll certainly want to pour them in under a layer of bedding. You can rest assured that they'll be happy if you care for them—red wrigglers don't mind living in captivity and are relatively tolerant of varying levels of temperature, moisture, and pH.

There are also other living organisms, as I mentioned above, that are part of the vermicomposting team. Though they are less visible than the worms, they play an important role in this ecosystem-in-a-box. Don't worry about them trying to escape—they too see the outside world as an inhospitable place and will be happy to stay where they are!

Step 4: The food

WHAT'S ON THE WORMY MENU?	
FOODS THAT MAKE WORMS HAPPY	**FOODS THAT MAKE WORMS REBELLIOUS**
most fruit and vegetable scraps (including juicer pulp)	onions and garlic
dead leaves from your houseplants	citrus
tea bags, coffee grounds (including paper filter)	fats/oils
sprouted or cooked grains (without oil, salt, or other seasonings)	seasoned foods (salty, vinegary, oily, etc.)
eggshells (if there are people in your house eating eggs)—dried and crushed very fine	any animal products or byproducts

The best way to offer worms their food is in small pieces so that the decomposers have a greater surface area on which to feed. Some people put scraps in the blender, but being in favor of avoiding extra dishes at all costs, I think chopping them into a small dice is fine. I rip up tea bags (discarding any tags, strings, or staples).

Give the worms a day or two to get used to their new environment before giving them any food scraps. When it's feeding time, I always bury the food scraps under a layer of bedding. There are two good reasons for this: one, because it is less likely to attract fruit flies, and two, because, unlike fish in a tank, worms don't like to come up to the surface to eat—they prefer to do it in the dark.

Visually divide the bin into quadrants. You can label each corner with your permanent marker: 1, 2, 3, 4. At each feeding, put the food in a different quadrant to help maintain balance in the vermi-bin and to encourage the worms to get a bit of a workout (ha, ha).

These worms are healthy eaters—they can consume up to half their weight per day (so half a pound of worms can eat about that much food in two days). I'd start off by offering them about 1½ cup of scraps at each feeding and see how it goes. You don't want to give your worms more than they can chew up and poop out in a few days or things might get smelly. The best approach I've found is to start by feeding them every four to five days and take it from there. If they're plowing through the food at a good rate, you might feed them more often. If there are always leftovers from the last feeding, give them a bit more time to finish their meal. I have a worm-feeding schedule with dates and quadrant numbers stuck on the side of my bin (so I'm sure to feed them every five days), but you might develop your own trick for keeping track.

Collect your chopped-up scraps in a well-sealed container (like one for yogurt) and keep it either on your countertop (the worms actually like slightly rotting food) or in the fridge (though it's best if the food is at room temperature when you offer it to the little critters). Just as you should be eating a broad range of foods, you'll help keep a healthy ecosystem in the bin and get the best vermicompost if you offer your worms a diverse range of food scraps.

Now is perhaps the time to say that if you live in a house with more than two people, you might find you need to get a second bin (and the worms and bedding to fill it) to accommodate more food waste. While upgrading to a larger bin might be considered, the worms and the organisms that help them need a decent amount of oxygen to do their work, thus making surface area (length x width) important. So more bins are your best bet (you can always stack 'em to save on space).

Step 5:

TROUBLESHOOTING		
PROBLEM	**CAUSE**	**SOLUTION**
Stinky	Too much food, not enough worms	Decrease amount of food, or get more worms
Ammonia smell	Too much fresh green matter (nitrogen-rich materials)	Add some shredded newspaper, dead leaves, dry straw (carbon-rich materials) to balance things out
Sulfuric smell	The bedding is too wet, and not enough air is getting to the bottom of the bin	Add dry, shredded newspaper and/or dead leaves to the bottom of the bin, and mix some in the bedding. Reduce food for a while
Worms are climbing the walls of the bin	Bedding is too moist	Add dry, shredded newspaper (see above)
Worms are climbing the walls of the bin	Bedding is too acidic	Add some dolomitic lime or powdered dry egg shells (and be sure you're not feeding the worms any citrus)
Worms are climbing the walls of the bin	Too many worms	Harvest the vermicompost and then start fresh with new bedding and fewer worms (give the rest of the worms away or start a second bin)
Fruit flies	Food is exposed to air, which attracts flies	Be sure to bury food under a layer of bedding (add more bedding if necessary)
Fruit flies	Too much food in the vermi-bin	Decrease the amount of food for a while

Step 6: Harvesting and using your vermicompost

Three to six months will pass and then it's time to harvest that precious, nutrient-rich soil conditioner we call vermicompost and invite the worms to start anew. There are two ways to harvest:

1. The donkey and carrot approach

This is the prissier of the two methods, as you don't really need to touch the worms at all. First, shift all the contents of the vermi-bin to one half of the box. Then fill the space you've just created in the other half with fresh new bedding. Give the worms about a week to chow down on any remaining food scraps in the first half.

After that time, you can start burying food scraps in the new bedding only. All the worms, lured by the food, will migrate over to the new bedding and set up shop there.

This pilgrimage should take a couple of weeks. You can then scoop out all the vermicompost in the first half and fill that side with new bedding too.

2. The down 'n' dirty approach

This method involves more human-worm contact and works on the principle that worms don't like light and will run away from it.

Stop feeding the vermi-bin for one to two weeks,

until all visible food scraps have been eaten up (you'll want to keep checking humidity levels during this time; if it seems dry, sprinkle them with just a little water so the worms don't dry up for lack of moisture).

Lay a large garbage bag or tarp on a flat surface under an intense light (or get yourself a good flashlight). Dump out the vermi-bin's contents and divide it into a few piles. Shine the light on one pile at a time, starting with the outside edges and working your way in. The worms will squirm away from the light and make a big worm ball in the center. Gently place this back in the vermi-bin with fresh new bedding.

Now take this amazing vermicompost, also known as black gold, and sprinkle it in your planters or toss it with soil you plan to use as a medium for growing veggies and herbs (a good ratio is one part vermicompost to four or five parts all-purpose soil). These worm castings will improve the quality of the soil, adding beneficial microbial activity and helping your plants resist parasites and disease.

You might also make some "worm casting tea" by putting a spoonful or two in a paper envelope (or coffee filter) and steeping it in some water overnight. Use this liquid to water your plants every few weeks. It makes for a much better option than any conventional, chemical fertilizer.

KIDS AND WORMS

Vermicomposting is a great project for kids. There are also teaching resources available. Get your hands on a copy of Worms Eat Our Garbage: Classroom Activities for a Better Environment *by Mary Applehof. It could also help to search around on the web for fun activities for kids and worms. Red wrigglers are certainly low maintenance compared to a puppy, hamster, or any other pet your little one desires!*

RESOURCES:

Appelhof, Mary. *Worms Eat My Garbage*. Kalamazoo, MI: Flower Press, 1982.
See also Appelhof's website: *wormwoman.com*
"Vermicomposting" article at New Mexico State University website *cahe.nmsu. edu/pubs/_h/h-164.pdf*
Urban Agriculture Notes: *cityfarmer.org/wormcomp61.html*
Compost Guide blogsite: *compostguide.com/vermicomposting-composting-with-worms/*
"Vermicomposting: Composting with Worms": *lancaster.unl.edu/pest/resources/ vermicompost107.shtml*

For vermicomposting kits:

Cathy's Crawly Composters: *cathyscomposters.com*
If you live in Ontario or anywhere within the reach of Canada Post, Cathy can
help you get started. And she's awfully friendly and helpful. You can order bits
and pieces from her (depending on how DIY you are) or the whole shebang.

(For more information, see pp. 255–257)

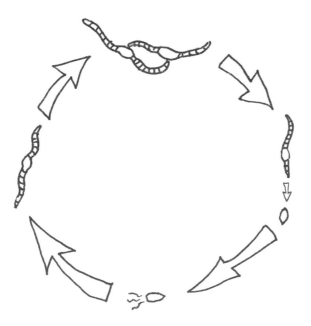

WINTER

You won't catch me claiming to be winter's biggest fan, no siree. Winter sports don't have huge appeal for me (I prefer yoga), and while I'm willing to strive for fashionable layering as much as the next gal, I don't appreciate the way long underwear squeezes my leg hair at uncomfortable angles, and I get frustrated that my toes still freeze up in my thermal socks and clunky boots. Most of all, it's the diminished amount of natural light during the day that really gets to me.

These coldest months aren't all bad news, though. We can cozy up in front of the fireplace with mugs of Hot Toddies (p. 92). There's bulky knitting to be done. I host a cookie exchange in mid-December each year, which is a great excuse to do a ton of baking and put on a pot of Mulled Cider (p. 90) to share with guests. That's also the month when many of us carry on traditions of celebrating with family and friends. And there's a sense of starting fresh that we have with the turn of the New Year.

Traditional Chinese medicine suggests that this is the season to care for your kidneys (which filter the blood and produce urine) and bladder (which collects the urine excreted by the kidneys). It is also the season to take on your fears and face them. Finally, this might be when you want to start taking better care of your bones.

- Enjoy eight to twelve cups (depending on your size and activity level) of filtered water each day. This can include lemon water and herbal teas. Drink warm liquids instead of ice-cold ones. Avoid tannic acid (found in black tea and wine), which is hard on the kidneys. Lay off soda pop and other carbonated beverages, and cut out sugar and coffee, all of which can leach minerals from your bones.

- Enlist the help of particular herbal allies for the kidneys and bladder such as marshmallow root (to soothe irritation and inflammation), ginger root (warming, supports circulation), and nettle (tones the kidneys). Make a tea of 1 tsp dried herb per cup of boiling water, and steep for fifteen to thirty minutes.

- Look into saw palmetto extract as another herbal ally if you have urinary system issues.

- Address or let go of the things that are freaking you out. Charge at them head-on with confidence, or work on developing acceptance for what is.

- Hibernate a little: keep warm, stay quiet, sleep well, be at home, and look within. It's natural to feel more emotional at this time of year.

- But don't hide yourself away completely: do still maintain the relationships in your life and keep doing things that stimulate, engage, and excite you.

- Avoid late nights, blow-out parties, overactivity, and inadequate rest and sleep.

- Indulge in head, chest, abdomen, back, butt, leg, and foot massages that will likely hit points on the bladder and kidney meridians.

- Ladies, if you develop a routine of daily Kegel (pelvic floor) exercises (repeatedly squeezing and relaxing those same muscles that stop the flow of urine), it could do wonders for those of you with weak bladders, who are pregnant, and/or want to hit a whole new level of sexual pleasure.

- For those who suffer from repeated urinary tract infections (UTIs), look for the root cause, and take a capsule of cranberry extract (proven to help with UTIs) daily.
- Make sure you're providing your bones with the nutrients they need: calcium, magnesium, phosphorus, and vitamin D. Enjoy bone-supporting foods like almonds, black beans, bok choy, broccoli, collard greens, navy beans, pumpkin seeds, sesame seeds, spinach, sunflower seeds, Swiss chard, and turnip greens.
- Take a liquid vitamin D supplement because you're not getting as much exposure to the sun, which allows your body to synthesize this vitamin.
- Enjoy foods that are said to nourish the Water element (ideally, if in season locally for you): buckwheat; adzuki, black turtle, kidney, and pinto beans; beets (both root and greens), mushrooms, nori, red cabbage; blackberries, blueberries, cranberries; chia and black sesame seeds; miso, sea salt, soy sauce, umeboshi plums and umeboshi vinegar, pickles (in brine).

COZIER, CLEANER HOME

Because winter is the season when we spend the most time indoors (I dunno about where you're living, but Canadian winters—even in southern and urban areas—can get painfully bitter!), this is a good time to look at how healthy your immediate environment really is.

Humble yet heroic house plants

Some people say they're not "plant people." They're often the same people who "can't cook." If you've been wary of keeping indoor plants in the past, or only have a token one or two that you picked up from IKEA when you moved into your home, this information is meant to get you into growing more of a jungle. (If you already have a bunch of plants in your house, feel free to read and gloat!)

Here's a short but inspiring list of facts in support of houseplants:

- They feed on the carbon dioxide we breathe out and release oxygen for us to breathe in.
- They don't require the electricity that plug-in air filters do, yet they help minimize airborne bacteria and mildew and mold spores and reduce the toxic effects of off-gassing of ammonia, benzene, and formaldehyde from synthetic materials found in our homes.
- They facilitate healthy humidity levels.
- Their lively green leaves are like cheerleaders' pom-poms when all you can see out your window is the white ground and bare tree branches against a grey sky.

- Studies have shown houseplants may even noticeably reduce stress and increase productivity.
- Fresh air is vital to our health and well-being. Plants quietly and effectively contribute to clean air in our homes, and they're attractive too!

To really reap the benefits of houseplants, you'll want to have at least three or four small to medium plants, or two large ones for every 100 sq ft/9.3 sq m. The more toxic items contained in your indoor environment (e.g., wall-to-wall carpeting, upholstery, printers, copying machines), the more plants you'll need. Here are a few suggestions:

- Rubber plants are superb at removing airborne chemicals, are easy to grow, and are quite resistant to insects. Weeping figs (*Ficus benjamina*) are a bit more challenging to grow. *Ficus Alii* also fall in this category, and are easier to grow than the weeping fig. All three prefer full sun, and to dry out thoroughly between good waterings. Feed them only between midsummer and fall.
- Boston ferns are great at removing chemicals from the air, are somewhat easy to grow, and are very resistant to insects. Kimberly Queen ferns are just as effective, but a little bit harder to grow. They both require partial sun and like to be moist but not soggy. Don't let them dry out; give them a bit of a mist, especially in drier months.
- Peace lilies are great at chemical removal and easy to grow. They're happy in partial sun (in low light they're still fine, but less likely to flower), and they like to dry out fully before being soaked. Feed only every few weeks in the spring to fall, but mist freely; they like that too.
- Gerbera daisies are impressive removers of chemicals, if you're skilled enough to grow 'em. They like to be in full sun, with kinda damp soil, and to be given fertilizer every few weeks in spring and summer.
- Golden pothos and philodendrons, with their heart-shaped leaves and vine-like penchant for travel, are very easy to grow and are quite resistant to insects. Golden pothos are very effective at chemical removal, philodendrons more moderately so. Also happy in just partial sun, both like to stay moist but not soggy. Be sure to mist often, and water less in winter. Feed them only once a month in the spring and summer.
- Bamboo palms, areca palms, and lady palms are more effective chemical removers than parlor palms, but all are easy to grow and quite resistant to insects. Keep them moist but not soggy, and mist away! Happy in partial sun, fertilize once a month from spring to fall.

What are you waiting for? Get growing!

Homemade potions for a truly cleaner home

In general, cleaning is not a skill that comes as naturally to me as cooking, which is why you will never catch anyone who truly knows me calling me a "domestic goddess" or anything to that effect. One of my goals in life is to be surrounded by people I can cook for in exchange for tasks that I really don't want to do—computer upkeep is on that list, but so is dishwashing. I imagine being happily married to someone who has no qualms about washing the dishes after I've served him/her a satisfying meal or a nice slice of cake.

Until the yin to my domestic yang appears, though, the cleaning's got to be done. And just like cooking, some of the best concoctions are made simply from scratch. What worries me about those brightly colored plastic bottles of sudsy potions that promise to make your entire home sparkle and shine—and not smell as though a human (or anything that breathes oxygen) has ever lived there—is that, first of all, some of them feature chlorine, which contains dioxin, a carcinogenic substance that is not safe no matter how small an amount gets into your body. Second, these cleaners don't completely disappear once they go down your drain, even though they may seem to not be your problem anymore. They make their way into the public water system and into our environment, throwing off the natural balance Mother Nature so kindly and relentlessly strives for. They are unnecessarily blended with dyes and scents (great, more synthetic chemicals). The most frustrating part is that ingredients are not required to be listed on the bottle or box.

Look for any cautionary labeling: a "warning" won't kill you but could make you pretty sick; "caution" indicates the product is somewhat toxic; and the terms "corrosive," "danger," or "poison" often indicate the most toxic ones.

The following "recipes" either came from my own trial-and-error or are borrowed from eco-authors Renée Loux and Adria Vasil (whose books are listed in the Resources section at the back of the book).

Cutting board sanitizer: 1 tbsp baking soda + ¼ cup hydrogen peroxide (three-percent dilution) + ¼ cup white vinegar + 4 drops grapefruit seed extract. Sprinkle the soda on your cutting board. Combine all remaining ingredients in a spray bottle or pitcher. Spritz or gently pour it on, and allow it to fizz like crazy. Give it a good rinse or wipe with clean water.

Drain clogs: Start by making a reminiscent-of-elementary-school-science-class "volcano" in the drain by pouring in ¼ cup baking soda, followed by 1 cup white vinegar. Give it about fifteen minutes to do its thing before pouring down a kettle's worth of just-boiled water. You can repeat this whole process a few times until the drain clears. If that's not enough, pick yourself up some washing soda from your local health food or environmental products store (or maybe a grocer's) and shake a cup's worth down the drain followed by 3 cups of just-boiled water. Adria Vasil says you can "repeat until you break on through to the other side," but cautions not to overdo it if you have PVC pipes. Prevent clogs in the first place by getting mesh sink-drain screens for your kitchen and tub—they'll only run you a coupl'a bucks at the hardware store.

Fruit and veggie wash: 1 cup filtered water + 1 tbsp white or apple cider vinegar + 2 tsp baking soda or 1 cup water + ⅓ cup hydrogen peroxide (three-percent dilution). Either mixture can be doubled, tripled, or quadrupled as needed. Combine all ingredients in a bowl or spray bottle. Dunk or spritz the mix all over your produce (except mushrooms—they're too absorbent). Wait ten to thirty seconds, then give it a good rinse with clean water.

Mineral deposits (like in your kettle): Bring 1 cup white vinegar + 1 cup water to a boil in your kettle, and keep it rolling for a few minutes (the vinegar will smell strong, so open a window), then dump it, and refill the kettle with fresh water. Bring to a boil again for another three minutes to rid the kettle of the vinegaryness. Repeat if needed.

Oven cleaner: 1–2 cups baking soda + ½–1 cup hot water (enough to make a spreadable but not runny paste) + time. That's the simple equation, and so much gentler than the store-bought stuff with the extreme warnings. Shake the soda over the bottom of your oven, then pour or spray on the water to get it wet but not yet runny. Let it sit for eight to twelve hours, then wipe it away, using a scrubbing sponge if needed. Elbow grease is likely not needed if you let it sit for all that time, but if you've got a huge job on your hands, Renée Loux suggests you make a more effective solution with soda and water as above, then add 2–4 tbsp Citra-Solv Degreaser Concentrate, stir it into a paste, and smear on.

Smells: Baking soda is great at absorbing odors and moisture. Place a semi-permeable box (poke some holes in your box) in your fridge, and change it every two to three months. Zeolite, a natural volcanic mineral, is another option for a fresh smelling fridge, bathroom, or garbage can. You can get it at health food or environmental products stores, and the cool thing is that it'll "recharge" itself. Once a year, just spread it on a baking sheet and lay it in the sun for a few hours to dry and *voilà!* For smelly Tupperware, dampen it, then shake in a bit of baking soda, allowing it to sit overnight before rinsing.

Stainless steel cleaner: Option 1: ½ cup baking soda + 1 cup club soda. Mix together in a bowl, then rub it onto the steel surface with a damp cloth or sponge. The baking soda is gently abrasive, but not enough to scratch. Option 2: equal parts cream of tartar + baking soda + hydrogen peroxide (three-percent dilution)—just a couple tbsp of each. Combine in a bowl and then rub onto the steel surface with a damp cloth or sponge. Allow it to dry completely before wiping off with a damp cloth. Cream of tartar has natural bleaching properties and will help your steel surfaces to shine.

Stain remover: Attack stains as soon as possible! Many stains (like blood) are most likely to come out when doused in cold water, though there are some exceptions, like strawberry stains, which will disappear from cloth when you pour just-boiled water on them from a decent height (lift your kettle about one foot above the affected fabric). "Green bleach" made from hydrogen peroxide is an effective alternative to the chlorine stuff and is usually color-safe! (Do a patch test first to be safe.)

Toilet cleaning: For the most challenging jobs, pour in 1 cup borax powder + ¼ cup white vinegar. Allow it to sit for a few hours before giving it a good scrub. I also hear calcium stains will lift off with a 1,000-mg tablet of vitamin C dropped in the bowl overnight (or for eight hours).

Window cleaner: Pour 1 part white vinegar and 1 part water in a spray bottle. You can also add a drop or two of essential oil (see sidebar) if you like. Spritz away, and wipe off with balled-up newspaper.

Wood polish: 1 cup olive or hemp seed oil + 1 tbsp lemon juice. Sounds like a mild salad dressing, but it isn't carcinogenic like those commercial furniture sprays. Pour small amounts on the surface that needs treating, then wipe in and off following the grain of the wood.

RESOURCES:

Colbin, Annemarie. *Food and Our Bones: The Natural Way to Prevent Osteoporosis.* New York: Plume, 1998.

Loux, Renée. *The Balanced Plate: More Than 150 Flavorful Recipes That Nourish Body, Mind, and Soul.* Emmaus, PA.: Rodale, 2006.

——. *Easy Green Living: The Ultimate Guide to Simple, Eco-Friendly Choices for You and Your Home.* Emmaus, PA.: Rodale, 2008.

Vasil, Adria. *Ecoholic: Your Guide to the Most Environmentally Friendly Information, Products, and Services.* Toronto: Vintage Canada, 2007.

(For more information, see pp. 255–257)

GOOD SMELLS AND BAD SMELLS

Synthetic scents give me a headache, can cause respiratory issues, and they're not doing anything great for the environment, either. Pure essential oils, on the other hand, are plant-derived and very potent. For home use I have lavender (relaxing, antibacterial), tea tree (medicinal-smelling, but antibacterial), sweet orange (uplifting), and peppermint (refreshing). Add just a few drops to unscented liquid soap or a homemade cleaning potion.

GF, SF, NF & R

WHAT THE SYMBOLS MEAN

I have included the following symbols with my recipes for you to be able to easily spot which recipes can be complementary to any of your dietary requirements. Note that the symbols may not apply to any suggested substitutions, side dishes, or accompaniments.

Gluten-free (GF)

Indicates recipes that are safe for those with Celiac Disease or others avoiding gluten.

You must, however, check that the brand of non-dairy milk, tamari soy sauce, pasta, and/ or vegetable stock called for in the recipe is gluten-free. I have not marked recipes containing oats as "gluten-free" because oats come from "contaminated sources" more often than not.

Soy-free (SF)

When this symbol is noted, you must, however, check that the brand of food, non-dairy milk, or margarine called for in the recipe is soy-free.

Nightshade-free (NF)

This means that recipes are free of tomatoes, potatoes, eggplants, and peppers (both bell and hot). For info on nightshades, check out The World's Healthiest Foods website (*whfoods.com*).

Raw/living (R)

Recipes denoted as raw/living food recipes may not be completely 100 percent living ingredients; it's up to you to ensure all your ingredients are, in fact, raw. For example, you have to make sure any non-dairy milk, nut butter, soy sauce, miso, sweetener, cocoa, or carob powder called for would be raw.

FALL

WINTER

SPRING

SUMMER

PART II: THE RECIPES

Drinks

me, with my haul of pears
at Two Century Farm

Nut Milk

½ cup raw almonds, cashews, hazelnuts (or another nut if it's local to you), soaked in filtered water overnight (4–10 hours)

3–4 cups filtered water (depending on how rich you want the milk to be)

up to 1 tbsp liquid sweetener (agave nectar, maple syrup or brown rice syrup) or 1–2 soft pitted dates or ½ tsp stevia (optional)

up to 1 tsp pure vanilla extract (optional, for "vanilla milk")

⅛ tsp sea salt (optional)

This recipe appeared in Get It Ripe, *but it's such a staple that I thought it also needed to be included here. Making your own "milk" allows you to use (hopefully filtered) water right from your own tap and a reusable glass jar for storage, while imported milks, which are mostly water in disposable tetra paks, are trucked or flown in before making it to your grocer's shelves. Homemade non-dairy milk also provides beneficial living enzymes, and allows you to tweak the various ingredients to your liking and vary the quantity—make a double batch for a breakfast party or a quart batch if you only need a splash.*

1 | Drain the soaking water off the nuts and discard.

2 | Place them in a blender along with the fresh, filtered water sweetener, vanilla, and salt (if desired), and give them a good whirl until the nuts have been completely pulverized, about 2 minutes.

3 | Strain out the nut pulp* if a smooth consistency is desired—you can use a fine mesh strainer, nut milk bag, or cheesecloth. Keeps in the fridge for up to 4 days. Give it another blend before each serving (or store in a glass jar and shake well).

Makes 3–4 cups (when strained of pulp).

GF, SF, NF, R

* Leftover nut pulp can be thrown into baked goods or sprinkled on cereal. Get creative!

Great Canadian Hemp Milk

It seems that most of us in North America are getting our hemp food products from Manitoba, Canada. While the plant itself would be happy to grow elsewhere, governments in other countries are not happy to have this impressive crop sprouting out of their soil! I find many of the hemp milks on the market contain sugar (evaporated cane juice). Make a creemy one at home that doesn't.

1 | Place the hemp seeds and water in a blender and give them a whirl for about 1 minute.

2 | Add the sweetener and salt if desired and whirl again.

3 | Give it a taste, and if the milk is too thick for your liking, dilute it with another ½–1 cup water and whirl again.

Makes 3½ cups.

GF, NF, SF, R

1 cup hulled hemp seeds

3 cups filtered water

up to 1 tbsp liquid sweetener (agave nectar, maple syrup, date syrup) or 1–2 soft pitted dates or ½ tsp stevia (optional)

up to 1 tsp pure vanilla extract (optional, for "vanilla milk")

⅛ tsp sea salt (optional)

Rice Milk

Rice milk is certainly thinner than other non-dairy milks, but I think those who love it appreciate that. If you want rice milk that's just ever so slightly on the richer side, add the optional oil to this recipe.

1 | Place the rice in a blender or food processor along with the water and give it a good whirl until the rice has been completely pulverized, about 2 minutes.

2 | Strain out the rice pulp*—you can use a fine mesh strainer, a nut milk bag, or cheesecloth. Return the milk to the blender, adding the sweetener and salt. Turn it on high, and while the milk is whirling around, slowly drizzle the oil into the vortex of the mixture. Keep it running for 10–20 seconds longer, then turn it off. Keeps in the fridge for up to 4 days. Give it another blend before each serving (or store in a glass jar and shake well).

Makes 3 cups (when strained of pulp).

GF, SF, NF

* Leftover rice pulp can be thrown into baked goods or sprinkled on cereal. Get creative!

⅔–1 cup cooked brown rice

3 cups filtered water

up to 1 tbsp sweetener (agave nectar, maple syrup, date syrup, Sucanat) or 1–2 soft pitted dates or ½ tsp stevia (optional)

⅛ tsp sea salt (optional)

1 tbsp almond or liquid non-hydrogenated coconut oil (optional)

up to 1 tsp pure vanilla extract (optional, for "vanilla milk")

Oat Milk

½ cup steel-cut oats

2–3 cups filtered water

up to 1 tsp liquid sweetener (maple syrup or agave nectar) or 1 pitted date (optional)

a pinch of sea salt (optional)

I find oats so comforting. This great milk is pretty thick—you have the option to water it down if you like. But why can't we call this recipe raw? As it turns out, because oats are such a soft and moist grain and can go rancid quite quickly, manufacturers typically steam them at around 212°F (100°C) so they won't go bad. This explains why whole oats won't sprout (unless you've bought oat kernels specifically labeled "raw" or "living").

1 | Soak the oats in the water in a covered bowl overnight (for 6–10 hours).

2 | Pour the soaked oats and 2 cups of the water into a blender and give it a whirl for about 1 minute.

3 | Strain out the oat pulp (you can eat it with syrup and seeds, toss it in baked goods, or discard it).

4 | Whisk in the sweetener and salt if desired. If the milk is too thick for your liking, pour it back in the blender and dilute with another ½–1 cup of water and whirl again.

Makes 1½–2½ cups.

GF (if oats are processed in a gluten-free facility look for this the label), SF, NF

❋ Watermelon Juice (or Popsicles)

I have never been to the deep south (Sarasota, Florida, doesn't count, right?), but I have read books and seen movies, and I always imagine people sitting on their porches on the hottest summer days drinking this.

1 watermelon

1 | Wash the watermelon and chop into chunks, discarding the rind.

2 | Press watermelon chunks through a fine mesh with the back of a spoon. This may take a while, but it's worth it. (If you're inclined to get bored, make sure someone's around for good conversation, or put on some favorite music. Or, if you have a seedless watermelon, you can throw the chunks into your blender until smooth.)

3 | It would be perfectly reasonable to pour this juice into popsicle molds and freeze until solid.

1½ cups makes 1 serving. Results depend on the size of your watermelon.

GF, SF, NF, R

Green Juice

1 medium apple or pear

1–2 stalks celery

1 large or 1–2 medium garlic cloves (very optional)

1–2 handfuls parsley or dandelion leaves

5 kale stems* (or 2–3 kale leaves) or 3 green cabbage leaves

1 small or ½ medium cucumber (optional)

This juice is an exhilarating source of easy-to-absorb vitamins, minerals, and enzymes! The addition of the optional garlic will make for a very different-tasting, but more nourishing, experience.

1 | Wash or scrub all produce well, and trim off any funky bits. Run each ingredient through your juicer according to the manufacturer's directions, in the order listed. Enjoy immediately.

Makes 1–1½ cups.

GF, SF, NF, R

You could use the stems you saved from Kale Krisps (p. 132) in this recipe!

Yellow Juice

3 medium apples or pears

1 small–medium golden beet (optional)

½ lemon (trimmed of peel)

thumb-sized piece fresh ginger

3 green cabbage leaves (optional)

A sweet and zingy juice packed with vitamins, minerals, and enzymes.

1 | Wash or scrub all produce well, and trim off any funky bits. Run each ingredient through your juicer according to the manufacturer's directions, in the order listed. Enjoy immediately.

Makes 1–1½ cups.

GF, SF, NF, R

Orange Juice

4 medium carrots

1–2 medium apples, any kind

thumb-sized piece fresh ginger

1 medium orange (optional, if available locally)

Carrot juice is high in beta-carotene, the apples (and optional orange) add sweetness, and the ginger makes it gently spicy!

1 | Wash or scrub all produce well, and trim off any funky bits. Run each ingredient through your juicer according to the manufacturer's directions, in the order listed. Enjoy immediately.

Makes 1–1½ cups.

GF, SF, NF, R

◈ Red Juice

Sweet, ruby red, and rich in vitamins, minerals, and enzymes!

1 | Wash or scrub all produce well, and trim off any funky bits. Run each ingredient through your juicer according to the manufacturer's directions, in the order listed. Enjoy immediately.

Makes 1–1½ cups.

GF, SF, NF, R

1 medium or 2 small red beets

thumb-sized piece fresh ginger

3–4 medium carrots

1 medium or 2 small apples, any kind

◈ Soothing Apple Juice

This is a great drink to prepare when you have a sore, scratchy throat. It thickens as it cools. The recipe is adapted from Aviva Romm's book Naturally Healthy Babies and Children—*but it's great for adults too! If you'd prefer, you can use pear juice instead of apple. But if juice straight-up is too sweet for you, dilute this with some warm filtered water. Find kudzu in health food stores or Asian markets—the packages I buy are small clumps of fine powder (about the size of rock salt).*

1 | Pour half the juice into a saucepan and heat on medium.

2 | Dissolve the kudzu root in the rest of the juice in a measuring cup or pitcher, or the 1L bottle of juice itself. Stir this into the saucepan, turn up the heat, and bring to a boil, stirring all the while.

3 | Reduce temperature to low and heat 2 minutes more. Cool until drinkable (removing the cinnamon stick, if used).

Makes 4 servings. You can drink up to 1 qt/L per day.

GF, SF, NF

1 qt/L unclarified apple juice

4 tsp powdered kudzu root

½–1 tsp ground cinnamon or 1 whole cinnamon stick

❋ Hemp Pro Smoothie

½–1 cup chopped local fruit (fresh or frozen)

⅓ cup blueberries (fresh or frozen)

1 cup non-dairy milk or more (or filtered water), to desired thickness

¼ cup hemp protein powder

½ tsp cardamom powder (optional—adds warmth and helps with digestion)

1 tsp maca powder (optional—nourishes the adrenals, though it usually comes from Peru!)

½ tsp probiotic powder (optional—helps with digestion and supports the immune system)

½ tsp slippery elm powder (optional—helps heal mucous membranes in the body)

I'm a big smoothie lover, and pretty content with a similar blend of ingredients day after day. I appreciate the boost of protein hemp gives me—either after exercise (helping to build muscle mass) or to help maintain blood sugar levels throughout the day (without the digestive issues that many of us experience from soy protein). When I asked on Twitter what people use to thicken their smoothies when bananas aren't local and yogurt's a no-go for vegans, one person responded to say that she knows her banana farmer (she lives in Hawaii), and when she's in non-banana-growing regions she chooses not to eat them. I don't see many of you (or me for that matter) moving to Hawaii anytime soon, so I've left most of the fruit selection here up to you. Switch it up depending on what's available from your local market or your kitchen freezer at various times of the year. Frozen fruit does make a thicker smoothie, but your body will need to spend extra energy warming it up in your stomach before it can digest it properly.

1 | Toss all ingredients into a wide-mouth 1 qt/L cup (if using a hand blender) or into your blender or food processor. I put a bit of liquid in before adding any of the powders to keep them from clumping at the bottom. Give it all a whirl until smooth. Enjoy immediately.

Makes 1 large serving.
GF, SF, NF, R

☼ Melon Smoothie

A refreshing summer drink for a hot afternoon in the garden. (You might even spike it with splash of vodka if you like.) This would be a great time to snatch up any and all heirloom varieties of melons from your farmers' market or local food co-op.

1 | Remove the rind and seeds from your melon (and add them to your compost pile), and chop up the flesh. Place it in a bowl or plastic bag in the freezer until frosty, but not frozen solid—about 30–60 minutes. Toss it all into a blender or food processor and whirl until smooth. Add the juice (apple, white grape, or peach juice with cantaloupe or honeydew: any berry juice would be nice with watermelon) or filtered water to thin if necessary. Add lemon or lime juice and sweetener if you think it's needed. Pour into 2 frosted glasses, garnish with the mint, and serve.

Makes 2 servings.

GF, SF, NF, R

1 small-medium melon (cantaloupe or other orange-fleshed melon; honeydew or other green-yellow fleshed melon; seedless watermelon—any variety)

½–1 cup juice or filtered water, as needed

1 tbsp fresh lemon or lime juice, or to taste (optional)

1 tsp liquid sweetener, or to taste (optional)

2 sprigs fresh mint, for garnish (optional)

Blueberry Green Drink

You can watch me making this on YouTube. I'm a little embarrassed by the video now that it's almost two years old, but it's still there for you to see me in my old kitchen, chatting away to help viewers get their daily dose of greens. Spirulina is an incredible superfood—it's 60 percent amino acids (the building blocks for protein), and it contains anti-inflammatory GLA and betacarotene.

Spirulina's color is intense, but the blueberry juice complements it—both visually and in terms of flavor—nicely.

1 | Put all ingredients into a 10-oz/300-mL or 1 pint/473 mL glass jar (for which you have a tight-fitting lid). Screw the lid on tight and give it a real good shake, making sure that all the powder is absorbed into the liquid. Drink immediately.

Makes 1 serving.

GF, SF, NF, R

¼ cup pure blueberry juice (or a blueberry/other juice blend)

½ cup apple juice

1 rounded tsp spirulina powder

1 tbsp high-quality greens powder (like New Chapter Berry Greens)

approx. ¾ cup filtered water

5–10 drops liquid trace minerals blend like Mineral Resources International ConcenTrace (optional)

✺ Dandelion Morning Tea

3 parts dandelion root (tones the liver and gallbladder, stimulates the appetite, aids with respiratory, digestive, and urinary issues)

2 parts anise seeds (tones the liver and gallbladder, stimulates the appetite, helps with bad breath)

2 parts lemon balm (alleviates indigestion, nervousness, restlessness)

2 parts nettle leaves (aids with urinary and respiratory issues, allergies)

1–2 parts of any of the following:

burdock root (helps balance blood sugar)

oat straw (used to treat inflammation, constipation, sore throat, anxiety, and depression)

schisandra berries (helps alleviate depression, fatigue, and thirst)

This tea is great-tasting, liver-supporting, and can stimulate your appetite. Dandelion in particular is a wonderfully nourishing herb—I like to make a tea with its roots on the mornings that I don't drink lemon water. Do use organic and locally grown herbs whenever possible.

1 | Combine all herbs together in a large bowl. Measure out 1 tsp of herb blend for each cup of water or a heaping tbsp for 4 cups of water, and add to mug or teapot.

2 | Bring desired amount of filtered water to a boil.

3 | Pour water over the herbs, cover, and allow to steep for 10–30 minutes before drinking.

4 | Strain out the herbs and rebottle the liquid—you can store the tea in a thermos to keep it warm throughout the morning.

5 | Transfer remaining dry herbs into a glass jar with a well-fitting lid, store in a cool, dark place, and use over the next few months.

Enjoy 1–4 cups daily.

GF, SF, NF

❀ ☀ Hippie Herb Garden Tea

I have this vision of back-to-the-lander wise-women goddesses, their hair and skirts long and flowing, their rustic homes cluttered with jars of various concoctions and bouquets of herbs and flowers hanging to dry by strings tied to the rafters. They, like me, drink most everything out of Mason jars and don't mow the lawn. I imagine these women diffusing the essence of nourishing herbs in water, making a tea with the help of the dazzling summer sun instead of the kettle on their stovetops.

1 | Pack a wide-mouth jar (say, 1 pint/500 mL or 1 qt/L) about a third to halfway full with whatever fresh herbs from the list you have available (or make a particular blend with just a few that you think you'll like) first thing in the morning on a sunny day.

2 | Fill the jar to the top with water and screw on the lid.

3 | Place the jar on a sunny windowsill and let steep for 6–10 hours.

4 | Drink as is, or strain out the herbs before serving.

Makes 1–2 servings.

GF, SF, NF, R

1 part packed fresh herbs (alfalfa, chamomile flowers, lavender flowers, lemon balm leaves, lemon verbena leaves, peppermint, red clover, red raspberry leaves, sage, and/or spearmint, etc.)

3–4 parts filtered water

Good Mood Winter Tea

3 parts St John's Wort (helps relieve anxiety, depression, indigestion, seasonal affective disorder SAD, congestion, flu, insomnia)

2 parts cardamom pods (or 1 part seeds) (helps relieve bronchitis, colds, fever, indigestion, infections, liver and gallbladder problems, sore throat)

2 parts cinnamon bark (helps relieve bronchitis, colds, fever, indigestion, infections, sore throat, balances blood sugar levels)

2 parts licorice root (helps relieve bronchitis, coughing, indigestion, nourishes adrenals)

1 part dandelion root (tones liver and gallbladder, stimulates the appetite, aids with respiratory, digestive, and urinary issues)

1 part black pepper (helps relieve bronchitis, colds, coughing, infections, inflammation)

1 part cloves (helps relieve bronchitis, colds, coughing, infections, inflammation)

I know I'm not the only one who gets a little blue when the days are colder and darker. St John's Wort is clinically recognized for improving moods (though if you're on anti-depressant meds, consult with a health practitioner before consuming it). Cinnamon, cardamom, black pepper, and cloves are all warming, and dandelion and licorice roots not only help you feel grounded, they also nourish your liver and adrenals, respectively.

1 | Combine all herbs in a large bowl. Measure out 1 tsp of herb blend for each cup of water or a heaping tbsp for 4 cups of water and add to mug or teapot.

2 | Bring desired amount of filtered water to a boil. Pour water over the herbs, cover and allow to steep for 10–30 minutes.

3 | Strain out the herbs and rebottle the liquid—you can store it in a thermos to keep it warm throughout the day.

4 | Transfer remaining herbs into to a glass jar with a well-fitting lid, store in a cool, dark place, and use over the next few months.

1 tsp herbs / 1 cup water makes 1 serving.
GF, SF, NF

Strawberry Daiquiris

I am not a big drinker by any means, but there's something about summertime that makes me want to sit on the balcony with something cold and festive.

1 | Mix all ingredients in a blender to achieve desired consistency.

2 | Rub the rim of two chilled cocktail glasses with a piece of lime, then dip the rims onto a plate of sugar.

3 | Distribute the blended drink evenly between the two glasses.

4 | Serve with a strawberry garnish.

Makes 2 servings.

GF, SF, NF, (R only if rum is omitted)

2 oz/60 mL amber rum

½ cup hulled and chopped strawberries, + 2 whole strawberries for garnish

¼ cup lime juice (from 2 limes)

2 tbsp sweetener (agave nectar, maple syrup, or organic sugar)

1 cup ice cubes (ideally made from filtered water)

sugar for coating rim of glasses

Pretty in Pink Lemonade

¼ cup liquid sweetener (agave nectar or maple syrup), or to taste

up to 1 tbsp finely grated fresh ginger

1 cup just-boiled water

2–4 thin slices raw beets

2½ cups cold filtered water

minced fresh peppermint leaves or lemon balm leaves (optional)

½ cup lemon juice (2 medium lemons—be sure to pick out the seeds!)

1 cup ice cubes

I don't know what I thought gave the pink lemonade from concentrate its color when I drank it as a kid. Maybe I believed that there were pink lemons, just as there are pink grapefruits. In any event, this is a festive and refreshing drink that takes just a moment to whip up. I like to bring it with me on sunny afternoons in the park. (You might even spike it with splash of vodka, if you like.)

1 | Place the sweetener and ginger, if using, in a 1 qt/L glass jar. Pour in the just-boiled water and let steep for 5–10 minutes before tossing in the beet slices. Add the filtered water, peppermint (or lemon balm), if using, and lemon juice. Screw on the jar's lid and give it a good shake to combine. Fish out the now-pale beet slices (or keep 'em in).

2 | Fill individual glasses with the ice, pour in lemonade, and enjoy immediately (unless it's a picnic and you're all drinking from the same jar—in which case, drop the ice in there).

Makes 1 qt/L or 2–4 servings.

GF, SF, NF, R

Mulled Cider

2 cups apple cider or unclarified apple juice

½ cup filtered water

1 cinnamon stick

1 tsp grated fresh ginger

4 green cardamom pods or 3–4 whole cloves

Try to get hold of cider pressed from locally and organically grown apples. I make larger quantities of this for winter gatherings (using about 2 qt/L cider for 10–12 people), adding a splash of amber rum or brandy (or even calvados, an apple brandy, if you can find it) to each serving if desired.

1 | Combine ingredients in a small saucepan. Heat on low for 30 minutes. It should gently simmer, but don't let it come to a boil. Pour through a strainer into mugs or fish out spices with a spoon or simply avoid swallowing the whole spices. Serve hot.

Makes 2 mugs.

GF, SF, NF

✸ Noël Nog

Again, here we have a recipe where the ingredients may not be locally sourced, but you have the opportunity to use homemade non-dairy milk (see pp. 78–80), which means at least the water (the bulk of the recipe, really) doesn't have to be shipped from far away.

1 | Pour the almond and coconut milks into a small saucepan and heat on medium-low.

2 | Whisk the syrup and spices together in a small bowl, until no clumps remain.

3 | Add the spice mixture to the saucepan and simmer for about 4 minutes, never allowing it to come to a boil as the milk may separate.

4 | If you want a smooth, velvety drink, pass the liquid through a fine mesh strainer (otherwise just leave it—some spice "grit" will settle at the bottom of each glass, but you can call it "rustic nog").

5 | Mix in your alcohol of choice if you fancy.

6 | Serve warm (non-traditional) or transfer to a jar and chill in the fridge for 1 hour before serving cold.

Makes 4–6 servings.

GF, SF (option), NF

4 cups unsweetened almond milk (soy milk will also do)

½–1 cup coconut milk (optional), to desired thickness and richness

2–3 tbsp maple syrup (to taste)

½ tsp nutmeg

¼ tsp turmeric

⅛ tsp cinnamon

⅛ tsp cloves

⅓ cup (or so) brandy or rum (optional)

✺ Tomato (or Zucchini) Herb Tofu Scram

1 lb/454 g medium or firm non-GM tofu, roughly chopped or crumbled

3 tbsp tamari soy sauce

2 medium or 1 large garlic cloves, pressed

1 tbsp non-hydrogenated coconut or olive oil

1 medium tomato or 1 small zucchini, diced

1 green onion, thinly sliced

2 tbsp chopped fresh herbs (a blend of parsley, cilantro, and/or basil; or rosemary, marjoram, and/or oregano) or 2 tsp blended dried herbs

1–2 tbsp nutritional yeast (optional)

½–1 tsp turmeric

A fresh and tasty alternative to scrambled eggs! While you're not going to be convincing any omnivores you may be brunching with that this is practically the same, it will indeed satisfy you! Serve with whole grain toast and fresh salad.

1 | Allow tofu to marinate in tamari and garlic for 5–20 minutes.

2 | Heat oil in a frying pan on medium-high. Throw in the diced tomato or zucchini and the green onion, and sauté for about 5 minutes until they begin to lose their juice (it'll start to get wet and steamy in the pan). Add tofu and marinade. Sprinkle in the herbs, nutritional yeast, and turmeric. Stir with a spatula until heated well through, about 6 minutes more.

Makes about 4 servings.

GF, NF (option)

Pretty in Pink Lemonade (page 90),
Plum Upside-Down Cake (page 217),
Tomato-Basil Amuse-Bouches (page 131),
Raw Mexican Stuffed Bell Peppers
(page 191)

Spring Sesame Noodles (page 186)

✸ Blueberry Peach Pancakes

I love these pancakes hot off the griddle, with warm juicy peach slivers and the burst of blueberry juice that stains the plate purple as it swirls with the maple syrup.

1 | Whisk together the flour, baking powder and soda, spice, and salt in a large bowl. Add the milk, applesauce, sweetener, and oil, and mix with a silicone spatula just until all the flour has been absorbed.

2 | Portion the batter out by ¼ cupfuls onto a hot and lightly oiled skillet and immediately sprinkle a few peach slices and blueberries onto each of the pancakes, smushing them in a little to allow some of the batter to cover them up.

3 | Cook on medium heat until golden on both sides, about 3 minutes on the first side and 2 minutes on the second.

4 | Serve with your favorite pancake toppings—maple syrup, chopped nuts or seeds, nut butter or non-hydrogenated/non-dairy/non-GM margarine, spices (ground cinnamon, cardamom or nutmeg) ...

Makes about 4 servings or 12 pancakes.
SF, NF

2 cups spelt flour

1 tsp baking powder

½ tsp baking soda

½ tsp ground cardamom or cinnamon

½ tsp sea salt

1 cup non-dairy milk

½ cup applesauce (p. 98 or unsweetened store-bought)

2 tsp liquid sweetener (maple syrup or agave nectar)

1 tbsp sunflower oil (coconut or olive are okay too), plus more for frying

2 medium ripe peaches, thinly sliced or diced

1 cup fresh blueberries

❦ Dried Fruit Compote

When I've attended meditation retreats where we sit in silence for 10 hours each day, fruit compote is always served at breakfast. It's mostly made of prunes, a laxative, as I'm sure the meditation center cooks must know we need this when we're sitting still all day long. It's sweet and tasty over oatmeal, yogurt, pancakes, or even ice creem. Enjoy this one regularly (no pun intended) when you're menstruating or pregnant, as these dark-colored dried fruits are fantastically iron-packed.

1 | Place the fruit and water in a saucepan, cover and heat on medium to medium-low. Cook for 45 minutes, stirring occasionally to prevent sticking and encourage even cooking, until mashable (of course you can chose to leave the compote as chunky as you wish).

Makes about 3½ cups. Store in a sealed jar in the fridge for up to 2 weeks.
GF, SF, NF

3 cups chopped dried fruit (including at least 1 ½ cup prunes, plus chopped unsulfured apricots, apples, figs, peaches, pears, and/or raisins, and no more than ½ cup dates)

3 cups filtered water

Roasted Applesauce

2 lb/1 kg apples (preferably 2 or more varieties, like Pink Lady, Granny Smith, Northern Spy)

¼ cup lemon juice (1 lemon) (optional, see note)

up to 1 tbsp ground cinnamon (optional)

½–¾ cup warm filtered water, as needed for desired texture

While applesauce is a staple in vegan baking, it's also a simple and delicious addition to many breakfasts: with yogurt and/or granola, on pancakes or waffles, or warm in a bowl on its own. Baking the apples amps up the flavor—and gives your house an incredible aroma! If you use just the peeled apples and water, the sauce will be simple and neutral enough to do anything with. Adding the lemon juice will brighten the flavor, make the sauce a little smoother, and likely help it keep longer in the fridge (ascorbic acid from the lemons being a preservative). Keeping the peels on the apples (if they're organic) makes the sauce more nutritious, but they won't dissolve completely—it won't be as smooth, though likely to blend in just fine if used in baking.

1 | Preheat oven to 350°F (180°C). Line a baking sheet with unbleached parchment paper and set aside.

2 | Peel the apples if they're conventionally grown, or, if they're organic, you can choose to leave the skins on. Core them and chop them into even-sized pieces (¼-in/⅔-cm slices or 1-in/2.2-cm bits).

3 | Toss the apples with the lemon juice and cinnamon (if using) in a large bowl. Scatter them across the prepared baking sheet in an even layer.

4 | Slide them into the oven and bake for about 50 minutes, turning them and giving them a bit of a stir with a silicone spatula about halfway through.

5 | Allow to cool for 5 minutes or so before scraping all the apples into your blender or food processor and giving it a whirl just until no apple chunks remain. Alternately, you could use a food mill to mash the apples.

Makes 2⅔ cups. Store in a sealed container or glass jar in the fridge for about a week (maybe 2 weeks if you used lemon juice) or can the applesauce (pp. 57–61) for up to a year.

GF, SF, NF

Apples

Nutritional virtues *Apples contain pectin, a great fiber that will be appreciated by your digestive tract. It is used in many medicines to treat digestive difficulties, including ulcers and diarrhea. It lowers cholesterol levels and also has antioxidant properties. Jonagold apples have the most pectin.*

Varieties *There are over 7,500 varieties of apples grown worldwide, though we are commonly exposed to only a few. Some common varieties include:*

For eating: *Go for crisp and juicy: Cortland, Fuji, Gala, Golden Delicious, Granny Smith, Jonagold, McIntosh, Pink Lady, Pippin, and Winesap*

For pie and sauce: *Go for tart and juicy: Cortland, Fuji, Golden Delicious, Granny Smith, Jonagold, McIntosh, Northern Spy, Pippin, and Rome Beauty*

For baking: *Go for those that will hold their flavor and shape when cooked: Rome Beauty (the best, I hear), Cropland, Golden Delicious, Granny Smith, Ida Red, Jonagold, Northern Spy, and Pippin.*

Get it *Firm. Where I live, I resist buying them in the early summer because they're more likely to come from Chile or Argentina instead of a nearby orchard. I eat apples liberally throughout the fall and winter, in part because they store well, but also because they tend to be one of the most affordable fruits when going organic.*

Eat it/Make it *Raw, juiced, dried, cooked or baked straight up, in soups, salads, baked goods, granola.*

Keep it *Apples will keep on your kitchen table for about a week, otherwise store them in the fridge (or cold storage).*

Apple Cinnamon Buckwheat GRAWnola

6 cups sprouted buckwheat (from about 2 cups dry, see sidebar, p. 101)

1 cup walnuts or almonds, soaked for 8 hours

1 cup sunflower or pumpkin seeds, soaked for 8 hours

1 cup raisins or chopped dried unsulfured apricots, soaked for 1–2 hours

3 medium apples, peeled, cored, and finely chopped

⅔ cup liquid sweetener

2 tbsp cinnamon

¼ tsp sea salt

This recipe will come together over the course of a few days (you can't rush soaking, sprouting, and dehydrating!), but the final product will likely become a staple in your kitchen. I've been really into eating raw foods in the morning (it's just what I crave), especially in the summer, so after I have some fresh fruit, this granola, with some non-dairy milk, makes for a substantial part of a good breakfast. I take this with me when I travel, and on otherwise unpredictable food days it can provide a whole-foods breakfast or a tasty dry snack.

1 | Combine all ingredients in a large bowl, stirring with a silicone spatula, making sure to evenly distribute the sweetener, cinnamon, and salt.

2 | If you have an Excalibur brand food dehydrator (which can be lined with Teflex [non-stick] sheets, mesh sheets, or unbleached parchment paper on the mesh sheets), portion the mixture evenly onto 3 sheets (about 4 cups per sheet). If you just want to use your oven, you'll need parchment-lined baking sheets. Smooth out mixture with a spatula so that it isn't more than ½-in/1.3-cm thick in any place. Slide into the dehydrator, set at 115°F (46°C) for 12–16 hours, or in your oven at the *lowest* possible setting (see sidebar on oven dehydrating) for about 3½–5 hours, until completely dry (humidity in your kitchen will affect the time).

Makes 12 cups or up to 20 servings. Keeps in a sealed container for up to 3 months.

GF, SF, NF, R

A note about oven dehydrating: If you don't have a dehydrator, you can use your oven to make this and other "raw" treats in the book. Just set it to the lowest temperature it goes to (typically 170°F/77°C or 200°F/93°C), and keep something heatproof (like a metal utensil or a ball of tin foil) wedged in the oven door so it always stays open a crack and lets out any humidity.

SPROUTING BUCKWHEAT

Step 1: Soak raw buckwheat groats (not kasha, which is toasted buckwheat) in enough filtered water to cover them by about an inch (2 cm), overnight or for about 8 hours.

Step 2: Drain it into a large colander (fine mesh preferred).

Step 3: Rinse well, ideally with the spray setting on your faucet. Place the colander on a plate or baking sheet to catch any dribbles.

Repeat step 3, 2 to 3 times daily (3 times in hotter weather/climates). The water that runs off sprouting buckwheat tends to be particularly slimy, which isn't a sign that something's wrong; just rinse it every time until the water runs through less gloppily.

Allow the grains to sprout for 2 to 3 days (up to 72 hours), until the tails (sprouted parts) are about double the length of the grain itself. If you start to see little wispy bits (off-shoots) on the end of the sprouts—that's enough sprouting! Use immediately, or store in a sealed container in the fridge for up to 3 days.

2 cups dry raw buckwheat should give you about 6 cups of sprouts.

Apple Spice Pancakes

I remember a lot of pancakes on weekend mornings when I was a kid. This is the recipe from my mum's most-used cookbook (I'm sure your mum or dad has one too— it's thick and old, the spine is probably broken, and the pages with the favorite recipes are splattered with all sorts of ancient ingredients), only veganized. Serve these with maple syrup or buttery spread and sugar and lemon juice, and roll 'em up in cigar shapes to eat with your hands (as I used to do).

1 | Whisk together the flour, baking powder and soda, nutmeg, and salt in a large bowl. Whisk in the grated apple, coating well with the flour mixture (this helps to keep the grated apple from clumping). Add the milk, applesauce, sweetener, and oil, and mix with a silicone spatula just until all the flour has been absorbed.

2 | Portion the batter out onto a hot and lightly oiled skillet and cook on medium to medium-high heat until golden on both sides, about 4 minutes on the first side and 2 minutes on the second.

3 | Serve with your favorite pancake toppings—maple syrup, chopped nuts or seeds, nut butter or non-dairy/non-GM/non-hydrogenated margarine, cinnamon ...

Makes about 4 servings or 10–12 pancakes.

SF, NF

1½ cups spelt flour

1 tsp baking powder

¼ tsp baking soda

¼ tsp ground nutmeg

½ tsp sea salt

1 medium apple, grated (about 1 cup) + 1½ tsp fresh lemon juice

1 cup non-dairy milk

½ cup applesauce (p. 98 or unsweetened store-bought)

¼ cup liquid sweetener, 1 tbsp sunflower, coconut or olive oil, plus more for frying

Flax Apple Pudding

3 medium or 4 small apples, chopped—go organic and keep the skins on! (about 4 cups chopped)

½ cup filtered water

2 tbsp flax seeds, very finely ground (makes about 3 tbsp ground flax seeds)

½ tsp cinnamon (and additional spice, if desired, to taste)

½ tsp pure vanilla extract (optional)

1 tbsp chopped almonds, walnuts, or pecans (optional)

non-dairy milk, to taste

I could eat pudding all day long, so why not start at breakfast? This is a recipe from my friend and colleague Julie Daniluk, nutritionista extraordinaire, and author of Meals that Heal Inflammation. *If you're using early harvest local apples that are on the tart side, you might want to add some raisins for sweetness.*

1 | Place the apples and water in a small saucepan, and bring to a boil. Reduce heat to a simmer, cover, and cook for 10 minutes, until mashable. Remove from heat.

2 | Stir in the ground flax, cinnamon, and vanilla until smooth.

3 | Serve hot, sprinkled with the chopped nuts (if desired) and drizzled with milk.

Makes 2 medium or 1 large serving.

GF, SF, NF

Stick-to-Yer-Ribs Porridge (Steel-Cut Oats)

4 cups filtered water

1 cup steel-cut oats

¼–½ tsp sea salt

Unconventional optionals:

up to ¼ cup raisins

up to ¼ cup chopped nuts or seeds or 2 tbsp nut or seed butter

up to 1 tsp cinnamon

When I go to Scotland for a visit, my diet always seems to be half oats—oatcakes, oat milk, and, of course, porridge. I think it might be my favorite grain. This breakfast is not for your in-a-rush morning, it's for the days you get up early, or don't have to race out of the house right away. I like my porridge on the thicker side, so I cook it for the full time, then drizzle on some maple syrup and almond milk. Leftovers heat up nicely (for your more rushed days); just add an additional splash of water to a small saucepan on medium-low heat.

1 | Pour the water, oats, and salt into a medium saucepan, and bring to a boil. Once boiling, turn heat down to low, partially cover, and cook for 30–40 minutes (depending on desired consistency), stirring every 10 minutes or so to prevent sticking. Serve hot.

Makes 4 servings.

GF (possibly), SF, NF

Whole Grain Waffles

It's now a tradition in my family to make these waffles every year on Christmas morning. This recipe is adapted from one by holistic practitioner and author Rebecca Wood, and it has a really great blend of flavors. Soaking the whole grains, instead of using flour, makes them easier to digest, and also allows them to provide you with a whole other level of nutrient bio-availability. They freeze well, so maybe make a double batch, and toast them one at a time on busier breakfast days.

1 | Drain and rinse the soaked oats and place them in a blender or food processor. Add the seeds, filtered water, coconut, squash, oil, sweetener, baking powder, orange zest, cinnamon, and salt. Give it a whirl until you've got a uniform batter. Add more water if needed for a pourable consistency.

2 | Pour the batter onto a hot and lightly oiled waffle iron, close and bake according to your iron's directions. Serve hot with any toppings you desire.

Makes about 4 servings or 10–12 waffles.

GF (option), SF, NF

2 cups whole oats (you can also use buckwheat, or ½ of either of those grains and ½ millet), soaked overnight in enough water to cover

¼ cup sunflower, pumpkin, or sesame seeds

1 cup filtered water, or more if needed

¼ cup unsweetened, shredded coconut

¼ cup cooked, mashed winter squash (or sweet potato) or applesauce (p. 98 or unsweetened store-bought)

2 tbsp non-hydrogenated coconut, sunflower, or olive oil, plus more for the waffle iron

2 tbsp liquid sweetener

1 tbsp baking powder

finely grated zest of 1 organic orange

2 tsp cinnamon, or more to taste

½ tsp sea salt

Home Sweet Homefries

2½ lbs/1¼ kg non-GM potatoes or sweet potatoes, scrubbed clean and chopped into bite-sized pieces

1 medium onion, minced

1 tsp paprika or dried rosemary (or up to 1 tbsp fresh)

1 tsp sea salt, or to taste

a few twists of the pepper mill

⅓ cup olive oil or sunflower oil (approx.)

Homefries are one of the few things a vegan can eat when out at a diner for brunch; this recipe puts the "home" back in the fries. I've found that the best homemade fries—the ones that are soft on the inside and crispy on the outside—are boiled before they're fried.

1 | Boil the potatoes in a pot of water until relatively soft (about 6–7 minutes). Drain and place in a large bowl. Toss the potatoes with the onion, paprika or rosemary, salt and pepper.

2 | Heat 2 tbsp oil in a medium or large skillet on medium. Add ⅓–½ of the potatoes at a time (depending on the size of your skillet, so that they can all rest in one layer), and sauté, watching for/avoiding fast browning (especially of the onions) by adjusting the temperature as needed. Do not cover the skillet, as they'll steam if covered and not get crispy like they should.

3 | Flip the potatoes around every 4 minutes so they are evenly crisped on all sides, about 16 minutes in all. (Resist flipping too often, which won't allow the taters to crisp up at all.) Serve hot with homemade ketchup (p. 132).

Makes about 8 servings. Leftovers can be reheated in your toaster oven or in a pan.

GF, SF, NF (option)

Grandmother Palmer's Baked Beans

Mother to two of the most fantastic kids I've ever cared for, Alisa Palmer put me in touch with her dad, Marven, who was willing to share this recipe of his mother's with me. (He'd made it once when visiting, and years later I still remembered the heavenly smell as the beans cooked for hours.) Of course, I had to find a replacement for the pork they used, but otherwise it's pretty true to the original.

This is slow food, New Brunswick (turned vegan-whole-foods) style. Serve with Oatmeal Soda Bread (p. 124) and a fresh salad.

1 lb/454 g (about 2⅓ cups) navy beans (or Maine yellow-eye or European soldier beans), soaked in cold water to cover, overnight (for 6–10 hours)

1 medium onion, finely chopped

½–¾ cup or 1 small can tomato paste (optional)

¼ cup unsulfured blackstrap molasses

¼ cup pumpkin seed butter

1 tsp mustard powder

1 tsp freshly grated ginger or ½ tsp ginger powder

1 whole chipotle pepper (or ½ tsp powder (optional but highly recommended)

1½–2 tsp sea salt

freshly ground black pepper, to taste

1 | Drain the soaking water off the beans and rinse. Put them in a 5-qt/L pot on medium heat, and add 6 cups fresh water. Bring to a boil, skim off as much of the foam as you can, then simmer uncovered for 30 minutes, until the beans begin to plump up (lose their wrinkled look).

2 | Preheat oven to 350°F (180°C).

3 | Add the onion, tomato paste, molasses, pumpkin seed butter, sweeteners, salt, mustard, ginger, and chipotle and black peppers. Stir, then pour in an additional 1½ cups filtered water. Cover and bake for 30 minutes.

4 | Reduce the heat to 300°F (150°C), and bake for about 4 hours longer (the original recipe says to be sure to check them "mid-afternoon"—it's likely that Grandmother Palmer always served dinner at 6 pm), until the beans are soft and there's just the right amount of sauce (which is, of course, up to you, but know that you can add water ½ cup at a time, as needed). Serve warm.

Makes 8 servings or about 8 cups.

GF, SF, NF (option)

Kathryn, one of my recipe testers, said this:

Brown gold. jae, stop whatever you are doing now. Whip up 10 batches of this and get thee to a cannery. Watch the money fly. You will make millions. You and Grandma Palmer. These are amazing: 1) my house smells incredible, 2) the ingredients leave a million little souvenirs on the palate, 3) you feel like a million bucks after nursing this dish all day to find out it is the most delicious thing you've ever made, 4) when your mom calls and you mention you're making from-scratch baked beans, pride will spill out of the phone receiver (excellent timing).

The texture is fantastic. Perfect. Goopy and warm and melty, yet the beans are still firm. I questioned the point at which the beans "plump up." I wondered if there was too much liquid in the pot before adding the rest of the ingredients. Never question anything with this recipe. Just proceed. It will be perfect.

Tempeh "Soysauge" Patties

1 9-oz (255-g) cake organic tempeh, cut in quarters

2 tbsp whole grain flour

2 tbsp tamari soy sauce

2 tbsp warm filtered water

1 tbsp olive or sunflower oil

1 tsp marjoram

½ tsp cumin

½ tsp sage

½ tsp thyme

½ tsp smoked paprika

additional oil (non-hydrogenated coconut or sunflower) for frying

In my family we make these for Christmas Day brunch and everyone loves saying the word "soysauge" with a forced New York accent as many times as they can fit it into the conversation. These patties have a great flavor and offer a satisfying dose of protein in a meal that may also be full of sugary waffles or French toast. If you like, serve with Herb Garden Biscuits (p. 119) and a fresh salad.

1 | Fill the bottom of a saucepan fitted with a steamer basket with 1 in/2.5 cm of water. Place on high heat, cover, and bring to a boil. Add the tempeh and steam until tender but not mushy, about 20 minutes.

2 | Allow to cool, then grate into a medium bowl.

3 | Add all the other ingredients, mix and press firmly into 8 patties.

4 | Fry in oil on medium heat until browned on both sides, about 4 minutes on the first side and 3 on the second.

Makes 4 servings.

GF (option), NF (option)

✹ Date-Almond Raw Bars in Three Variations

You can buy some pretty tasty raw bars, but they tend to cost a couple bucks each, and have traveled to the store shelf from far away in glossy packaging. Here's a tasty alternative.

2 cups almonds, soaked overnight, drained and rinsed

3 cups packed pitted dates

1 cup raw cacao nibs, ground

1 cup pumpkin seeds, partially ground

½ cup gogi berries, soaked overnight and drained

¼–½ tsp sea salt (optional)

1 | Place the almonds in your food processor and give it a good whirl to break them up, until just a few chunks remain. Add the dates, ground cacao, pumpkin seeds, gogi berries, and salt, and process until it comes together in a sticky lump. You will likely need to do this in batches in order to control the texture of your dough. Scrape the mixture out onto a Teflex sheet (or a parchment-lined baking sheet), and form into a square about ½-in/1-cm thick. Score with a sharp knife—2 lengthwise cuts and 6 or 7 widthwise cuts.

2 | Dehydrate at 115°F (46°C) for 12–18 hours in your dehydrator, or 6–8 hours in your oven at the lowest temperature (170–200°F/77–93°C), with the oven door propped open with something heatproof like an all-metal spatula or ladle. Flip the bars around ⅔ of the way through, until they are dry to the touch, but not yet crumbly.

Makes 21–24 bars.

GF, SF, NF, R

Other flavor combinations:

APPLE HEMP

2 cups almonds, soaked overnight, drained and rinsed

2 ½ cups packed pitted dates

2 cups cored, peeled, and finely chopped apple

2 tsp finely grated fresh ginger root

1 tsp cinnamon

¼ tsp sea salt (optional)

1 cup hulled hemp seeds

Follow directions above, but fold in the hemp seeds by hand before spreading mixture to dry.

POPPYSEED APRICOT

2 cups almonds, soaked overnight, drained and rinsed

2 cups packed pitted dates

2 cups dried unsulfured apricots, soaked overnight, drained, and finely chopped

¼–½ tsp sea salt (optional)

½–⅔ cup poppy seeds

Follow directions above, but fold in the poppy seeds by hand before spreading mixture to dry.

Lemon Poppyseed Pancakes

2 cups spelt flour

¼ cup poppyseeds

1 tsp baking powder

½ tsp baking soda

½ tsp sea salt

1 cup non-dairy milk

3 tbsp liquid sweetener

1 tbsp non-hydrogenated coconut or sunflower oil, plus more for frying

1 tsp pure vanilla extract

finely grated zest of one lemon

¼ cup lemon juice (1 lemon)

Nice and cake-like, with a satisfying crunch, these are for Dominika, who is not only one of my favorite brunch dates, but tries to get me to put poppy seeds in everything. (Poppy seeds are actually a good source of calcium and help to calm the nervous system.) These are also for all of you lucky ducks who live in regions where lemons grow. Remember to zest your lemon before slicing it open to juice it.

1 | Whisk together the flour, seeds, baking powder and soda, and salt in a large bowl. Add the milk, sweetener, oil, and vanilla, and mix with a silicone spatula just until all the flour has been absorbed. Quickly stir in the lemon zest and juice.

2 | Portion the batter out by ¼ cupfuls onto a hot and lightly oiled skillet and cook on medium heat until golden on both sides, about 3 minutes on the first side, and 2 minutes on the second.

3 | Serve with your favorite pancake toppings.

Makes about 4 servings or 10 pancakes.

SF, NF

Muffins, Scones, & Breads

apricots at a Parisian farmers' market

✾ Strawberry Rhubarb Muffins

2½ cups spelt flour

1 tsp baking powder

1 tsp baking soda

½ tsp cinnamon

½ tsp sea salt

1 cup diced rhubarb (about 1 large or 2 thin stalks, sliced down the middle and cut in ½-in/1-cm pieces)

⅔ cup maple syrup, to taste

⅓ cup applesauce (p. 98 or unsweetened store-bought)

⅓ cup buttahmilk (1 tbsp apple cider vinegar + non-dairy milk)

¼ cup sunflower oil

1 tsp pure vanilla extract

⅔ cup sliced strawberries

optional topping: 1 tbsp organic sugar + ¼ tsp cinnamon

There's a fantastic time late in the spring where the rhubarb's been out for a few weeks and the first strawberries appear. How can you not immediately celebrate this perfect pairing with some muffins? Pay particular attention to the size of the pieces of rhubarb you cut—if they're too big, their sourness will be quite a contrast in the muffin; if they're too small, they won't be noticeable.

1 | Preheat oven to 375°F (190°C). Prepare a 12-cup muffin tray with liners or a light coating of oil and set aside.

2 | Whisk together the flour, baking powder and soda, cinnamon and salt in a large bowl. Add the rhubarb. Pour in the maple syrup, applesauce, buttahmilk, oil, and vanilla. Mix together just until all the flour has been absorbed. Gently fold in the berries. Portion evenly into the prepared muffin cups. Bake for 25 minutes, until the tops are domed and a toothpick inserted in the center comes out clean.

Makes 12 muffins. Keeps in an airtight container for 2 days or in the fridge for up to a week.

SF, NF

✳ Anyberry Muffins

This is your basic berry muffin. Soup it up as you like (see suggestions below), depending on what's available and in season. If you have larger berries (like blackberries), you may want to break them up a bit for better distribution.

1 | Preheat oven to 375°F (190°C). Prepare a 12-cup muffin tray with liners or a light coating of oil and set aside.

2 | Whisk together the flour, sugar (if using), baking powder and soda, salt, and any spices or zest (if using) in a large bowl. Add the milk, maple syrup (if using), applesauce, oil, and vanilla. Gently mix together just until all the flour has been absorbed. Gently fold in the berries. Pour evenly into the prepared muffin cups. Bake for 25 minutes, until the tops are domed and a toothpick inserted in the center comes out clean.

Makes 12 muffins. Keeps in an airtight container for 3 days or in the fridge for up to a week.

SF, NF

2½ cups spelt flour

½ cup organic sugar or liquid sweetener (maple syrup, agave nectar)

2 tsp baking powder

1 tsp baking soda

½ tsp sea salt

1¼ cups non-dairy milk (only 1 cup if using liquid sweetener)

½ cup applesauce (p. 98 or unsweetened store-bought)

⅓ cup sunflower oil

2 tsp pure vanilla extract

1½ cups berries (fresh or frozen but not thawed)

Optionals:

1–2 tsp ground anise, cardamom, cinnamon, ginger, or nutmeg

zest of one organic lemon or orange

☼ Raspberry Millet Muffins

2 cups spelt flour

⅔ cup millet (dry, not cooked)

2 tsp baking powder

1 tsp baking soda

½ tsp sea salt

1 cup non-dairy milk

½ cup applesauce (p. 98 or unsweetened store-bought)

½ cup liquid sweetener (maple syrup, light agave nectar)

⅓ cup sunflower oil

1 tsp pure vanilla extract

1½ cups raspberries (fresh or frozen but not thawed)

I like the contrast of the sourness of the baked raspberries with the sweetness of the muffin, but if you're not into that, hold back a tbsp or 2 of the sweetener (that would otherwise go into the batter) to mash in with the raspberries (creating more of a mush), and gently fold this mixture into the batter just before you portion it into the tray. Oh, and the millet adds great texture.

1 | Preheat oven to 375°F (190°C). Prepare a 12-cup muffin tray with liners or a light coating of oil and set aside.

2 | Whisk together the flour, millet, baking powder and soda, and salt in a large bowl. Add the milk, applesauce, sweetener, oil, and vanilla. Mix together just until all the flour has been absorbed. Gently fold in the berries. Pour evenly into the prepared muffin cups. Bake for 25 minutes, until the tops are domed and a toothpick inserted in the center comes out clean.

Makes 12 muffins. Keeps in an airtight container for 3 days or in the fridge for up to a week.

SF, NF

✳ Double Corn Muffins

I seem to always have a ton of cornmeal in my pantry, which is fine by me because I really enjoy the texture it adds to baked goods, and it's a nice warming grain in the cooler months. These muffins are sweet, but the sweetness is subtle enough that they can go either way— serve them with a soup or stew, or a nice smear of jam at breakfast or tea time.

1 | Preheat oven to 350°F (180°C). Prepare a 12-cup muffin tray with liners or a light coating of oil and set aside.

2 | Whisk together the flour, cornmeal, baking powder and soda, salt, and cinnamon (if using) in a large bowl. Add the buttahmilk, oil, maple syrup, applesauce, and corn kernals. Gently mix together just until all the flour has been absorbed. The batter will seem pretty thin, but the cornmeal will absorb a decent amount of liquid as it bakes. Pour into the prepared muffin cups, filling them about a ¼ in (⅔ cm) from the top.

3 | Bake for 25 minutes, until the tops are domed and a toothpick inserted in the center comes out clean.

Makes 12 muffins. Keeps in an airtight container for 3 days or in the fridge for up to a week.

SF, NF

1⅓ cups spelt flour

1 cup organic or non-GM cornmeal

2 tsp baking powder

½ tsp baking soda

½ tsp sea salt

½ tsp cinnamon (optional)

1¼ cups buttahmilk (1 tbsp apple cider vinegar + non-dairy milk)

⅓ cup olive oil or sunflower oil

¼ cup maple syrup

¼ cup applesauce (p. 98 or unsweetened store-bought) or 1 "flax egg"

½ cup corn kernels (fresh or frozen) or substitute raisins or dried cranberries

✸ "South-in-Your-Mouth" Peach Pecan Muffins

2½ cups spelt flour

½ cup roughly chopped pecans, toasted

2 tsp baking powder

1 tsp baking soda

½ tsp cinnamon

½ tsp sea salt

1 cup non-dairy milk

½ cup applesauce (p. 98 or unsweetened store-bought)

½ cup liquid sweetener (maple syrup, light agave nectar)

⅓ cup sunflower oil

1 tsp pure vanilla extract

1½ cups peeled and diced peaches (fresh or frozen but not thawed—from about 3 medium fruits)

These are mid-summer muffins for a mid-summer morning. You could certainly try out nectarines, apricots, plums, pears, or peeled apples in place of the peaches, and almonds or walnuts in place of the pecans, depending on what's more seasonal or readily available.

1 | Preheat oven to 375°F (180°C). Prepare a 12-cup muffin tray with liners or a light coating of oil and set aside.

2 | Whisk together the flour, pecans, baking powder and soda, cinnamon, and salt in a large bowl. Add the milk, applesauce, sweetener, oil, and vanilla. Mix together just until all the flour has been absorbed. Gently fold in the peaches. Pour evenly into the prepared muffin cups. Bake for 25 minutes, until the tops are domed and a toothpick inserted in the center comes out clean.

Makes 12 muffins. Keeps in an airtight container for 2 days or in the fridge for up to a week.
SF, NF

Kristin, one of my recipe testers, had this to say:

The "South in your Mouth." Seriously! Sweet burst of summer peaches, toasty pecan flavor, spicy cinnamon, with vanilla rounding it all out. These are all tastes reminiscent of my childhood in the southeastern US. Took me back to the days of sneakily picking pecans at the house down the road from my grandparents, then coming home and shelling them.

These muffins are moist, but not overly so. So many textures to appreciate: cakey muffin, soft and juicy peaches, crunchy pecans. Love it. My favorite ever.

🍁 Love Muffins

Gluten-free (option), gooey love in the center. I dedicate these to everyone I know with sensitive systems who (vegan or not) needs to avoid gluten, sugar, dairy, and/or eggs. Especially Julie.

1 | Preheat oven to 375°F (190°C). Prepare a 12-cup muffin tray with liners or a light coating of oil and set aside.

2 | Drain and rinse the grains, then place in a food processor or blender, add the applesauce, syrup, oil, vanilla, ground flax seeds, cinnamon, and salt, and give it a whirl for about a minute, until you can no longer see any whole buckwheat (or oat) kernels. Add the baking powder, soda, and vinegar, and whirl again for another 10 seconds or so.

3 | Fill the muffin cups half way, then drop a tsp of apple butter into the middle of each one, then portion the rest of the batter evenly on top—you're pretty much filling them to the top here. Bake for 25 minutes, until the tops are domed and a toothpick inserted in the center comes out clean (of course, the toothpick won't be completely clean, as it'll go through the apple butter).

Makes 12 muffins. Keeps in an airtight container for 2 days or in the fridge for up to a week.
GF, SF, NF

2 cups whole buckwheat or (gluten-free) whole oats, soaked in 3 cups filtered water for 2–8 hours

½ cup applesauce (p. 98 or unsweetened store-bought)

½ cup maple syrup

¼ cup softened non-hydrogenated coconut or sunflower oil

1 tsp pure vanilla extract (optional)

1 tbsp flax seeds, ground (makes 2 tbsp)

1 tsp cinnamon

½ tsp sea salt

2 tsp baking powder

1 tsp baking soda

1 tbsp apple cider vinegar or lemon juice

¼ cup apple butter

Sweet Potato Date Muffins

2½ cups peeled and cubed sweet potatoes (approx.)

2 cups spelt flour

1 cup oat bran

1 cup rolled oats

1 tbsp baking powder

1 tsp baking soda

2 tsp cinnamon

1 tsp sea salt

1 cup chopped pitted dates

1 cup applesauce (p. 98 or unsweetened store-bought)

¾ cup maple syrup

⅔ cup sunflower or softened non-hydrogenated coconut oil

If you like to make a muffin your meal, these are the ones for you. They are dense and delicious, and might just become one of your favorite muffins ever. When you look at the ratio of dry to wet ingredients or the high baking temperature, you might think, "This can't work!" but trust me—it does! Pile the thick batter high in those muffin cups (yes, just 12) and you'll get crunchy tops and moist interiors—yum!

1 | Preheat oven to 410°F (210°C). Prepare a 12-cup muffin tray with liners or a light coating of oil and set aside.

2 | Fill the bottom of a saucepan fitted with a steamer basket with 1 in/2.5 cm of water. Place on high heat, cover, and bring to a boil. Add the cubed sweet potatoes and steam until tender but not mushy, about 6–8 minutes.

3 | Whisk together the flour, bran, oats, baking powder and soda, cinnamon, and salt in a large bowl. Add the dates and stir to coat with the flour. Pour in the applesauce, maple syrup, and oil. Mix together just until all the flour has been absorbed. Gently fold in the sweet potatoes. Portion evenly into the prepared muffin cups. Bake for 28 minutes, until the tops are domed and a toothpick inserted in the center comes out clean.

Makes 12 large muffins. Keeps in an airtight container for 3 days or in the fridge for up to a week.

SF, NF

Sweet potatoes

Nutritional virtues *Sweet potatoes are high in carotenoid antioxidants and vitamins A and C. They also offer some thiamine (vitamin B1) and calcium.*

Varieties *Sweet potatoes come from South America. They are sometimes called yams, but true yams come from Africa. In addition to the traditional orange-fleshed Beauregard, Jewel, and Garnet varieties, there are white fleshed boniato sweet potatoes (which can make a fine, though a bit sweet, replacement for white potatoes in recipes, as they are dryer than their orange-fleshed cousins).*

Get it *In fall and winter, and look for firm tubers. Smooth and unblemished is a plus but not required.*

Eat it *Raw (in very thin slices) or cooked (baked, mashed, steamed, boiled, puréed, fried, or creamed), sweet potatoes are delicious. Make sure you cover them when boiling so that they don't discolor.*

Keep it *Buy only what you plan to cook. They will keep a few weeks in your fridge, but not as long as regular potatoes.*

Morning Glory Muffins

Yay! A muffin sweetened with dates instead of sugar. Carrots, raisins, and pumpkin seeds—how else would you want to start your morning?

1 | Preheat oven to 375°F (190°C). Prepare a 12-cup muffin tray with liners or a light coating of oil and set aside.

2 | Whisk together the flour, grains, baking powder and soda, spices, and salt in a large bowl. Stir in the carrots, raisins, and pumpkin seeds until well coated in flour.

3 | Toss the dates and soaking water into a food processor or blender and give it a whirl. While it's running, drizzle in the oil, then the orange juice and zest, if desired.

4 | Scrape this sweet mixture into the large bowl and stir just until all of the flour is absorbed. Add the vinegar and stir just until evenly distributed.

5 | Portion the batter evenly into 12 muffin cups and bake for 22–24 minutes, until the tops are domed and a toothpick inserted in the center comes out clean.

Makes 12 muffins. Keeps in an airtight container for 2 days or in the fridge for up to a week.

SF, NF

2 cups spelt flour

¼ cup rolled oats (or other rolled grain)

2 tsp baking powder

1 tsp baking soda

1 tsp cloves

½ tsp nutmeg

½ tsp sea salt

1½ cups grated carrots (I use my food processor with the grater attachment for this)

¾ cup organic raisins

⅓ cup pumpkin or poppy seeds

1 cup packed chopped and pitted dates, soaked in ½ cup just-boiled water for at least 20 minutes

½ cup softened non-hydrogenated coconut or sunflower oil

1 cup orange juice (apple or pear juice is okay, too)

zest of one organic orange (optional)

2 tbsp apple cider vinegar

Oatmeal Raisin Muffins

1½ cups oat flour

1 cup rolled oats

½ cup oat bran

⅓ cup ground flax seeds (from about 2½ tbsp whole flaxseeds)

1 tbsp baking powder

½ tsp baking soda

1 tbsp cinnamon and/or nutmeg and/or cloves (1 tbsp spice in all)

½ tsp sea salt

¾ cup raisins

½ cup applesauce (p. 98 or unsweetened store-bought)

½ cup maple syrup

½ cup buttahmilk (1 tbsp apple cider vinegar + non-dairy milk)

½ cup sunflower oil

I baked these up once when I was feeling the need for a break from spelt flour. When talking to people about oats, I'm always sure to remind them that oats nourish the nervous system. They sure are a comfort food to me. The spice in these muffins isn't a wussy undertone; it's pretty prominent, so if that makes you nervous, feel free to scale it back to 1–2 tsp of spice. The raisins can be replaced with other dried fruits (chopped dates, cranberries, etc.) or chopped nuts (walnut or pecan would be nice).

1 | Preheat oven to 375°F (190°C). Prepare a 12-cup muffin tray with liners or a light coating of oil and set aside.

2 | Whisk together the flour, oats, bran, ground flax, baking powder and soda, spices, and salt in a large bowl. Add the raisins and stir to coat in the flour. Pour in the applesauce, maple syrup, buttahmilk, and oil. Gently mix together just until all the flour has been absorbed. Portion evenly into the prepared muffin cups. Bake for 25–28 minutes, until the tops are domed and a toothpick inserted in the center comes out clean.

Makes 12 muffins. Keeps in an airtight container for 3 days or in the fridge for up to a week.

GF (possibly), SF, NF

✷ Herb Garden Biscuits

I just can't think of a better accompaniment for soup, can you?

1 | Position the rack in the upper-middle portion of the oven, and preheat it to 450°F (230°C).

2 | Line a baking sheet with unbleached parchment paper.

3 | Whisk together the flour, baking powder and soda, and salt in a large bowl. Add the herbs and whisk again. Cut in the oil using a pastry cutter or 2 knives, until you get a coarse meal with a few larger lumps of oil. Stir in the buttahmilk and sweetener with a silicone spatula, just until it all comes together in a sticky lump.

4 | Turn it out onto a clean, lightly floured work surface (I often use a large cutting board) and form into a rough ball. (No overworking the dough!) Cut the ball in half, roll out to about 1-in (2.5-cm) thick, and cut 3–4 biscuits out of each half using a 2½–3-in (6–7-cm) biscuit cutter or an inverted glass. Place biscuits on the cookie sheet and bake until the tops are golden, about 10–12 minutes. Serve right away.

Makes about 8 biscuits. Keeps in an airtight container for 3 days or in the fridge for up to a week.

SF, NF

2 cups spelt flour

2 tsp baking powder

½ tsp baking soda

½ tsp sea salt

1 tbsp minced fresh parsley (or 1 tsp dried)

1 tbsp minced fresh basil (or 1 tsp dried)

2 tsp minced fresh rosemary leaves (or 1 tsp dried)

1 tsp marjoram leaves (or ½ tsp dried)

½ cup cold non-hydrogenated coconut oil (or non-dairy, non-GM margarine), chopped into ¼-in (⅔-cm) cubes

¾ cup buttahmilk (1 tbsp apple cider vinegar + non-dairy milk—use something rich like almond milk)

1 tsp dry or liquid sweetener

Apricot Oatbran Scones

1¾ cups spelt flour

¾ cup oatbran

2 tsp baking powder

1 tsp baking soda

½ tsp sea salt

½ cup cold non-hydrogenated coconut oil (or non-dairy, non-GM margarine)

½ cup buttahmilk (1 tbsp apple cider vinegar + non-dairy milk)

3 tbsp maple syrup or agave nectar

1 tbsp pure almond or vanilla extract

1 cup chopped pitted fresh apricots (about 2 medium)

The inspiration for recipes can really come from anywhere. I was watching one of my favorite corny summer romance movies, The Love Letter (starring Kate Capshaw, Ellen DeGeneres, and Tom Selleck). Jennifer, a university student who works at the bookstore where many of the movie's scenes take place, brings the other employees fancy café treats every morning. It was muffin-recipe creation week in my test kitchen when I was watching, and when I heard her say, "Apricot Wheatgerm Scone," I knew she was onto something (only wheat-free). I find fresh apricots can be hit or miss, so if you come across a few mealy ones this summer, set them aside for a baking recipe such as this one.

1 | Preheat oven to 425°F (220°C). Line a baking sheet with a piece of unbleached parchment paper or lightly oil it.

2 | Whisk together the flour, oatbran, baking powder and soda, and salt in a large bowl. Cut in the coconut oil (or marg). Add the buttahmilk, sweetener, vanilla, and apricots. Mix them in until all the dry ingredients have been absorbed. The dough should be able to hold its own—it shouldn't be super sticky, nor crumbly at all (add more flour/oatbran, or milk/oil to make any needed adjustments).

3 | Lightly grease a ⅓ -cup measuring cup. Fill with dough, then thwack out onto the prepared baking sheet. Repeat 7 times to make 8 scones. Bake for 22–25 minutes, until the bottoms are golden and there's not a bit of gooeyness inside when you break one open.

Makes 8 scones. Keeps in an airtight container for 2 days or in the fridge for up to a week.

SF, NF

Oatmeal Scones

Do you pronounce it "scONes" or "scOnes"? I used to say the former, which is more British, but now I tend to say the latter, which is more popular in North America. Fortunately, everyone seems to pronounce "yum!" the same way.

1 | Position the rack in the upper-middle portion of the oven, and preheat it to 375°F (190°C).

2 | Line a baking sheet with unbleached parchment paper. Place the oats on the baking sheet and toast them in the oven until fragrant and lightly brown, about 7 minutes. Transfer them to a bowl to allow them to cool. Increase the oven temperature to 450°F (230°C).

3 | Whisk the buttahmilk, applesauce, and sweetener together in a small bowl. Spoon 1 tbsp out into another small bowl and set aside.

4 | Place the flour, baking powder, and salt together in the work bowl of a food processor and pulse about 4 times to combine. Drop in the cold oil, and pulse 12–14 more times, until the flour mixture resembles coarse cornmeal. Scrape this into a medium bowl and stir in all but 2 tbsp of the cooled oats.

5 | Fold in the buttahmilk mixture with a silicone spatula or a fork just until the dough begins to come together. Knead into a cohesive lump, adding the remaining oats to prevent/minimize stickiness (don't knead it till it's super-smooth or your scones will be tough).

6 | Form the dough into a 7-in (18-cm) round, about 1 in (2.5 cm) high. Place it on the baking sheet, cut into 8 even wedges, and separate them out about 2 in (5 cm) apart. Brush them with the remaining tbsp of liquid, and slide the baking sheet into the oven to bake until golden brown, about 12–14 minutes. Allow to cool on the sheet or on a rack for 20 minutes before enjoying.

Makes 8 scones. Keeps in an airtight container for 3 days or in the fridge for up to a week.

SF, NF

1½ cups rolled oats

½ cup buttahmilk (2 tbsp cider vinegar + non-dairy milk—use something rich like almond milk)

¼ cup applesauce (p. 98 or unsweetened store-bought) or 1 "flax egg"

¼ cup liquid sweetener

1½ cups spelt flour

2 tsp baking powder

½ tsp sea salt

¾ cup cold non-hydrogenated coconut oil (or non-dairy, non-GM margarine), chopped into ¼-in (⅔-cm) cubes

Cranberry Almond Loaf

2½ cups spelt flour

½ cup organic sugar or Sucanat

2 tsp baking powder

1 tsp baking soda

1 tsp cinnamon

½ tsp sea salt

1¼ cups non-dairy milk

½ cup applesauce (p. 98 or unsweetened store-bought)

⅓ cup softened non-hydrogenated coconut or sunflower oil

1 tsp pure vanilla extract

1 tsp almond extract

1½ cups frozen or fresh cranberries

¾ cup chopped almonds

1 tbsp cider vinegar

The tartness of the cranberries and the sweetness of the almonds make for a nice blend of flavors here. These loaves are pretty enough that I like to wrap them up nice and give as gifts. (In the summer, you might use halved and pitted cherries in place of the cranberries.)

1 | Preheat oven to 350°F (180°C).

2 | Prepare an 8.5- x 4.5-in (22- x 11.4-cm) loaf pan or 4 mini-loaf pans with a light coating of oil and a dusting of flour or line with unbleached parchment paper for greatest ease of removal at the end.

3 | Whisk together the flour, sugar, baking powder and soda, cinnamon, and salt in a large bowl. Add the milk, applesauce, oil, and vanilla and almond extracts, and stir just until all of the flour is absorbed. Fold in the cranberries and almonds and then quickly stir in the vinegar just until it's evenly distributed.

4 | Portion batter evenly into the loaf pans and bake for about 30 minutes (mini-loaves) or 45–50 minutes (medium loaves), until the tops are domed and a toothpick inserted in the center comes out clean.

Makes 1 medium or 4 mini-loaves. Keeps in an airtight container for 2 days or in the fridge for up to a week.

SF, NF

Cranberries

Nutritional Virtues *Fresh cranberries have a high level of nutrients. They are an excellent source of vitamin C and a very good source of dietary fiber. They are a good source of manganese and vitamin K. Cranberries are famous for their ability to help prevent and treat urinary tract infections. They make it difficult for bacteria to adhere to the urinary tract and are being studied for a variety of other health benefits.*

Varieties *They grow wild on bushes, but most of the ones you find in the stores have been cultivated in sandy bogs.*

Get it *Look for plump, firm, dark red berries.*

Eat it *Cranberries are harvested from September to November and are available until December in the stores. If you can't find them fresh, try frozen or dried. Most American cranberries come from Massachusetts, but they are cultivated across the northern US. British Columbia is the world's third largest producer of cranberries after Massachusetts and Wisconsin, responsible for about 95 percent of the cranberries grown in Canada.*

Make it *Best to cook with fresh cranberries. They are tart, so can be used to add a zing to a sweet dish. They are delicious when combined with a sweet fruit in a salad. Dried cranberries can replace raisins in recipes.*

Keep it *Fresh cranberries keep well in a container in the refrigerator and can last for months. Make sure you get rid of any spoiled ones before you store them. Dried cranberries retain most of their antioxidant properties.*

◈ Sunflower Nutmeg Bread

This is a quick-bread that is great served with soup.

1 | Preheat oven to 400°F (205°C). Lightly oil and flour 2.5 x 9-in (13 x 23-cm) loaf pans.

2 | Combine the flour, seeds, millet, baking powder and soda, nutmeg, and salt in a large bowl. Add the buttahmilk, oil, applesauce, and sweetener, and stir just until all of the flour is absorbed.

3 | Pour batter equally into the loaf pans. Bake for about 40–50 minutes, until the tops are domed and a skewer inserted into the center comes out clean.

Makes 2 loaves. Keeps in an airtight container for 3 days, or in the fridge for up to a week.

SF, NF

3 cups spelt flour

⅔ cup sunflower seeds

¼ cup millet (dry, not cooked)

1 tbsp baking powder

1 tsp baking soda

2 tsp nutmeg

1 tsp sea salt

1 ¾ cups buttahmilk (2 tbsp apple cider vinegar + non-dairy milk)

½ cup olive or sunflower oil

½ cup applesauce (p. 98 or unsweetened store-bought)

2 tbsp liquid sweetener

Oatmeal Soda Bread with Walnuts

2½ cups rolled oats (not quick oats), divided

1½ cups buttahmilk (2 tbsp cider vinegar + cups non-dairy milk)

1 cup whole walnuts

2 cups whole spelt flour

1 cup oat flour

2 tsp baking soda

1½ tsp cream of tartar

1½ tsp sea salt

2 tbsp olive or sunflower oil + 1 tbsp for brushing top of the loaf

¼ cup liquid sweetener (maple syrup or barley malt)

There's nothing like freshly baked bread. And if you are phobic about baking with yeast—as I am (it just so rarely works out for me!)—then this recipe is for you. Eat a slice warm, slathered with buttah. My dad says that when he was a child his Gran Burns made soda bread that would be "as hard as a door stop" by the next morning. The same may not exactly be true for this recipe, but it is best fresh or sliced and toasted on the second day.

1 | Place 2 cups of the oats in a medium bowl, and pour in the buttahmilk. Set aside to soak for an hour.

2 | Position the rack in the upper-middle portion of the oven, and preheat it to 400°F (205°C). Line a baking sheet with unbleached parchment paper. Place the walnuts on the sheet and toast them in the oven until fragrant, about 5 minutes. Be sure to set a timer! It's so easy to burn toasting nuts. Allow them to cool before roughly chopping.

3 | Whisk together the flours, remaining ½ cup oats, soda, cream of tartar, and salt in a large bowl. Drizzle in 2 tbsp of the oil and work it into the flour mixture with your fingertips until you get a coarse crumb texture.

4 | Pour in the buttahmilk-soaked oats and sweetener, and stir with a silicone spatula or a fork just until the dough begins to come together. Knead in the walnuts, just until the dough is cohesive and lumpy (12–14 turns should do it; don't knead it till it's smooth or your bread will be tough).

5 | Form the dough into a 7-in (18-cm) round, about 2–2½ in (5–6.4 cm) high. Place it on the baking sheet and score it with an "X", about 5 in (13 cm) long, and ¾-in (2 cm) deep.

6 | Bake until the loaf is firm on the outside and a toothpick inserted into the center comes out clean—about 40–45 minutes. Remove loaf from the oven and brush with the remaining tbsp of oil.

7 | Let cool to room temperature before digging in—30–40 minutes.

Makes 1 loaf. Keeps in an airtight container for 2 days or in the fridge for up to a week.

SF, NF

Dips, Spreads, & Appetizers

Barrett checks out the tomatoes

❀ Superhero Spinach Dip

2 cups tightly packed spinach

1½ cups cooked or canned white beans (baby lima, cannellini, great northern, navy)

up to ⅓ cup filtered water (to desired thickness)

2 tbsp flax seed or olive oil

1–2 tbsp nutritional yeast (optional)

1–2 medium garlic cloves (roasted garlic will give a mellower flavor)

½ tsp sea salt, or to taste

With a focus on the mineral-rich greens (and not the beans), this very simple dip retains a fresh mighty color. Dip in your favorite veg or spread it on some crusty bread.

1 | Combine all ingredients, starting with just 2 tbsp water and the smaller amount of salt, in a food processor and give it a whirl until desired consistency is reached, adding more water as necessary. Adjust seasonings to taste.

2 | Chill for at least 30 minutes, though it's best when not cold straight from the fridge.

Makes 2 cups. Keeps in the fridge for up to 1 week.

GF, SF, NF

✿ Classic Veg Pâté

This version is adapted from a recipe given to me by my dear friend Elise. Don't be deterred by the length of the method; the detail is meant to help you save time and energy. Using a food processor to prepare the vegetables makes short work of this pâté. You can, however, prepare the vegetables by hand, in which case you might want to pull out a box grater for the carrots and potato instead of chopping them. If you're not into mushrooms, Elise assures me you can leave them out, and the end result will still be tasty. Serve Veg Pâté with crackers or sliced thinly in a sandwich.

1 cup sunflower seeds

1 medium onion, chopped

2–3 medium garlic cloves, chopped

2 tbsp olive oil + ⅓ cup olive oil

6–8 oz (about 2–3 cups) cremini or white mushrooms

1½ cups just-boiled filtered water

1 fist-sized potato or sweet potato, chopped

1 medium carrot, chopped (again, peel only if not organic)

¾ cup nutritional yeast flakes

½ cup whole grain flour

2 tbsp lemon juice

1 tbsp fresh (or 1 tsp dried) basil, thyme, or sage leaves

½ tsp dried marjoram

1 tsp sea salt, or to taste

freshly ground black pepper, to taste

2–3 tbsp wheat germ (optional, if tolerant)

1 | Preheat oven to 350°F (180°C). Lightly oil an 8 x 8-in (21 x 21-cm) baking pan (or line it with parchment). If you only have a larger pan, the layer of pâté will be thinner, and it will bake faster.

2 | Grind sunflower seeds in a food processor until there are no whole seeds remaining. Scrape into a large bowl and set aside. (Keep the food processor handy—there's no need to wash it before the next step.)

3 | Place the onions and garlic in the food processor and whirl it to a mince.

4 | Heat the 2 tbsp of oil in a skillet. Add the minced onions and garlic (don't put the food processor bowl in the sink yet!), and sauté for about 5 minutes, until the onions begin to soften.

5 | Place the mushrooms in the food processor and chop them up before adding them to the skillet. Sauté veggies for 5 minutes more.

6 | Add the contents of the skillet to the bowl with the sunflower seeds. Using the water, deglaze the pan, then pour off into the bowl. Prepare the potato and carrot, either chopping them together in the food processor or using a grater, and add them to the bowl as well, along with the nutritional yeast, flour, additional oil, lemon juice, herbs, salt, and pepper. Mix into a relatively uniform texture with clean hands or a silicone spatula. Scrape the mixture into the baking pan and press into a smooth layer. You might sprinkle wheat germ on top for a nice, slightly crispy crust.

7 | Bake for 35–45 minutes, until it begins to brown on top and feels slightly firm to touch.

It's pretty delicious warm, but once cooled it will keep in the fridge for up to a week.

Makes up to 12 servings.
GF (option), SF, NF (option)

🌼 Savory Stuffed Mushroom Caps

¼ cup raw walnuts or hazelnuts

2 tbsp breadcrumbs (gluten-free is fine)

freshly ground pepper, to taste

14 medium organic cremini or white button mushrooms

1 tbsp olive oil, plus more for the pan

2–3 medium garlic cloves, minced

¾ tsp dried basil

½ tsp dried thyme

¼ tsp dried marjoram

1 tbsp tamari soy sauce

1 tbsp red wine, red wine vinegar, or balsamic vinegar

Lauren passed this delicious recipe on to me; it originally came from Jess of the vegan blog Get Sconed! I just made a few tweaks, really. Serve these mushroom caps at any point in the day, from brunch to dinner. Organic mushrooms are certainly preferable; see opposite for more info.

1 | Preheat oven to 400°F (205°C). Toast the whole nuts on an ungreased baking sheet for 7–10 minutes (being sure to use a timer, as these babies can burn fast!). Remove from the oven and set aside to cool for 5–10 minutes. Coarsely chop the nuts.

2 | Transfer the nuts to a small bowl and stir in the breadcrumbs and freshly ground black pepper.

3 | Remove the mushroom stems with a gentle but meaningful joystick wiggle. Set the caps aside. Finely chop the stems.

4 | Preheat a pan on medium heat with the olive oil. Add the garlic and cook for 2 minutes, being careful not to burn. Add the chopped mushroom stems and sauté for 2–3 minutes more; you will see them start to juice.

5 | Add the herbs, tamari, and red wine or vinegar. Sauté for 3–4 minutes, until the liquid is absorbed. Stir the sautéed mixture into the breadcrumbs, mixing well with a fork.

6 | Lightly grease an 8 x 8-in (21 x 21-cm) baking pan (large enough to fit the mushrooms cosily in one layer) with olive oil, or line with unbleached parchment paper.

7 | Portion the filling evenly amongst the mushroom "bowls," pressing the mixture with the back of the spoon or your finger so it is tightly packed.

8 | Place the stuffed mushrooms next to one another in the prepared pan. Once assembled, drizzle more extra virgin olive oil and red wine or vinegar over the mushrooms, enough so a thin layer of liquid sits on the bottom of the pan.

9 | Bake for 15–18 minutes, until browned. Broil for 1 minute, if desired (being sure to set that timer again!).

Makes about 4 servings.

GF (option), NF

Mushrooms

Nutritional virtues *It is important to remember that not all mushrooms are edible, but the edible ones are really good for you. They are high in selenium (an antioxidant), riboflavin (vitamin B$_2$), pantothenic acid (vitamin B$_5$), copper, niacin (vitamin B$_3$), potassium, and phosphorus. They are also a good source of iron. Shiitake, oyster, king oyster, and maitake mushrooms contain the highest amounts of ergothioneine, a powerful antioxidant. Shiitakes are also considered a complete protein. But white button mushrooms contain antioxidants, so you don't have to spend a fortune to get those health benefits.*

Varieties *The light brown cremini mushrooms are richer in flavor and have more nutrients than the white button mushrooms that are commonly available. The others mentioned above are considered specialty mushrooms and may not be so readily available.*

Get it *Choose mushrooms that are plump and fresh. Dried and withered or slimy ones are to be avoided. You may have heard that mushrooms are grown in horse manure, but more specifically, the manure is pasteurized and then a layer of peat moss is placed on top; the mushrooms grow in that. If your mushrooms are organic, the manure is from organically raised animals. Fresh mushrooms are available all year round.*

Eat it *You can eat your mushrooms raw or cook them.*

Eat it/Make it *They are lovely fried or roasted or in soups. Stuffed mushroom caps are delicious. Large portobello caps make great burgers. When cleaning them, don't soak in water or they will get spongy. Simply wipe with a damp cloth or mushroom brush and slice off the bottom of the stem.*

Keep it *They will keep in the fridge in a paper bag. You probably want to eat them within a few days, but if they dry and don't get slimy they will still be good.*

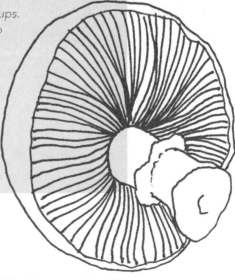

☀ Herb Garden Hummus

2 cups cooked chickpeas (garbanzo beans) or white beans (or 1 19-oz/540-mL can, drained and rinsed)

½ cup packed fresh herbs (basil, parsley, or cilantro, or a blend of any of those along with some fresh lovage, marjoram, oregano, or rosemary)

3 tbsp tahini

2 tbsp lemon juice (about ½ lemon)

2 tbsp flax seed or olive oil

2 medium garlic cloves (roasted garlic gives a mellower flavor than raw) or 1 green onion, sliced

1 tsp sea salt

freshly ground black pepper, to taste

½ cup filtered water

Hummus is a much appreciated go-to spread or dip in my kitchen. This version gets a green boost from your garden or windowsill herb box, and bumps up the nutritional value with vitamin C (parsley), or detoxifying (cilantro), anti-fungal (oregano), or anti-inflammatory (rosemary) properties.

1 | Toss all ingredients in a blender and give it a whirl, adding more water as necessary (be careful not to let it get too runny, though it does thicken up once refrigerated).

Makes 2 cups. Store in an airtight container in the fridge for up to 5 days.

GF, SF, NF

☀ Salsa Verde

1 lb/454 g tomatillos (about 6–10 fruits), husked and quartered or diced

½ medium onion, chopped or minced

⅓ cup chopped cilantro

3 garlic cloves, chopped or pressed

1 serrano chili, seeded and finely chopped

½ tsp sea salt

Tomatillos appear at my local farmers' markets in August—green tomatoes cutely wrapped in individual husks (I still wash them before eating, though). You can enjoy them in this salsa fresh or roasted, it's up to you. If the latter, roast them whole in an oven preheated to 450°F (230°C) for about 20 minutes, until tender. Heck, roast the garlic called for in the ingredients while you're at it.

1 | Place all ingredients in a food processor and pulse to desired consistency, or mix together with a silicone spatula in a medium bowl.

2 | Allow flavors to meld for 1–4 hours before serving.

Makes 2 cups.

GF, SF, R (option)

✺ Tomato-Basil Amuse-Bouches

These raw appetizers, reminiscent of a Caprese salad (without the bocconcini cheese), are a delicious way to "amuse the mouths" of your guests before dinner is served on a hot summer evening. Use about 1 tomato per person; if you have less than 8 people to serve, you may end up with leftover cashew creem (which wouldn't be such a bad thing, would it?).

1 cup raw cashews, soaked in filtered water to cover for 4–8 hours

½ cup filtered water

¼ tsp sea salt

5–8 cocktail tomatoes (larger than cherry tomatoes, rounder than plum tomatoes)

1 medium clove garlic

½ cup fresh basil leaves

additional sea salt and freshly ground pepper, to taste

1 | Drain and rinse the cashews and put them in a blender or food processor (fitted with the smaller work bowl if you have one), along with the fresh water and salt. Give it a whirl until the cashews are as smooth as they're ever gonna be. You'll need to stop the motor, scrape down the sides of the work bowl with a silicone spatula, and whirl again at least twice. Scrape into a small bowl or container and allow it to set in the fridge.

2 | Cut the tomatoes widthwise into almost ½-in/1-cm slices, discarding the ends. Place the slices in one layer on your serving plate. Use a garlic press to squeeze the clove of garlic over the tomatoes so that just a little bit of crushed garlic hits each slice. Dollop about a heaping teaspoon of cashew creem onto each slice. Press 1–3 basil leaves (depending on their size) onto the creem. Season with salt and fresh pepper to taste.

Makes up to 8 servings. (They don't keep all that well once prepared, so try to make just enough for all your guests.)
GF, SF, R

Homemade Ketchup

¼ cup apple cider vinegar

¼ cup filtered water

2 tbsp liquid sweetener (maple syrup, rice syrup, barley malt, or agave nectar)

½ tsp sea salt

1 tsp fresh oregano leaves (or ½ tsp oregano)

¼ tsp mustard powder

¼ tsp nutmeg

freshly ground pepper, to taste

1 clove garlic, grated or pressed

⅔ cup (or 1 5.5-oz/156-g can) tomato paste

Ketchup you make yourself doesn't take long, and it often has a whole other dimension of flavor that store-bought bottles lack. Make a large batch of this to freeze or can in small jars (see p. 57).

1 | Place all ingredients but the tomato paste in a small saucepan and bring to a boil. Turn the heat down to low, stir in the paste, cover and cook for about 8 minutes before removing from heat.

Makes 1 cup. Keeps in a jar in fridge for up to 2 weeks, or in freezer for up to 3 months.
GF SF

Kale Krisps

1 bunch green or curly kale (about 8 oz/227 g), stemmed and chopped into 3-in (7-cm) pieces (or so)

3 tbsp prepared salad dressing (see pp. 136–138)

Wouldn't it be super if you could make yourself a snack that had the crispy and flavorful satisfaction of potato chips, but wasn't so caloric and fatty and was actually a good source of greens? Here you go! Use any dressing that you like; perhaps something with tahini and lemon for that sour-cream-and-onion effect, something with a spicy kick like ginger or cayenne, or simply pesto straight up!

1 | Toss the chopped kale leaves with the dressing in a large bowl until the dressing is evenly dispersed.

2 | Spread the seasoned leaves in a single layer (if they get piled they'll steam instead of crisping up) over 3 dehydrator sheets, or baking sheets lined with unbleached parchment paper. Dehydrate at 115°F (46°C) for 3–5 hours, or in the oven at 150°F (66°C) or 175°F (79°C) (with the door propped open) for 1½–2 hours, until the kale is dry.

Makes 2–4 servings. Will keep in a sealed container for up to a month.
GF, SF, NF

◈ Root Chips

If you choose to buy organic root vegetables, you don't need to peel them; merely scrub them before slicing. Sure, you can remove any imperfections, but otherwise the skin is very nutritious. Slice them into "chips" with even thickness, and in a size that's right for you (so you might cut carrots and parsnips on a bias). A mandoline or the slicing attachment on your food processor will make short work of the preparation, though this may be a good opportunity to practice your knife-wielding skills.

8 cups thinly sliced (no more than ⅛-in / ¼-cm) root vegetables (beets—both red and golden—carrots, celery root, Jerusalem artichokes, parsnips, sweet potatoes, turnips)

¼ cup olive oil

1 tsp sea salt

freshly ground pepper, to taste

1 medium garlic clove, pressed (optional)

1 | Toss the sliced roots with the oil and salt in a large bowl until the oil is evenly dispersed. Grind in the pepper (and press in the garlic, if desired) and toss again.

2 | Spread the seasoned roots in a single layer over 3 dehydrator sheets, or baking sheets lined with unbleached parchment paper. Dehydrate at 115°F (46°C) for 6–8 hours, or in the oven at 150°F (66°C) or 175°F (79°C), with the door propped open, for 2–3 hours, until they are dry.

Makes 4–6 servings. Keeps in a sealed container for up to a month.
GF, SF, NF, R

Sunny Flaxtastic Crackers

1 cup golden flax seeds

1 cup sunflower seeds

2 cups filtered water

1 small or ½ medium zucchini, chopped

¼ cup lemon juice

1 tsp liquid sweetener (like agave nectar) or ¼ tsp stevia powder

1 tbsp grated garlic or ginger root (optional)

1 tsp turmeric powder

1 tsp sea salt

These are an adaptation of a recipe from my friend and colleague Julie Daniluk, author of Meals That Heal Inflammation. *The turmeric is in there for both its color and its anti-inflammatory properties, but you can leave it out if you have a more sensitive palate.*

1 | Soak the seeds in the water in a glass jar or bowl overnight or for at least 6 hours.

2 | Place the seed mixture (along with the water it was soaking in) into a food processor. Add the zucchini, lemon juice, sweetener, garlic or ginger, turmeric, and salt. Process until you get a uniform mixture.

3 | Spread mixture evenly onto Teflex sheet or fruit roll trays to no more than ¼-in (⅔ cm) thick, and dehydrate at 110°F (43°C) for about 9 hours.

4 | Cut with kitchen shears into desired-sized pieces (I make 4 cuts widthwise, and 3–4 cuts lengthwise, then cut those squares in half on the diagonal) and return to trays (removing Teflex sheets) to dehydrate for 3 hours more, until no longer moist in the middle and crisping at the edges.

Makes 80–100 2 x 2-in (5 x 5-cm) crackers.

GF, SF, NF, R

Salads & Dressings

Michelle and her CSA box loot

Maple Apple Cider Vinaigrette

½ cup flaxseed and/or olive oil

⅓ cup apple cider vinegar

2 tbsp apple cider

2 tbsp maple syrup

2 medium garlic cloves, pressed, or 2 tsp finely grated ginger root

½ tsp sea salt

When maple sap is harvested and boiled down in early spring in my part of the world to create maple syrup, it's hard not to use it in everything! Here you've got both sweet and tangy—a good staple salad dressing if you're looking for a change. It's yummy on fresh salad greens or grilled veggies.

1 | Place all ingredients in a 1 pint (473-mL) glass jar. Cover with a tight-fitting lid and give it a good shake to combine.

Makes about 1 cup. Keeps in the fridge for at least 2 weeks.

GF, SF, NF

Creemy Ramp Dressing

1 cup olive oil

½ cup chopped wild leeks (bulbs and leaves)

⅓ cup red wine vinegar

¼ cup light miso paste

1 tsp prepared mustard

You'll want to take advantage of the short time that wild leeks (a.k.a. ramps) are available in the spring (for those of you who are lucky enough to live in a region where they grow). You can use this dressing as a green hollandaise sauce (or just put it on salad—one tester said it actually got her eating more salads than usual!). If it's too thick for your liking, feel free to add a tbsp or 2 of filtered water.

1 | Place all ingredients in a blender or food processor (or hand blender jar/cup) and blend till very smooth (about 1 minute). Serve over veggies, cooked grains, or salad.

Makes 2 cups. Best used immediately, but will keep in the fridge in an airtight jar for up to 5 days.

GF, NF, R

✺ Berry Vinaigrette

There's something very summery about a berry dressing. And summer's the season when I crave huge fresh salads every day, so it all works out!

1 | Place all ingredients—except for the water—together in a blender or food processor and whirl until all the berries are puréed. Add some or all of the water to desired consistency.

Makes about 1 cup. Keeps in the fridge in an airtight jar for up to a week.

GF, SF, NF, R

⅔ cup olive and/or flax seed oil

½ cup berries (fresh or frozen)

⅓ cup red wine vinegar or apple cider vinegar

up to 1 tbsp liquid sweetener (agave nectar, maple syrup) or ¼ tsp stevia powder, to taste

¼ tsp sea salt, or to taste

freshly ground black pepper, to taste

up to 3 tbsp filtered water

✺ Pesto Dressing

Sometimes I get on these pesto kicks, and I want the stuff on everything! Here's a way to get the flavor to disperse evenly over salad, roasted vegetables, pasta, grains, or legumes.

1 | Place all ingredients in a 1-pint (473 mL) jar. Cover with a tight-fitting lid and shake well to combine.

Makes about 1 cup. Store any leftover dressing in the fridge for up to a week.

GF, SF, NF, R

⅔ cup olive oil

½ cup non-dairy pesto (p. 146 or you can use store-bought)

⅓ cup lemon juice (from about 1½ lemons)

1 large or 2 medium garlic cloves, grated or pressed

½ tsp sea salt

freshly ground black pepper, to taste

✺ Lemon Dill Dressing

What do you do with fresh dill? Here's one option. Serve this dressing over potatoes, white beans, pasta, or anything else that inspires you.

1 | Place all ingredients in a 1-pint (473-mL) glass jar. Cover with a tight-fitting lid and shake well to combine.

Makes ¾ cup. Any leftover dressing will keep in the fridge for up to a week.

GF, SF, NF, R

½ cup olive oil

¼ cup lemon juice (about 1 lemon)

1 packed tbsp minced fresh dill (or 1 tsp dried)

1 medium garlic clove, pressed

½ tsp sea salt, or to taste

freshly ground black pepper, to taste

Better than Balsamic Vinaigrette

2 tbsp fresh miso paste (any kind—light and darker varieties both work)

¾ cup olive oil (and/or flax seed oil or hemp seed oil)

⅓ cup balsamic or red wine vinegar

2 medium-large garlic cloves, pressed or grated

1 tsp maple syrup or agave nectar

1 tsp dried oregano or rosemary

½ tsp sea salt

freshly ground black pepper, to taste

up to ⅓ cup minced fresh parsley (optional)

For those of you who couldn't get enough of the House Dressing in Get It Ripe, *this is what I came up with when I'd eaten it for so long that I was in need of a change.*

1 | Place the miso in a small bowl and pour in a splash or two of the oil, stirring until you've got a smooth, liquidy consistency. Scrape this into a 1-pint (473-mL) glass jar. Add the rest of the ingredients, cover with a tight-fitting lid, and shake well until combined. (Alternately, you could just throw all the ingredients in a blender and give them a whirl.)

Makes about 1½ cups. Store leftover dressing in the fridge for up to a week.

GF, NF, R

❀ Pesto Potato Salad

I've always been turned off by potato salad (or egg salad or tuna salad) with mayo. Bleh. (No offense if you're into it.) This, however, is great. You could also throw in up to a cup green peas or chopped green beans, though you might want to up the amount of pesto and/or salt if you do. Serve with a fresh green salad or steamed greens.

1 | Bring a 3-qt/L saucepan of salted water to a boil, plunk in the potatoes, and cook uncovered until the taters are soft but not yet falling apart, about 10–12 minutes. Drain into a colander, rinse well with cold water, and place in a large bowl to cool.

2 | Add the pesto, onions, salt, and pepper, and mix gently (a silicone spatula works well). Serve at room temperature.

Makes 6–8 servings.

GF, SF

2 lbs/1 kg potatoes: scrubbed well, funky bits peeled off, and chopped into bite-sized pieces (about 1-in/2.5-cm cubes)

½ cup non-dairy pesto, any kind—basil, cilantro, garlic scape (p. 146), parsley (p. 146), wild leek, whatev ...)

5 spring red onions (or 6 green onions), thinly sliced

1 tsp sea salt

freshly ground black pepper, to taste

Green onions (also called scallions)

Nutritional virtues Like other onions, they are antifungal and antimicrobial. Green onions are said to be an effective digestive aid. The green tops are high in vitamin A, while the bulbs contain vitamins A, B complex, and C.

Varieties Along with onions, garlic, and leeks (members of the Allium family), green onions come from the same seeds as yellow or red onions; they're just planted closer together and harvested earlier.

Get it Fresh, crisp and bright green in the springtime.

Eat it Raw in salads, sandwiches, or as a flavorful garnish on pastas, soups, or stews. They're also nice grilled. Chop off the hairy root end and the drier top end. Some recipes may specify discarding most of the green top.

Keep it In a container or plastic bag for up to 2 weeks after harvesting. Sometimes the outer layers will get funky or dry but you can just peel them down to the fresher inner layers.

Springtime Tabouleh

1 cup millet

2 cups filtered water

2 cups chopped asparagus

1 cup finely chopped lemon balm

1 cup finely chopped mint

1 cup finely chopped parsley

5 spring red onions (or 6 green onions), thinly sliced

6 small radishes

2 tbsp to ¼ cup lemon juice

2–3 tbsp olive oil

½–1 tsp sea salt, to taste

freshly ground black pepper, to taste

Bulgur wheat, the traditional grain in tabouleh, is replaced here by gluten-free millet (or you could use quinoa). Asparagus and radishes are an early-in-the-season variation on the classic tomatoes and cukes. Fresh lemon balm is well worth picking up at your farmers' market when it's available (or plant it in your garden)—it makes a unique replacement for some of the parsley. If you can't find it though, just double the amount of parsley called for below. This filling salad tastes best on the first day, but will be fine on day 2 or 3. Serve with a fresh green salad or steamed greens.

1 | Combine the millet and water in a 2-qt/L saucepan, bring to a boil, reduce heat to low, and cook covered for 20 minutes, just until all the water has been absorbed. Set aside and let cool.

2 | Steam the asparagus for 2 minutes, until *al dente*, then transfer to a colander. Run cold water over them to stop the cooking process, and set aside to cool completely.

3 | Toss all the ingredients together in a large bowl (you can even use your clean hands) until everything is well distributed. Adjust seasonings to taste. Serve at room temperature.

Makes about 8 servings.

GF, SF, NF

✸ Warm Mushroom and Spinach Salad

This is a springtime salad for when the weather's still not warm enough for all-raw ingredients.
You might choose to add Heart Beets (p. 182), Braised Fennel (p. 179), Ginger Glazed
Carrots (p. 177), marinated and grilled tempeh or a cup of sunflower sprouts.

1 | Heat the oil on medium in a medium skillet. Add the onion, mushrooms, and garlic, and sauté until the onions and mushrooms soften, about 7 minutes.

2 | Toss the spinach, vinegar, salt, and pepper together in a large bowl. Add the still-hot sautéed veg and toss again to encourage the spinach to wilt. If it's not wilting as much as you like, scrape it all back into the warm pan and stir for a minute or 2.

3 | Portion onto 4 plates, garnish with the toasted nuts or seeds, and serve immediately.

Makes 4 servings.

GF, SF, NF

¼ cup olive oil

1 medium red onion, thinly sliced

8 medium cremini or shiitake mushrooms, thinly sliced

2 medium or 1 large garlic clove, minced

1 lb/454 g spinach (stemmed and chopped if mature

⅓ cup balsamic vinegar

½ tsp sea salt, or to taste

freshly ground black pepper, to taste

¼ cup lightly toasted nuts (chopped almonds, walnuts, pecans) or seeds (sunflower or pumpkin seeds or pine nuts)

Sesame Arame Broccoli Salad

¼ cup arame (a dark sea veggie)

1 medium bunch broccoli, chopped into bite-sized pieces (both florets and peeled stems, about 5 cups chopped)

2 tbsp tamari or shoyu soy sauce

2 tbsp toasted sesame oil

1 large garlic clove, pressed, or 1 tsp grated fresh ginger

½ tsp dulse powder or flakes (optional)

freshly ground black pepper, to taste

3 tbsp unhulled sesame seeds (brown or black)

Here's a quick and simple way to get some liver-loving broccoli and mineral-rich sea vegetables in your diet. It tastes great warm or cold. Serve over brown rice, maybe with some marinated and grilled tempeh or tofu, and some natural pickled ginger (avoid the stuff that's been dyed pink).

1 | Fill a large saucepan fitted with a steamer basket with about 1 in/2.5 cm of water. Cover and place on high heat.

2 | Place the arame in a small bowl and cover with water. Soak for about 10 minutes, until soft, then drain (discarding soaking water or saving it for a soup stock).

3 | When the water in the saucepan has come to a boil, add the chopped broccoli, cover again, and steam for 2–4 minutes, until tender. Remove from heat and transfer the broccoli to a large bowl.

4 | Combine soy sauce, oil, garlic (or ginger), dulse, and pepper in a small bowl. Pour the dressing over the broccoli.

5 | Toss gently with the arame and sesame seeds and serve.

Makes about 4 servings.

GF, NF

Fennel and Pink Pearl Barley Salad

Not only is this satisfying to eat, but it's wonderfully festive looking. Leftovers make a nice packed lunch.

1 | Fill a small saucepan fitted with a steamer basket with about 1 in/2.5 cm of filtered water, and bring to a boil. Add the beets and steam for about 4 minutes, until tender. Remove them from the pot and set aside, pouring the steaming water into a 4-cup measure.

2 | Add more water (or veg stock) to make 2½ cups. Pour this back in the saucepan, along with the barley, bring to a boil, reduce heat to simmer and cover. Cook barley until tender, about 50 minutes.

3 | Once cooked, smooth the barley out in a medium-sized bowl to allow it to cool a bit.

4 | Whisk together the lemon juice, olive oil, salt, and pepper in a small bowl. Pour this over the barley, add the fennel, and allow it to stand at room temperature for 30 minutes to 2 hours to allow the flavors to meld.

5 | Add the beets, spinach, and pine nuts and gently toss. Serve immediately.

Makes 5–6 servings.

SF, NF

1 cup julienned red beets

2½ cups filtered water (and veg stock), as needed

1 cup pearl barley, rinsed

1 tbsp fresh lemon juice

¼ cup olive oil

1 tsp sea salt, or to taste

freshly ground black pepper, to taste

2 cups finely sliced fennel bulb

2 cups chiffonade (thinly sliced) spinach

¼ cup lightly toasted pine nuts or sunflower or pumpkin seeds

Roots and Shoots

1 cup packed grated carrots, beets, sunchokes, daikon, and/or celery root

1 cup sprouts—mung bean, alfalfa, clover, sunflower, pea shoots, and/or a mix

2 tbsp flax seed or hemp seed oil

2 tbsp fresh lemon juice (from ½ lemon) or apple cider vinegar

½ tsp sea salt

freshly ground black pepper, to taste

In winter, when the only local produce available seems to be hearty storage crops, fresh sprouts can be as locally grown as your own kitchen! Enjoy this on its own or over a bowl of (unlikely to be local in the winter) organic mixed baby greens or chopped lettuce and/or spinach.

1 | Toss all ingredients together in a medium bowl. Adjust seasonings to taste.

Makes 1 large or 2 smaller servings.

GF, SF, NF, R

PART II: THE RECIPES

Pestos, Sauces, & Gravies

at the Edinburgh farmers' market

Garlic Scape Pesto

1 cup chopped garlic scapes (about 10 scapes)

⅔–¾ cup raw nuts or seeds (walnuts, cashews, almonds, sunflower or pumpkin seeds, or a combination)

¾ tsp sea salt

freshly ground black pepper, to taste

½ cup olive, flax seed or walnut oil

¼–½ cup filtered water

You may recognize scapes as the crazy green shoelace-looking things at farmers' market stands. They can replace both the basil and the garlic in a traditional pesto recipe. Serve over pasta, on pizza, in salads, as a dip … whatevah!

1 | Add the scapes, nuts (or seeds), salt, pepper, and oil into a blender or food processor and give them a good whirl. Stop the machine, scrape down the sides with a silicone spatula, and whirl again until a pretty uniform paste is achieved (you may need to stop and scrape again).

2 | While the machine is still running, pour in the amount of water needed to get the desired pesto consistency (it's up to you, but I use the larger amount). Adding the water in this way makes the pesto nice and creamy.

Makes about 2 cups. Keeps in an airtight container in the fridge for up to a week, or in the freezer for up to 3 months.

GF, SF, NF, R

✻ Parsley Pesto

1 bunch roughly chopped flat-leafed parsley—about 2½ packed cups (including some stems)

⅔ cup pumpkin or sunflower seeds

⅓ cup olive oil

3 medium-large garlic cloves, roughly chopped

½ tsp sea salt

¼ cup warm filtered water

Parsley, for all its nutritional benefits, needs to move way past garnish status in your kitchen. It's an excellent source of vitamins A, C, and K, as well as being a good source of folate (vitamin B$_9$) and iron. And considering parsley is so easy to find, you really have no excuse not to make this. If you're certain this glorious green sauce won't be heated at anytime (this means no putting it on pasta and then heating up the leftovers the next day), you can substitute flax or hemp oil for the olive oil.

1 | Add all ingredients except the water into a food processor or blender and give them a whirl for about 10 seconds. Stop the machine, take off the lid, and scrape down the sides of the work bowl. Whirl again, slowly pouring in the water while the machine is running, until the mixture has an even consistency.

Makes 1⅔ cups. Keeps in the fridge for up to a week, or in the freezer for up to 3 months.

GF, SF, NF, R

✹ All-Out Tomato Sauce

You know that a good tomato sauce doesn't come out of a can. It's something that simmers on the stove top for an afternoon, the flavors deepening all the while. Mine is more vegetable-packed than you may be used to (but, hey, I'm a nutritionist!). Pour this over cooked pasta or baked spaghetti squash, use it as a layer in lasagna, or exclude the herbs (except for the oregano) and use it as a base for chili. Make a triple batch in a larger soup pot and do some canning (if you're up to it—directions are on p. 57).

1 | Heat the oil in a 3-qt/L saucepan on medium heat. Add the onions and sauté for about 8 minutes, until softened. Add the garlic and mushrooms and sauté for another 5 minutes before adding the bell pepper, zucchini and/or spinach, and sauté for 5 minutes more. Pour in the tomatoes and vinegar (or wine), and simmer for 10 minutes. Stir in the herbs, salt, and pepper.

2 | Cover and simmer on lowest heat for another 20 minutes to an hour, depending on how much time you have to spare. Adjust seasonings to taste, and thin with a splash of water if desired. Remove the bay leaves before serving hot.

Makes 6 cups. Keeps in a sealed glass jar in the fridge for up to a week or in freezer for up to 2 months.
GF, SF

3 tbsp olive oil

2 medium or one large onion, chopped

2–4 medium garlic cloves, minced or pressed

3½ cups sliced cremini or button mushrooms)

1 medium bell pepper, chopped

1 medium zucchini, chopped

1 cup chopped, packed spinach (optional, or to replace the bell pepper or zucchini)

3–4 cups finely diced ripe tomatoes or 1 28-oz/796-mL can crushed tomatoes

1–2 tbsp balsamic or red wine vinegar (or ¼ cup red wine)

1 tbsp fresh oregano leaves (or 1 tsp dried)

1 tbsp fresh basil leaves (or 1 tsp dried)

1 tbsp fresh rosemary leaves (or 1 tsp dried)

¼ tsp fennel seeds (optional)

2 bay leaves

1 tsp sea salt, or to taste

freshly ground black pepper, to taste

Barbecue Saucy

⅓ cup tomato paste (about ½ a 5.5-oz/163-mL can)

2 tbsp natural almond butter (or organic peanut butter, in a pinch)

2 tbsp apple cider vinegar

1 tbsp chili powder

1 tbsp organic blackstrap molasses or barley malt

1 tbsp maple syrup or agave nectar (optional)

2 tsp prepared mustard

4 medium garlic cloves, pressed

½ tsp sea salt

¼ tsp cayenne pepper, or to taste

freshly ground black pepper, to taste

2 tbsp–¼ cup filtered water, to desired consistency

You'll likely encounter lots of sugar in store-bought barbecue sauces, but here you can control both the sweetness and the quality of your ingredients. You could easily double this recipe and freeze half of it.

1 | In a food processor or blender or in a large bowl, mix together all the ingredients. Set aside and let all those flavors get to know each other.

Makes 1 cup. Keeps for up to two weeks in the fridge or 3 months in the freezer.

GF, SF

Summer squash

Nutritional virtues *An excellent source of manganese and vitamin C. Very good source of magnesium, vitamin A, dietary fiber, potassium, copper, folate, and phosphorous. A good source of omega-3 fatty acids, vitamins B_1, B_2, B_6, calcium, zinc, and niacin. Loses some of its antioxidant action when cooked.*

Varieties *Zucchini, classic green or golden, is the best known summer squash. (When they're small the British and the French call them courgettes; when large they call them marrows.) Middle Eastern zucchini is a pale green and stays firm when baked. There is also a round zucchini or globe squash, which is also firm, and has very few seeds. Patty pans are yellow and bell-shaped.*

Get it *Available summer and fall, choose summer squash with firm shiny skin. Avoid limp ones with any soft areas. The smaller ones (6 in/15 cm or so) tend to have more taste than the large ones. Often delicate-skinned, zucchini can be scratched—don't let this worry you.*

Eat it/Make it *Almost all summer squash can be prepared the same way. Wash the surface with a small brush, trim off the stem, and cut into slices or leave whole. Very versatile, summer squash can be steamed, fried, grilled, roasted, stuffed, and baked, or used in soups or sauces. Spiralize summer squash as a raw gluten-free pasta alternative. I often find it to be a good replacement for nightshades (like bell peppers) in recipes.*

Keep it *Will store for several days in the vegetable storage section of the fridge.*

❀ 🍃 Balsamic-Roasted Vegetable Sauce

Okay, so there's tomato sauce, but then there's this ... rich balsamic goodness. Serve it over greens, grains, legumes, or pasta (even as a lasagna layer).

1 | Preheat oven to 400°F (205°C). Line 2 baking pans with unbleached parchment paper or given them a light coating of oil.

2 | Toss the vegetables with the vinegar and oil in a large bowl.

3 | Spread out onto the baking sheets, making sure that the vegetables are laid out in a single layer.

4 | Slide the trays into the oven to bake. Pull them out every 15 minutes or so to stir. After about half an hour, evenly sprinkle on the basil, salt, and pepper, toss again, and return to the oven. The vegetables will likely take the better part of an hour to be done (they should be nice and soft, but not falling apart or burnt).

5 | Remove from the oven and let cool for about 15 minutes before transferring to a food processor or blender and whirling to a purée. Add a splash of filtered water or two if needed for desired consistency. Serve hot over pasta, grains, steamed vegetables.

Makes about 6–8 servings or about 5 cups. Keeps for up to a week in the fridge or 2 months in the freezer.

GF, SF, NF (option)

* For goodness' sake, go ahead and use organic produce so you don't have to fret about pesticides; if so, you can simply scrub and rinse the veggies thoroughly instead of having to peel 'em. Use a good head or 2 of the garlic; peel the cloves and leave 'em whole.

16 cups cubed vegetables* (golden beets, carrots, sweet potato, Jerusalem artichoke, yellow zucchini/summer squash, onions, garlic, and, if nightshades aren't an issue, red, orange, and/ or yellow bell peppers—best of all, use all of them!)

¼ cup balsamic vinegar

¼ cup olive oil

2 tbsp chopped fresh basil leaves (or 2 tsp dried)

1 tsp sea salt (or more to taste)

freshly ground pepper, to taste

Rosemary Mushroom Gravy

2 tbsp olive oil

3½ cups button mushrooms, sliced or chopped (depending on your size preference)

3 tbsp tamari soy sauce

1 tbsp minced fresh rosemary (1–2 tsp dried)

freshly ground black pepper, to taste

1½ cups filtered water

2 tbsp organic cornstarch dissolved in an additional ½ cup water

I love this gravy—it's got great flavor and fits in nicely at a holiday feast. Serve over roasted or steamed vegetables or with Zucchini Boats (p. 201).

Heat the oil in a small-medium skillet on medium. Stir in the mushrooms, tamari, rosemary, and pepper. When mushrooms are tender, add the water and bring to a boil. Slowly stir in cornstarch mixture and cook at a low boil, continuing to stir, until the gravy is clear and thick, about 5–10 minutes.

Makes 2½ cups. Keeps in the fridge for up to 4 days.
GF, NF

Ginger Miso Almond Sauce

Take a peanut sauce, give it a nutritional boost, and this is what you get. Peanuts can be pretty moldy, while almonds are a great source of calcium. Serve over grains, grilled tempeh or tofu, or grilled or fresh veggies.

Heat the oil in a medium saucepan on medium. Toss in the onions and garlic and sauté for 5 minutes, until they begin to soften (if necessary, add a splash of water to prevent sticking). Whisk in the almond butter, hot water, tamari, and curry powder, until a smooth consistency is reached. Remove the pan from the heat after 2 more minutes and whisk in the miso mixture and grated ginger. Stir in cayenne, if using.

Makes 2 cups. Keeps in the fridge for up to a week, or in the freezer for up to 3 months.

GF, NF (option)

1 tsp non-hydrogenated coconut or grapeseed oil

1 small onion, 2 shallots or 6 green onions (green tops removed), minced

2 large or 4 medium garlic cloves, minced

½ cup almond butter

¾ cup just-boiled water (or enough for desired consistency)

1 tbsp tamari soy sauce

½ tsp curry powder

1 tbsp miso paste dissolved in ¼ cup filtered water

2 tsp finely grated ginger

⅛–¼ tsp cayenne pepper, to taste (optional)

Cheesy Sauce

¾ cup red lentils, rinsed

1½ cups filtered water

1 medium garlic clove, chopped

½ tsp dry mustard powder

¼ tsp thyme

½ tsp sea salt

½ cup unsweetened non-dairy milk (almond or soy, not rice)

½ cup nutritional yeast

¼ cup tahini

freshly ground black pepper, to taste

2 tbsp olive oil

When I was a kid, I was more likely to eat celery, broccoli, or baked potatoes if they were drizzled with Cheez Whiz. I shudder at the thought now. Of course, I also loved my mum's from-scratch cheese sauce that she served with pasta and sometimes in crêpes with broccoli and sautéed mushrooms. It's the latter I was trying to recreate, sans dairy, when I came up with this. It's significantly higher in protein than the Red Star Sauce from Get It Ripe.

1 | Cover the lentils with the water in a 3-qt/L saucepan and bring to a boil. Reduce heat and skim off any foam that's risen to the surface.

2 | Stir in the garlic, mustard, thyme, and salt, cover and simmer for 20 minutes, until lentils are tender to the point of falling apart.

3 | Combine lentil mixture with the milk, nutritional yeast, tahini, and pepper in a food processor and blend just until smooth. Pour the oil in a steady stream while the processor is running (in order for it to effectively emulsify). Adjust seasonings to taste.

Makes 2⅓ cups. Store in an airtight container in the fridge for up to five days.
GF, NF, SF

PART II: THE RECIPES

Soups

beans and rice at a Santiago market

✿ White Bean and Lovage Soup

2 tbsp olive oil

1 large or 2 medium onions, chopped

2 new/green garlics, chopped or 6–8 garlic cloves, minced

4½ cups cooked white beans (Cannellini, navy, or Great Northern)

4 cups vegetable stock (p. 169 or 170) or filtered water

1 bunch lovage (to make ¾ cup chopped stems and 2 cups lightly packed leaves) or 2 cups flat parsley leaves and 2 stalks celery, chopped

2 tsp fresh rosemary or 1 tsp dried

1½ tsp sea salt, or to taste

freshly ground black pepper, to taste

This soup is heavy on the lovage (if you go for all the recommended ingredients), but it's nice for something different. If you don't have or want some of the ingredients, you'll be pleased with the more commonly found options and still get a satisfying soup.

1 | Heat the olive oil in a large saucepan on medium. Add the onions and sauté on medium-low heat until they begin to caramelize, about 20–30 minutes, stirring every so often to prevent sticking. Add the garlic, sauté on medium heat for 5 minutes more, then add the beans, stock (or water), and lovage stems only (or celery).

2 | Cover, and cook for 5 minutes, then use a hand blender to purée to the desired texture (alternatively, use a food processor or blender and combine in batches).

3 | Stir in the lovage (or parsley) leaves, rosemary, salt, and pepper, cover and cook for a final 5 minutes before serving.

Makes about 6 servings.

GF, SF, NF

☀ Favorite Summer Gazpacho

Summertime soup is especially for those scorching days (the easily digested vegetables help to replace the minerals and vitamins we lose when we sweat a lot). It relies on the best of summer tomatoes—boring tomatoes will make for boring soup. And yes, avocados come from afar for many of us, so you could leave them out (and add an extra tbsp or 2 of oil), but I really think they help make the dish.

1 | Place all but 1 cup of the chopped tomatoes and the cuke, onion, avocado, garlic, oil, salt, pepper, and fresh herbs in a blender or food processor. Blend to desired consistency (shorter time = chunkier, longer time = smoother).

2 | Transfer to a medium bowl or large pitcher and stir in the remaining chopped tomato and herb(s) of choice. Serve cool or at room temperature.

Makes about 6 servings or 5 cups.

GF, SF, R

Note: You can opt not to peel your cuke; it'll certainly be more nutritionally beneficial to keep the peel on—but I can't promise you'll love the color of the soup.

2 lb/1 kg ripe tomatoes (about 4–5 medium fruits), chopped

1 medium cucumber (about 8–10 in/20–25 cm long), peeled*

½ medium red onion, chopped

1 ripe avocado, roughly chopped

·1 medium garlic clove, pressed

3 tbsp olive oil

1 tsp sea salt

freshly ground black pepper, to taste

¼ cup chopped fresh basil, cilantro, or parsley leaves + 2 tbsp for garnish

☀ Chilled Borscht

This is another great chilled soup for summer. When I prepare beets, I trim them, scrub them, and peel only the scabby bit around the tops. (If they weren't organic, I'd probably peel the whole thing.)

1 | Place the beets, sweetener, and salt in a large heat-proof bowl, pour the hot water over them, and cover for 5 minutes. Add the green onions and dill, cover again, and place in the fridge to chill (about 30 minutes to 1 hour). Stir in the milk and cucumber. Adjust seasonings to taste.

Makes 6 servings.

GF, SF, NF, R

4 large beets (about 3-in/7-cm in diameter), grated

2–3 tbsp liquid sweetener (like agave nectar)

1 tsp sea salt

3 cups just-boiled filtered water

3 green onions, finely chopped

1–2 tbsp minced fresh dill weed

2 cups non-dairy milk (like Nut Milk, p. 78)

1 medium cucumber, peeled, seeded, and grated or sliced

freshly ground black pepper, to taste

❖ Simple and Smooth Squash Soup

1 medium-large butternut squash (about 2–2.5 lb/1 kg), roasted

1 tbsp non-hydrogenated coconut or olive oil

2 medium onions, chopped

2 large or 4 medium garlic cloves, minced

1 tbsp freshly grated ginger

1–2 tsp ground cardamom

1–2 tsp ground cinnamon

1–2 tsp ground turmeric

1–2 tsp sea salt

¾–1 cup coconut milk (or 1 13.5-oz/400-mL can light coconut milk)

3½–4½ cups filtered water or vegetable stock (p. 169 or 170)

⅓–½ cup pumpkin seeds, lightly toasted (garnish)

I love the subtlety of the flavors in this soup—not too much spice so that the squash can shine though. And there's just enough coconut milk in there to make it creemy, but not too rich.

1 | Scoop the soft, roasted squash flesh out of its skin and set aside (discarding the skin).

2 | Heat the oil in a large soup pot on medium. Add the onions and sauté until they begin to soften, about 5 minutes. Add the garlic, ginger, and other spices (weighting each one as your taste buds dictate—and if you want this to be a curried soup, throw in a tsp each of ground cumin and coriander, too). Stir to evenly distribute the spices and make sure nothing's sticking to the bottom of the pot (if it is, though, a splash of water and/or a slight adjustment of the heat should do the trick). After a few more minutes (everything should be lovely and fragrant), add the roasted squash, salt, coconut milk, and about half the water or stock.

3 | Using a hand blender, blend the soup until it is nice and smooth. You can also use a food processor or blender, in batches (just be careful when blending hot liquids).

4 | Mix in the rest of the water or stock (to reach desired consistency) and serve. Try it over fresh baby spinach or steamed kale, topped with the pumpkin seeds.

Makes about 8 servings.

GF, SF, NF

Polish Neighborhood (Cabbage Potato) Soup (page 164)
with Herb Garden Biscuits (page 119)

White Wine-Braised Fennel Bulbs (page 179),
Heart Beets (page 182), Squash Au Gratin (page 180),
Sweet and Salty Delicata Rings (page 179),
Ginger-Glazed Carrots (page 177),
Balsamic-Roasted Brussels Sprouts (page 181)

Pad Thai in the Raw (page 199)

Basic Onion Stock

I'll admit it—I'm lazy and often find myself without stock for soups and stews, even though I know they'd give my recipes more depth—both in terms of flavor and nutrition. Stocks don't get any easier than this, though, so just make some already! (This really is the most versatile stock you can make.) You can use the onions raw to make the stock, but it's tastier if you roast them first.

4 lbs (1.8 kg) onions (any kind you like—yellow, white, red, or a mix), peeled and roughly chopped

¼ cup olive oil (optional)

12–16 cups filtered water

1 | Preheat oven to 350°F (180°C). Toss the onions with the oil on two baking sheets, and bake for about 40 minutes, until tender.

2 | Place the onions (raw or roasted) in a large stock pot, and add the water. Bring to a boil, then cover and simmer for at least 1 hour. (The longer they simmer, the richer the flavor.)

3 | Allow the stock to cool before straining out the onions. Place a sieve over a large bowl, pour the stock through, and press the onions with a spatula or the back of a spoon to extract as much liquid as you can.

Makes 11–15 cups. Store in glass jars in the fridge for up to 4 days, or in non-glass containers in the freezer for up to 3 months.
GF, SF, NF

STOCK OPTIONS

You don't have to set out to make a stock in order to have a cooking liquid that will add nutrients and flavor to your soups, stews, and sauces. Salvage the water from steamed or boiled vegetables, or the soaking water from softening sea veggies. Store in a sealed jar in the fridge and use within 4 days.

Anything-Goes Veg Stock

1 part organic veg scraps (potato peels, carrot peels, corn cobs, leek greens, tougher/papery onion layers, celery leaves, mushroom stems, parsley stems, etc.)

about 2–3 parts filtered water

This is for the cook who doesn't want to be too busy in the kitchen, but still possesses a bit of organization or foresight. Say you're home at 4 or 5 pm, and you want to have dinner on the table by 7. Prep the veg for your recipe, set them aside, and use your scraps as follows. The fresh stock will even be ready for the meal you're making that night, should you require it!

1 | Place the vegetable scraps in a saucepan or soup pot. Pour in water so it covers the veg by about 2 in/5 cm. Bring to a boil and reduce heat to simmer. Cover and cook for as little as 15 minutes or as long as an hour.

2 | Allow the stock to cool (even just for 10 minutes; you don't want to burn yourself!) before straining out the veg scraps (which your compost will love). Place a sieve over a large bowl, pour the stock through, and press the veg with a spatula or the back of a spoon to extract as much liquid as you can.

Store in glass jars in the fridge for up to 4 days, or in non-glass containers in the freezer for up to 3 months.

GF, SF, NF (option)

Quick Miso Broth

1 cup just-boiled filtered water

1 tbsp miso paste

2–3 tbsp filtered water

1 large clove garlic

1–3 slices fresh ginger

1 green onion, finely sliced (optional)

$\frac{1}{8}$ tsp cayenne, or to taste (optional)

tamari soy sauce, to taste (optional)

Let's say you are sick and feeling crappy. You know you need to put something nourishing in your body, but you don't have the energy to go to the store or cook up anything major. Make this quick and satisfying soup, and get well soon.

1 | Boil the cup of water in a kettle.

2 | Mix the miso and the 2–3 tbsp of water in small bowl or cup. (There, now the most effortful part is over!)

3 | Press the garlic into a large mug, and add the ginger, green onion (if you have it), and cayenne (if you want it). Pour in the just-boiled water and let steep for 3–5 minutes. Scrape in the miso mixture and stir. Add a dash of tamari if you like. Cozy up under a warm blanket and drink it hot.

Makes 1 large mug.

GF, NF (option)

Mix 'n' Match or on the Side

Ryan mulches around the plants at Whole Village Farm

✺ Roasted Fiddleheads with Garlic

3 cups fiddleheads, trimmed

3 new/green garlic, chopped, or 12 medium garlic cloves, halved lengthwise

2 tbsp olive oil

¾ tsp sea salt

If you haven't discovered fiddlehead ferns before, now's the time! They're a cute spring delicacy somewhat similar to asparagus in flavor. And in this recipe, I think they turn out a little like olives in their succulentness. You must wash and blanch/boil fiddleheads before eating them to release a natural toxin that is sometimes present when they are raw. I'm glad Lisa, my cooking companion, warned me about this—turns out she hadn't done it when preparing some a few days earlier and got a pretty bad stomach ache!

I highly recommend topping these with Creamy Ramp Dressing (p. 136).

1 | Preheat oven to 450°F (230°C).

2 | Put a 3-qt/L pot of water on to boil, and once boiling, add the fiddleheads and blanch them for 4 minutes. Drain, run under cold water, and transfer to a roasting pan (one where they'll all fit nicely in one layer). Add the garlic, olive oil, and salt and toss.

3 | Slide them into the oven and roast for 10–15 minutes, until the fiddleheads begin to brown. Serve hot.

Makes 3 servings.

GF, SF, NF

Fiddleheads

Nutritional virtues *Low in cholesterol and sodium, they are a good source of vitamins A and C.*

Varieties *Fiddleheads are unfurled ostrich ferns. Get them from someone who knows their ferns, as other similar-looking plants are carcinogenic.*

Get it *During the small window of time that they're available in the early spring (or as late as July in colder climates). They should be under 2 in (5 cm) in diameter.*

Eat it *In place of asparagus, in moderation.*

Eat it/Make it *Give them a good wash, then boil them for at least 5 minutes, or blanch for 4 minutes prior to sautéing or roasting.*

Keep it *In a container or plastic bag for up to a week after harvesting.*

❀ Citrusy Roasted Asparagus

Love these! Just can't get enough asparagus this time of year, really!

1 | Preheat oven to 425°F (220°C).

2 | Place the asparagus in a roasting pan (one where they'll all fit nicely in one layer). Add the tsp olive oil, toss, and roast in the oven for 20–30 minutes (depending on their thickness), until the skin begins to blister and they are tender when pierced with a sharp knife.

3 | While the asparagus is roasting, pour the lemon juice into the smallest of saucepans and warm on medium heat to reduce to half the amount (so 1 tbsp remains). Remove from heat and whisk in the remaining 2 tbsp oil, zest, and salt. Pour this over the roasted asparagus (once they've come out of the oven) and season with pepper to taste. Serve hot.

Makes 3 servings.

GF, SF, NF

1 lb/450 g asparagus, trimmed (see Prep tips)

1 tsp + 2 tbsp olive oil

2 tbsp lemon juice (about ½ lemon)

1 tsp lemon zest (organic preferred)

¼ tsp sea salt

freshly ground black pepper, to taste

Prep tips:

- *Pencil-thin asparagus will just snap at the bottom, naturally breaking at the woodier part that you won't want to eat. With thicker shoots, cut off the bottom ½ in (1 cm) or so, then peel the skin off just the bottom inch (2.5 cm) of the remaining shoot.*

- *Be sure to zest your lemon before you cut it open and juice it! (You could also try this with lime or orange.)*

Wild Rice with Wild Leeks

1–2 tbsp olive oil

12 wild leeks (to make 1 cup sliced bulbs and 1 cup packed sliced leaves and stems)

1 new/green garlic, chopped, or 4 garlic cloves, minced

2 tsp chopped fresh (or 1 tsp dried) rosemary leaves

2 tsp dried sage leaves

2 tsp dried thyme leaves

½ tsp sea salt

1 cup brown rice, rinsed

½ cup wild rice, rinsed

½ cup amaranth or millet (or additional brown rice)

3½ cups hot vegetable stock or just-boiled water

freshly ground black pepper, to taste

This is a wild rice dish that makes use of wild leeks (known also as ramps) in the short time that they're in season. (I can't promise results if you use regular leeks, but you can try.) Brown rice may not be local for many of us, but wild rice grows near me! I like the texture of the amaranth, but if you're apprehensive, go for the millet or additional brown rice.

1 | Heat the oil in a 3-qt/L saucepan on medium. Add the wild leek bulbs (not the leaves, yet!) and garlic and sauté for 5 minutes, reducing heat if needed to prevent browning. Mix in the herbs and salt, followed by the grains. Stir.

2 | Pour in the hot veg stock or water, increase the heat, and bring to a boil. Once boiling, reduce heat to a simmer, cover and cook about 40 minutes, until the wild rice is *al dente*. Remove from the heat, stir in the chopped wild leek leaves and stems, add black pepper to taste, and serve hot, perhaps with something like marinated and grilled tempeh.

Makes about 6 servings.

GF, SF, NF

☀ Tomato Chard Bake

Swiss chard in bunches, with a rainbow of colored stalks, sure are beautiful to look at. When it comes to flavor, however, I'll admit chard is not at the top of my list of leafy green favorites. It's an impressive source of vitamins A, C, and K, as well as magnesium, manganese, potassium and iron, so it's worth finding ways to enjoy it. I like to serve this topped with nutritional yeast and along with cooked lentils or beans and steamed grains or potatoes.

1 | Preheat oven to 375°F (190°C).

2 | Place the onions, garlic, tomatoes, liquid, and vinegar in a 9 x 13-in (23 x 33-cm) glass baking pan. Bake for 30 minutes.

3 | Pull the pan out of the oven and fold in the chard, oil, salt, and pepper, making sure all the chard (or as much as possible) is under the liquid. Return to the oven and bake for about 30 minutes more, until the onions are soft.

Makes about 6 servings.

GF, SF

2 medium onions, chopped

3–5 medium cloves garlic, chopped

3 cups chopped fresh tomatoes (canned are okay in a pinch)

1 cup liquid (from vegetable stock, canned tomatoes, or filtered water)

2 tbsp balsamic vinegar

6 packed cups Swiss chard, chopped (about 1 large bunch)

2 tbsp olive oil

½ tsp sea salt

freshly ground black pepper, to taste

Swiss chard

Nutritional virtues *Swiss chard, nutritional powerhouse that it is, is a very good source of vitamins A, C, E, and K, magnesium, manganese, potassium, iron, and dietary fiber as well as copper, calcium, vitamins B$_2$ and B$_6$, and a good source of protein, phosphorus, vitamin B$_1$, zinc, and folate—yes!*

Varieties *Red-stalked, white-stalked, or rainbow (a variety of colors—pink, yellow, orange). Their leaves may be crinkly or flat.*

Get it *Locally available in the summer and fall. It should look perky and the leaves should be a nice rich green.*

Eat it/Make it *You can eat both the stems and the leaves, separately or together. If together, cook stems until almost done and then add leaves. Leaves can be used in recipes that call for spinach (like a layer in a lasagna). Stalks are nice braised, slow cooked, or roasted.*

Keep it *Store in a ventilated plastic bag in the fridge for 2–3 days. Don't store with fruits that emit ethylene gas as they ripen (apples, bananas, pears, plums, and most tropical fruits), as that will cause chard to decay.*

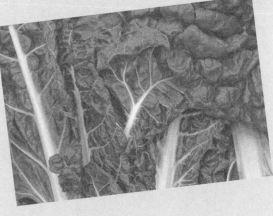

✸ Roasted Bell Peppers

2–4 medium-large red, orange, or yellow bell peppers (whole)

Slices of roasted peppers make a sweet addition to salads, sandwiches, pizzas, and pasta dishes. You might marinate them afterwards in some olive oil, garlic and salt.

1 | Preheat oven to 400°F (205°C).

2 | Place the peppers on their sides on a rimmed baking sheet. Roast, turning them every 10 minutes or so, until all sides are blistered, collapsing and even a bit charred, about 45 minutes.

3 | Remove them from the oven, transfer them to a bowl, cover (with a pot lid or an inverted plate), and allow them to steam for 5 minutes or so. Uncover and peel them with ease. (Reserve any juice that may have collected at the bottom of the bowl—it makes a sweet addition to salad dressings or sauces.)

4 | Slice into whatever-sized pieces you wish, discarding the stem, core, and seeds.

Makes about 4–8 servings.

GF, SF

Ginger-Glazed Carrots

Renée Loux is absolutely one of my favorite cookbook authors, who I (unfortunately) have yet to meet. This is a recipe from her second cookbook, The Balanced Plate. *It's simple, and I didn't really mess with it because I like it just how it is. Buy organic carrots so you can just scrub them well instead of having to peel them.*

1 | Preheat oven to 375°F (190°C).

2 | Mix together the oil, ginger, garlic, soy sauce, and sweetener in a small bowl. Place the carrots in a glass casserole dish, drizzle the glaze over top, and toss to coat.

3 | Cover the dish with a lid or a piece of foil and bake for 15 minutes.

4 | Uncover the carrots, stir them, and return them to the oven to bake, uncovered, for another 7–15 minutes, until tender (as tender as you'd like them, really). Season with salt to taste. Serve hot.

Makes 4 servings.

GF, NF

1–2 tbsp olive or raw sesame oil (not toasted)

2 tbsp finely grated ginger

2 medium garlic cloves, pressed

2 tbsp tamari or shoyu soy sauce

1 tbsp brown rice syrup (or 2 tsp maple syrup or agave nectar)

1 lb (454 g) young carrots, sliced in half lengthwise (or 4 medium carrots)

½ tsp sea salt, or to taste

Carrots

Nutritional virtues Carrots are a rich source of vitamin A, which is important for your vision (though the relationship between eating lots of carrots and thereby gaining better night vision is questionable). They also provide a small amount of vitamin C and some B vitamins. Eating too many carrots (usually done by carrot juice enthusiasts) can cause carotenemia—an orange tinge to your skin.

Varieties Originally from Afghanistan, the most common carrot sold in North America today is the Imperator, which is long and orange. Yellow, red, and purple varieties are less commonly available.

Get it Carrots start to become available in July and are fresh and seasonal until after the first frost (when they actually become sweeter). Select firm carrots that are dark orange, for the most vitamin A. Avoid "baby cut carrots," which are typically big broken carrots whittled down that may have been rinsed in chlorine as an antimicrobial treatment.

Eat it/Make it Carrots can be eaten raw, either whole or chopped or grated in salads and slaws. Grated raw carrots can also be added to cake or muffin batter. Chopped or julienned, they can be added to stir fries or soups, and they can also be roasted.

Keep it Baby carrots (the real ones, not the cut packaged ones) may be stored with their green tops on, but it is better to cut the greens off the larger carrots, as they will stay firmer and retain more of their nutrients in the root. Carrots can be stored in the fridge for at least a month.

☀ 🍁 Roasted Romanesco

1 head Romanesco broccoli

up to ¼ cup olive oil

sea salt and freshly ground black pepper, to taste

Is there a more beautiful and strange member of the Brassica family than Romanesco broccoli (also known as Roman cauliflower)? Sure, you can cook with it any way you'd use cauliflower or broccoli, but simply roasting it in large chunks really shows off its fractal-like appearance. Serve with Warm Mushroom and Spinach Salad (p. 141), Baked Sweet Potatoes (p. 181), Roasted Ratatouille (p. 197), or Zucchini Boats (p. 201).

1 | Preheat oven to 375°F (190°C).

2 | Trim the leaves and bottom of the stalk off the head of Romanesco, then slice it from the top down into even quarters. Place it on an un-oiled baking sheet, and drizzle with oil to coat as evenly as you can.

3 | Bake for about 45 minutes, until the tips begin to brown, the stalk looks caramelized, and it's tender when pierced with a fork. Serve hot.

Makes 4–8 servings.

GF, SF, NF

🍁 Roasted Spiced Cauliflower

1 medium head cauliflower, chopped into smallish florets

¼–⅓ cup melted non-hydrogenated coconut oil, or grapeseed or olive oil

6 medium garlic cloves, pressed or grated

1 tbsp garam masala

2 tsp mustard seeds (yellow or black)

1 tsp turmeric (optional)

½ tsp sea salt

I often like to add my own organic dishes to amazingly flavorful but not as healthy Indian take-out. Allowing some fresh organic baby spinach or steamed broccoli to soak up some of the flavor of the baigan bharta (a roasted eggplant dish) from my fave Indian restaurant balances things out a bit. But here's a simple and flavorful dish, requiring little effort, which you can make at home. The cauliflower and turmeric are great for your liver, and the other spices are good for digestion. (You may choose to omit the turmeric from this recipe if you've got a lot of other yellow, turmeric-heavy dishes on your plate).

1 | Preheat oven to 425°F (220°C). Line a baking sheet with unbleached parchment paper and set aside.

2 | Toss all the ingredients together in a large bowl. Spread evenly on the baking sheet so everything fits in one layer.

3 | Bake for 25–30 minutes, stirring once with a spatula halfway through the roasting time. Serve hot.

Makes about 4 servings.

GF, SF, NF

PART II: THE RECIPES
Entrées

the CSA shed at Whole Village Farm

🍁 White Wine-Braised Fennel Bulbs

Fennel is a delicious and warming herb, and is in peak season from fall until spring. I first made this when there was white wine left over from my birthday party the night before, so I sloshed some on—to delicious effect! Also try fennel raw, grated into salad or sliced in wedges and dipped in hummus; it's good for digestion.

1 | Preheat oven to 400°F (205°C). Rinse the bulb well and trim off the thread-like leaves and any dried stalk ends. Also slice off the dry (and possibly brownish) root end, but just enough to expose the white beneath it (you'll need most of the root intact to complete the next step with ease).

2 | Using a large chef's knife (no paring knives here!), slice the bulb from stalk to root, lengthwise (meaning you'll have fewer but wider slices than if you cut down widthwise), about ¼-in (⅔-cm) thick. Lay slices on a baking sheet in one layer. Whisk together the wine, oil, and salt in a small measuring cup and drizzle evenly over the fennel. Grind on generous amounts of fresh pepper.

3 | Roast for 30–40 minutes, until fennel is soft, with roasted-looking edges. Serve warm as an attractive side dish.

Makes about 4 servings.
GF, SF, NF

2 sweet fennel bulbs (about 14 oz/400 g each)

¼ cup white wine (optional, but highly recommended)

2 tbsp olive oil

½ tsp sea salt

freshly ground black pepper, to taste

🍁 Sweet and Salty Delicata Rings

I always think of delicata squash as the single girl's squash—one of them is just enough for 1 or 2 servings. Serve these cute little rounds on a bed of fresh greens with Maple Apple Cider Vinaigrette, or as part of a more harvest-type meal with, say, White-Wine Braised Fennel Bulbs (above) and Heart Beets (p. 182).

1 | Slice the peeled squash widthwise into rounds, about ½-in (1-cm) thick. Gently scrape out the seeds and stringy bits. Lay them down flat on a baking sheet in a single layer. Whisk together the syrup, oil, herb or spice, and salt in a small bowl, and pour this over the rings.

2 | Bake for about 45 minutes, turning about at about 25 minutes, until they are golden brown, crispy at the edges, and soft in the middle. Serve hot.

Makes 2 servings.
GF, SF, NF

1 delicata squash (about 1 lb/454 g), peeled

1 tbsp maple syrup

1 tbsp olive oil

½ tsp dried thyme leaves or ¼ tsp cinnamon or ¼ tsp chipotle powder

¼ tsp sea salt

Turmeric Tofu Triangles

1 tbsp grated fresh ginger

1 large or 2 medium garlic cloves, pressed or grated

2 tbsp lime juice (from 1 lime)

2 tbsp tamari soy sauce

2 tsp turmeric

1 tsp curry powder (get a good blend)

¼ tsp cayenne (or to taste)

1-lb/454-g block firm non-GM tofu, sliced width-wise into ¼-in (⅔-cm) squares

2–3 tbsp non-hydrogenated coconut, or high-oleic sunflower oil, for frying

My friend Elise and I made these one night u *everything in my kitchen bright yellow. As El* *that goes nicely with the color." I agree. Ser* *with Seasonal Veg (p. 204), or Easy Curri* *Cauliflower (p. 178).*

1 | Mix the ginger, garlic, lime juice, a paste in a small bowl.

2 | Slice all the tofu squares in half Lay them out on a glass or ceramic p

3 | Add the turmeric paste and co marinate from 15 minutes to a coup

4 | Heat the oil in a cast iron or ot

5 | Place as many triangles down up till they start to brown in parts a side and 2–3 minutes on the secon

Makes 4 servings.

GF, NF (option)

Corn

Nutritional Virtues *In addition to the carbohydrates and protein available in corn, it is a good source of dietary fiber. Corn provides vitamin B1, vitamin B5, folate, vitamin C, phosphorus, and manganese. Fresh corn offers higher nutritional value than canned or frozen.*

Varieties *Corn available in most grocery stores is usually yellow or white, though the peaches-and-cream variety has become very popular recently. Blue corn is often used for tortillas and corn chips. Blue corn tortillas contain about 20 percent more protein and 8 percent less starch than the more common version made with white corn, giving them a lower glycemic index. Plus, blue corn tortillas have a softer texture and sweeter flavor.*

Get it *I recommend that you buy organic corn so that you can avoid the genetically modified, conventionally grown ones. Buy it as soon as corn becomes available in the summer, which will depend on where you live. You want to buy fresh corn that has been kept cool. Heat turns corn's sugars to starch, so it will be sweetest if has been kept refrigerated or, if you are getting it from a farmer's stand, at least kept out of the sun. The husks should be soft and green and the silk should look lovely and silky. I always peel back the husk so that I can see the kernels at the top of the cob. They should be plump and pop when poked with a fingernail. If they are dented in at all the corn will be tough. Delicious, freshly picked corn is still available in late September in Ontario but by October, you will want to think about getting frozen.*

Eat it/Make it *You can eat raw corn, but many people like to cook it until it is heated through. It can be husked and then steamed or boiled or roasted in its husk on an open fire. A lovely East Indian treat is husked corn that has been rolled in spices cooked on a barbecue. My grandfather grew corn in his backyard garden; when it was ripe he would make sure he had the table set and a pot of boiling water ready on the stove before he picked the ears and ran into the kitchen with them. He swore that corn cooked this way was better than any other.*

Keep it *Corn is best eaten on the day it's picked. It can be kept in the fridge in its husk for a few days but you will notice that the kernels become less plump and firm and the corn will become tough as time goes by. At this point you might want to cut it off the cob and throw the kernels in with other vegetables that you are cooking; it provides a nice texture.*

Rainbow Dragon Bowl (page 203)

rutabaga

parsnip

carrot

black radish

red
beet

daikon

golden
beet

celery root

turnip

☀ Baked Mexican Stuffed Bell Peppers

Olé! Vegetables, protein (the beans), and starch (the corn) in one bell pepper package. Serve with a fresh green salad.

1 | Slice off the top ½ in (1 cm) of the bell peppers. Discard the stems, then chop the top slices into small pieces. Clean out the insides of the peppers gently with your fingers, discarding the veins and seeds.

2 | Heat the oil in a large skillet on medium. Add the onion and garlic and sauté for 5 minutes, until the onions begin to soften. Add the chopped pepper tops, tomatoes, jalapeño pepper, oregano, chili powder, cumin, and salt, and cook for 5 more minutes before adding the corn, black beans, and cilantro. Heat for another 10 minutes, stirring as needed to prevent sticking. Preheat oven to 350°F (180°C).

3 | Fill the peppers with the veg and bean mixture. Carefully pour about 1 in (2.5 cm) of water into the bottom of the baking dish. Bake for about 30 minutes, until the peppers begin to soften. Serve warm.

Makes 4 servings as an entrée or 8 servings (half a pepper per person) as a side.

GF, SF

4 medium bell peppers (any color)

1 tbsp olive oil

1 small onion, chopped

2–4 garlic cloves, minced

2 cups diced tomatoes

1 jalapeño pepper, minced

1 tbsp fresh oregano (or 1 tsp dried—Mexican oregano preferred)

1 tsp chili powder

1 tsp cumin

½ tsp sea salt, or to taste

2 cups corn kernels (fresh preferred, but frozen is okay too)

1½ cups cooked black beans

¼ cup minced fresh cilantro or parsley

☼ Easy Curried Eggplant

5–6 cups eggplant (small Indian eggplants, halved, are best, but a large Italian eggplant, cubed, will do just fine)

½ tsp sea salt, or to taste

2–3 tbsp non-hydrogenated coconut, sunflower, or olive oil

2 tbsp curry powder

1 medium onion, minced

1 small tomato, diced or 2 tbsp fresh lemon juice, to taste

¼ cup filtered water

This recipe is from my friend Dan Olsen, who I never see anymore (except on Facebook) because he lives in Vancouver. You'll find the texture of the eggplant is great here. Serve this with a lentil dal and a dish that includes spinach, broccoli, or another green veg.

1 | Throw the eggplant pieces in a colander, shake a little sea salt on 'em and allow to drain for 20–30 minutes.

2 | Heat the oil in a large skillet on medium. Add the curry powder and sauté for about 30–60 seconds, until fragrant. Add the onion and sauté for a few more minutes until onion becomes translucent.

3 | Add the eggplant and cook for another 4–5 minutes. Toss in a bit of salt and the diced tomato (or lemon juice) and the water. Cover and simmer for 7–8 minutes, until eggplant is tender. Serve hot.

Makes 2 main-dish servings or 4 as a side.
GF, SF.

☼ Pasta e Fagoli

1-lb (454-g) package brown rice pasta (or kamut or spelt noodles for the gluten-tolerant), any shape

1 cup pesto (p. 146 or store-bought)

2–3 cups cooked cannellini beans (or 2 15-oz/444 mL cans, drained and rinsed)

2 medium tomatoes, diced

1 tbsp olive oil (optional)

½ tsp sea salt, or to taste

freshly ground black pepper, to taste

2 tbsp chopped fresh parsley (optional garnish)

2 tbsp toasted pine nuts (optional garnish)

When I went to Italy in 2005, I learned the words for "hi" and "bye," "thank-you," "left," "right," "strawberry," and "mixed salad." I wish someone had told me that "fagoli" means beans, as I would have had a more adequate source of protein on my trip!

Serve this dish on a bed of fresh baby spinach or other steamed greens. It makes a fine packed lunch.

1 | Bring a large pot of salted water to a boil. Add the pasta and cook as per the package directions. Once *al dente*, drain the pasta and give it a quick rinse with cold water to stop the cooking.

2 | Transfer the pasta to a large bowl, add the pesto, and toss to coat. Throw in the beans and tomatoes, oil, salt, and pepper. Taste and adjust seasonings as needed. Garnish with parsley and pine nuts and serve.

Makes about 6 servings. Will keep in the fridge for up to 3 days.
GF (option), SF

☼ Lemongrass, Chinese Eggplant, and Tomato Stew

Amazing Emilie of the Conscious Kitchen writes: "Lemongrass was a feature flavor of my childhood in Southeast Asia and has always seemed like an exotic ingredient back here in the States. Last summer, however, I found that this citrusy herb grows quite happily in my backyard container garden, so grow it I did. By late summer, its flavor is deeply developed and it's perfect along with some fresh new garlic, hot peppers, and heirloom tomatoes in this flavorful Southeast-Asian-style stew. Slender purple Chinese eggplants are a great addition, but any eggplant, cut to approximately 1-in (2.5-cm) cubes serves as a fine substitute." Serve with cooked brown rice or quinoa or steamed broccoli.

2 tbsp olive oil

⅓ cup diced shallots

5 medium cloves garlic, smashed and chopped

1 large or 2 small lemongrass stalks, outer leaves removed, trimmed to pale purple core, minced

1–3 green Thai chilies, trimmed and chopped

1 large red bell pepper, diced

1 lb/454 g eggplant, sliced in 1-inch rounds or diced

1 lb/454 g heirloom tomatoes, diced

¼ cup tamari soy sauce

¼ cup filtered water

2 tbsp apple cider vinegar

1 tbsp maple syrup or agave nectar

juice of 1 lime

1 | Heat the oil in a large saucepan on medium. Add the shallots and sauté for 6–8 minutes or until translucent and very soft. Add the garlic, lemongrass, and chilies and sauté for 5 minutes or until softened and slightly caramelized. Add the bell pepper and eggplant and sauté for 6–8 minutes, until the eggplant is slightly softened. Add the tomatoes, tamari, water, vinegar, maple syrup, and lime juice.

2 | Cook covered on low heat for 30 minutes or until eggplant is very soft. Serve hot.

Makes 3–4 servings.
GF

✳ Sesame-Baked Tofu with Cashews and Snow Peas

1 1-lb/454-g block non-GM firm tofu, cut into 1-in (2.5-cm) square cubes

2 tbsp tamari soy sauce

2 tbsp olive oil

⅓ cup raw cashews

1½ cups trimmed snow peas, blanched in boiling water for 30 seconds and drained

Dressing:
2 tbsp rice vinegar

1 tbsp flax seed or olive oil

1 tbsp toasted sesame oil

2 tsp grated fresh ginger

1 tsp brown rice syrup (or agave nectar or maple syrup)

½ tsp tamari soy sauce

½ tsp ground coriander seed

½ tsp dulse powder (optional)

Optional garnishes:
2–3 thinly sliced green onions

2 tbsp unhulled sesame seeds

This dish is great served on a bed of fresh or steamed bok choy and brown rice. If you like, broccoli florets can replace the snow peas, and almonds can stand in for cashews.

1 | Preheat oven to 400°F (205°C).

2 | Place the tofu in a baking pan large enough to spread out the cubes in a single layer. Add the tamari and olive oil and toss to coat tofu evenly.

3 | Bake in the oven for 30 minutes, gently turning once or twice with a silicone spatula (to prevent breaking the cubes), until the edges of the tofu cubes are slightly browned and crispy.

4 | Toast the cashews in a dry skillet on medium heat for about 5 minutes, until they become golden and fragrant. Remove from the heat and set aside.

5 | Combine all the dressing ingredients in a small bowl and toss gently with the tofu, blanched snow peas, and cashews.

6 | Garnish with the sliced green onions and sesame seeds and serve hot. The snow peas will retain the brightest green color if the dish is served just after the dressing goes on.

Makes about 4 servings.

GF, NF

☀ Roasted Ratatouille

I adapted this recipe from the one in Moosewood Restaurant Simple Suppers, *and I just can't get enough of it—even for breakfast! Serve this with steamed quinoa, millet, brown rice, or polenta and steamed greens or a fresh green salad.*

1 | Preheat oven to 450°F (230°C).

2 | Cut all the vegetables into 1-in (2.5-cm) chunks (chop the garlic roughly). Place in a large bowl and toss with the oil, basil (only if using dried), thyme, salt, and pepper. Spread evenly on a baking sheet or two baking pans and bake for 15 minutes.

3 | Pull the vegetables out to stir and then return to the oven for another 25–30 minutes (stirring once more), until fork-tender and juicy.

4 | When vegetables are done, remove the sprig of fresh thyme (if used), and toss in the basil (if using fresh). Serve hot.

Makes at least 6 servings.

GF, SF

* You might choose to pour some of the tomato juice into the dish before roasting, but don't add all of it, as it would be too soupy. Save it to flavor another dish.

12–14 cups of vegetables in all, consisting of:

1 medium or 2 small zucchini

2 medium–large onions

1 large eggplant

2 medium–large tomatoes (or 1 14-oz/398-mL can whole tomatoes, drained* and halved)

2 bell peppers (red, yellow, orange, or green)

6 large (or 8 medium) garlic cloves

⅓ cup olive oil

1 cup packed fresh basil leaves, chopped or 1–2 tbsp dried basil

1 sprig of fresh thyme or ½ tsp dried

1 tsp sea salt

freshly ground black pepper, to taste

Collard Greens

Nutritional virtues *Collards are very high in vitamins A and C and in calcium. They are being studies for their role in helping boost detoxifying enzymes in the liver.*

Varieties *Part of the Brassica family (along with broccoli, Brussels sprouts, cabbage, cauliflower, and kale).*

Get it *Local collard greens are available in mid-summer to fall, and in the Pacific Northwest, throughout much of the winter, too. They are best in the cooler months. Choose leaves that are deep green and moist.*

Eat it/Make it *Cooked or raw. The more you cook them, the softer they become. With small leaves just slice and cook the whole thing. For larger leaves, cut out the tough stem and steam the rest. I like using big broad collard leaves as a wrap (in place of a tortilla, see p. 205). They're also tasty chopped and braised or stewed.*

Keep it *Store in a ventilated plastic bag in the fridge for 3–4 days. Don't store with fruits that emit ethylene gas as they ripen (apples, bananas, pears, plums and most tropical fruits.) as that will cause chard to spoil.*

Okra

Nutritional virtues *Okra, which arrived in North America from Africa, is high in carotene and contains vitamins C and B complex. Its slippery gel lubricates the intestines, easing constipation.*

Varieties *You can get red or green varieties, but the red type turns olive green when cooked.*

Get it *Locally available in full summer. Pods should be firm and, if you're going to steam them, uniformly colored. Avoid dry, stringy, or floppy okra. Okra with dark tips is okay for stewing.*

Eat it/Make it *Wash and dry the pods before trimming. Just trim off the stem but not enough to expose the seeds. If the recipe calls for sliced okra, just cut off the top and slice up the pod. You can balance its slippery nature by cooking it with something acidic like tomatoes, lemon, or vinegar. Okra takes on the flavors of the spices it is cooked with, so spice it up! Braise it with other vegetables. Okra will thicken clear soup and sauces if you pop it in during the last 10 minutes of cooking.*

Keep it *Okra perishes quickly and will keep a few days at most in the fridge. Store in a paper bag in a warmer part of the fridge. Blanch and freeze to enjoy during the rest of the year.*

☀ 🍁 Pad Thai in the Raw

I adapted this from a recipe in my dear friend Caroline Dupont's book, Enlightened Eating. If you have a spiralizer and a mandoline, you'll easily be able to make this dish. Others will have to get creative with peelers and be really skilled at very thin slicing (and julienning) with a chef's knife to get the "noodles" you need to make this dish work.

1 | Toss all the prepped veggies, fruit, and shredded coconut in a large bowl.

2 | Blend all the sauce ingredients until smooth, adding the water only if the sauce needs it for a smooth, pourable consistency (this would be the case if, say, your nut butter was quite thick).

3 | Pour sauce (as needed, there may be some left over) over veggies just before serving. (If you don't plan to eat it all in one go, only pour on enough sauce to eat right away, or it'll get too watery.) Toss and then garnish with the tomato, cilantro, and nuts/seeds.

Makes 4–6 servings.

GF, R

2 medium zucchini, spiralized or julienned

1 large or 2 medium carrots, julienned

½ cup thinly sliced red or green onion

1 medium bell pepper (or 2 halves of different colors—red, orange, yellow, purple), cut into bite-sized triangles or julienned

1 cup finely sliced red cabbage

1 medium green apple, julienned

1 cup finely chopped cauliflower florets

3 tbsp shredded coconut

Nutty Chili Sauce:
4 dates, soaked for about an hour (save water to use, below)

½ cup raw almond or cashew butter

3 tbsp raw liquid sweetener

3 tbsp Nama Shoyu (raw) soy sauce

juice of 1 lime

1 tbsp grated or minced fresh ginger

¼ tsp cayenne

up to ¼ cup date-soaking water or fresh filtered water (optional; to thin, if needed for desired consistency)

Garnishes:
1 small tomato, cut into thin wedges

¼ cup chopped cilantro

1–2 tbsp raw chopped almonds or unhulled sesame seeds

☼ 🍃 Dinner Party Pad Thai

1½–2 cups snow peas, trimmed and halved

1-lb/454-g package rice noodles, medium width

½ cup tamari soy sauce

¼–⅓ cup filtered water

¼ cup tomato paste

3 tbsp organic blackstrap molasses

2 tbsp "just peanuts" (no added sugar, oil, etc.) peanut butter (or almond butter)

1 tbsp sambal oelek (Asian chili paste)

¼ cup non-hydrogenated coconut or sunflower oil

1-lb/454-g block firm, non-GM tofu, cubed (use only ⅔ of the block)

8 medium cloves garlic, minced

1–2 whole dried red chilies, crushed

3 cups mung bean sprouts (home-sprouted if you can!)

6 green onions, sliced

⅔ cup chopped cilantro

1 medium lime, sliced in wedges

⅓ cup roasted peanuts (or almonds or cashews), crushed

Ooh, my goodness, I have never tried a Pad Thai I liked better! Often times, I've ordered a dish by the same name in a restaurant and been offered a plate of what tastes like simple rice noodles and ketchup (or can't order it because it has eggs and fish sauce—yikes!). This recipe, however, is quite a treat, showing off sweet summer snow peas, fresh cilantro, and home-sprouted mung beans. It's good for a dinner party because it's amazing fresh, and only so-so the next day.

1 | Bring a large pot of water to boil. Once boiling, add the snow peas and blanch for 1 minute, until bright green. Remove from water with a slotted spoon and set aside. Turn off heat and add the noodles to the water. Cover, and let 'em soak until they're tender, about 5 minutes. Drain in a colander, rinse with cold water, and set aside.

2 | Whisk together the tamari, water, tomato paste, molasses, nut butter, and sambal oelek in a small bowl. Set aside.

3 | Heat 1 tbsp of the oil in a large skillet or wok on medium. Add the tofu and gently sauté until golden. Remove from skillet and set aside. Be sure you've got all your other ingredients prepped so that they're easily available once the stir-frying starts.

4 | Heat 3 tbsp of the oil in the skillet or wok on medium-high. Toss in garlic and chili(es) and sauté, stirring constantly, until golden. Add the noodles and keep stirring for 5 minutes to mix thoroughly. The noodles will clump into a big mass; you may get frustrated and want to give up, but continue stirring for 5 minutes. (Quitting sooner means the final dish won't be warmed through.)

5 | Increase the heat and add the sauce, tofu, bean sprouts, and snow peas, and continue stirring for a few minutes. Add the green onions and cilantro and continue stirring, until the dish is absolutely steamy.

6 | Dish it out onto plates, squeeze on some fresh lime juice, sprinkle on some nuts, and serve it up with a li'l extra sambal on the side for those who like it.

Makes about 6 servings.
GF

☼ 🍁 Zucchini Boats

The first zucchini I can remember is a large one that grew in my dad's front garden. He gave it to me as a gift, and I brought it home to my mum's house where my stepfather (a puppeteer, and one of this book's illustrators) immediately carved it into a rustic Loch Ness monster. Later my mum baked Nessie into bread. (Yes, this is what my childhood was like.) So, what can you do with a huge zucchini? They're not ideal in many recipes as they're more watery than their smaller (ideally 8-in/20-cm) counterparts. But you'll often find them cheap at your farmers' market (or growing in your own garden). I say, stuff 'em. Serve this with a side of lentils and a fresh salad.

1 | Preheat oven to 425°F (220°C). Prepare a baking sheet with unbleached parchment paper or a light coating of oil.

2 | Slice the zucchini lengthwise and scoop out the seeds in the center, creating a trough for your tasty stuffing. Place on the baking sheet and set aside.

3 | Heat the oil in a medium skillet on medium. Add the onions and sauté until they are softened, about 10 minutes (alternatively, sauté them on low heat for about 30 minutes to caramelize them). Add the tomatoes (or mushrooms), garlic, coriander, sage, nutmeg, salt, and pepper, and allow to cook for about 5–10 minutes more (you may need to turn up the heat a bit to get those tomatoes/mushrooms to start releasing their juices).

4 | Remove the skillet from the heat and mix in the quinoa and parsley. Portion this evenly into the zucchini boats, packing in as much stuffing as you can. Bake for about 45 minutes, until the zuke is soft. Serve warm. Sprinkle with yeast as a garnish.

Makes 4–6 servings.

GF, SF, NF (option)

1 2-lb/1-kg zucchini

1–2 tbsp olive oil

1 medium-large onion, diced

1½ cups diced tomato or mushrooms

4 medium or 2 large garlic cloves, pressed or minced

1 tsp ground coriander

1 tsp minced fresh sage leaves (½ tsp dried)

⅛ tsp nutmeg

½ tsp sea salt

freshly ground black pepper, to taste

1 cup cooked quinoa (or other grain)

¼–½ cup chopped fresh parsley (or cilantro)

2 tbsp nutritional yeast (optional garnish, Red Star brand preferred)

West African Groundnut Stew

2 tbsp non-hydrogenated coconut, sunflower, grapeseed, or olive oil

2 medium onions, chopped

2 fist-sized sweet potatoes, diced to 1-in (2.5-cm) cubes (to make about 3 cups)

2 cups chopped cabbage (any kind)

1–2 medium garlic cloves, pressed

¼–½ tsp cayenne (or other dried and ground chilies), or to taste

3 cups vegetable stock (pp. 169 or 170) or filtered water

1 cup apple juice

2 medium tomatoes, chopped

2 tbsp to ¼ cup chopped cilantro

1 tsp finely grated ginger

1½ tsp sea salt, or to taste

1½ to 2 cups chopped okra (or zucchini or green beans if okra's unavailable)

½ cup organic, naturally processed peanut butter (or other nut butter)

I don't eat a lot of peanuts; despite their popularity they don't win the award for most-health-promoting nut. That being said, there are times when I get a real hankering for peanut butter. If you are intolerant to it, almond butter in this recipe would do just fine. This dish can rely on fresh okra and tomatoes in the summer when they're most abundant or frozen okra and canned or frozen tomatoes in the cooler months.

1 | Heat the oil in a large soup pot on medium. Add the onions and sauté until soft, about 10 minutes. Stir in the sweet potatoes, cabbage, garlic, and cayenne and cook, covered, for another 3 to 5 minutes. Add the stock (or water), juice, tomatoes, cilantro, ginger, and salt. Cover and simmer for 15 minutes, until the sweet potatoes are tender. Add the okra and cook for another 5 minutes.

2 | Ladle out a bit of the warm soup broth into a small bowl, and mix in the peanut butter to create a smooth paste, then return it to the pot and stir well to incorporate. Simmer on lowest heat for a minute longer to allow flavors to meld. Serve hot.

Makes 6 servings.

GF, SF

✦ Rainbow Dragon Bowl

An array of colors on your plate is visually stimulating, but the variety also suggests that you're getting a broader range of micronutrients to fuel your bod. In this recipe, we also get a beautiful blend of flavors. Many of these ingredients (except for the greens) can still be found locally, even in the winter. I like the contrast of the warm cooked grains and tempeh with all the raw veggies and sprouts, and the sweetness of the Dragon Sauce complements tempeh nicely. The ingredients listed are in rough per-person measurements.

1 | Layer the ingredients in the order they're listed in a decent-sized eating bowl. (No hard and fast rules; it's up to you.)

2 | Combine all ingredients for the Dragon Sauce in a bowl with a hand blender, or in a blender or food processor. Makes enough for 3 Dragon Bowls.

Makes 1 serving. Store any leftovers in a sealed glass jar in the fridge for up to 1 week.

GF, NF

* To prepare the tempeh, I just slice it however I want, splash on about 2 tbsp tamari and a pressed clove of garlic, and fry it up in about 1 tbsp non-hydrogenated coconut oil or raw sesame oil until browned on both sides.

½ to 1 cup cooked grain (brown rice, millet, quinoa)

1–2 good handfuls chopped romaine lettuce or baby spinach

1 handful finely shredded red cabbage

1 handful spiralized red beet

½ medium carrot, grated

a few pieces marinated and grilled tempeh*

1 small handful sunflower or mung bean sprouts

1 tbsp brown and/or black sesame seeds

⅓ recipe Dragon Sauce, or to taste

Dragon Sauce:

¼ cup nutritional yeast

3 tbsp grapeseed or olive oil

2 tbsp maple syrup

2 tbsp tamari soy sauce

2 tbsp filtered water

1 large or 2 medium garlic cloves, crushed

Coconut Curry with Seasonal Veg

2 tbsp coriander seeds

2 tbsp cumin seeds

1 tbsp cardamom seeds (remove husks if whole)

1 3-in (7-cm) cinnamon stick

6–7 whole cloves

2 bay leaves

4–5 whole chilies

2 tbsp + 2 tbsp non-hydrogenated coconut or sunflower oil

¼ cup shredded coconut

¼ cup filtered water

1 medium-large onion, puréed

5 medium cloves garlic, puréed

2-in/5-cm piece fresh ginger, puréed

2 13.5-oz (400-mL) cans coconut milk

6 cups vegetables (squash, potato, green beans, and/or peas, etc.), cut into bite-sized pieces

1 tsp sea salt, or to taste

2 tbsp fresh lemon juice (from ½ a lemon), or to taste

While the coconuts and the spices in this recipe sadly aren't local to many of us, this is a flavorful way to use up any seasonal veg that you're not sure what to do with. We have friendly Dan Olsen (former Toronto chef, now school teacher in Vancouver) to thank for it. The list of ingredients may seem long, but it takes only a short time to throw together.

1 | Grind the spices and chilies roughly in a coffee grinder (ideally used only for spices or cleaned very well) or mortar and pestle until broken but still grainy. Heat 2 tbsp of the oil in a small-medium skillet on medium-high. Add the spice mixture and cook until fragrant but not burnt. Add the shredded coconut and cook for a few minutes more. Add the water and set aside.

2 | Heat the remaining 2 tbsp oil in a 3-qt/L saucepan on medium. Add the onion purée and sauté for a few minutes. Add the garlic and ginger purées, and sauté for a few minutes more. Put in the spice paste and the coconut milk and simmer for about 20 minutes, until the coconut milk starts to thicken. Add the vegetables to the coconut sauce, allowing for an adequate cooking time for each (e.g., 20 minutes for potatoes, 12 minutes for winter squash, 5 minutes for green beans or summer squash, etc.)

3 | When vegetables are tender and the sauce is thick, add salt and lemon juice and serve.

Makes 4 main-dish servings or 6–8 as a side.

GF, SF, NF (option)

Build a Sandwich

The sandwich can be a simple everyday deal or something that bursts with flavor and pops with contrasting textures. I'm sure you've been making sandwiches since you learned how to pack your own lunch, but maybe you're looking for some fresh ideas?

> Tips
> * *Get something sticky (from the "fat" category) on the bread or wrap that can act a little like glue.*
> * *Avoid putting on something from the "freshness" category—like tomatoes or cucumber—either well before serving, or putting it right next to your base (unless you're using a collard wrap), as it'll make the wrap/ bread soggy.*

PLT (GF option, SF)
Whole grain toast, marinated and grilled portobello mushroom, sliced heirloom tomato, butter/ Boston lettuce, tahini or Cashew Creem (p. 131).

Roasted! (GF option, SF)
Whole grain toast, grilled eggplant, bell pepper, and zucchini, caramelized onions, pesto, olive tapenade, sprouts.

Garden Wrap (GF option, NF)
Tortilla or collard green leaf, grilled tempeh, caramelized onions, Herb Garden Hummus (p. 130), sliced cucumber, sprouts.

Fresh Thai (GF, NF option, R option)
Collard green leaf, grated carrots and beets, sliced cucumber and tomato, Ginger Miso Almond Sauce (p. 151), sprouts.

Choose 1 or 2 (as appropriate) from each of the following category:

Base:
whole grain bread—fresh or toasted; tortilla wrap; a large collard leaf (with base of stem cut off)

Substance or Protein:
hummus (p. 130); veg pâté (p. 127); sliced and grilled tempeh or tofu; sliced and grilled beets; bell peppers; eggplant; mushrooms; sweet potato; zucchini

Flava:
pesto; sun-dried tomato or olive tapenade; fresh miso; mustard; caramelized onions

Fat:
(creamier flavor): avocado (or guacamole); almond butter; tahini; Cashew Creem (p. 131); Ginger Miso Almond Sauce (p. 151)

Freshness:
fresh butter lettuce or romaine; sliced cucumber or ripe tomato; grated carrots or beets or daikon; sprouts of any kind

DIY Stir-fry

My stepfather David has been making me stir-fries almost my whole life. Of course, I asked him to share his wisdom here.

Lots of different vegetables can be stir-fried—use as many or as few vegetables as you would like. Your own taste buds will tell you what combinations you prefer (what's in your fridge might also have something to do with it). You do need to know which ones need how much cooking, however. If you add them in the right order (see below), they will all be cooked to perfection at the end. If you would like to include tempeh or tofu in the dish, fry them up first and then add them to the veggies at the end.

Be sure to prep all the vegetables you are going to use before you start cooking. It often works out best to cover the veggies while they cook, lifting the lid every minute or so to stir, until the last couple steps when you can uncover. Here are some guidelines:

Onions take the longest to cook. They should be thinly sliced and cooked for two minutes before adding veggies from the next group.

Garlic and ginger just get a few seconds to fry before adding some liquid and your next toughest veggies, the carrots (julienned) and cauliflower florets, celery root (sliced thinly), and fennel bulb (sliced thinly), if you want them. Cook covered for about 3 minutes before stirring in the next group.

The next group can contain mushrooms, bell peppers, broccoli stalks (julienned), broccoli florets, white cabbage, green beans, and/or celery stalks. Cook for 2–3 minutes before adding the veggies from the next group.

Now you can add snow peas, leeks, bok choy, kale, collard greens, Swiss chard, and/or mustard greens. Cook for 4 minutes before adding the veggies from the next group. (Here's where you throw in your pre-cooked tempeh or tofu, if using.)

The last group, which you need to cook only for a minute or so, includes mung bean sprouts, green onions (thinly sliced), and chopped spinach and/or celery leaves.

I'd suggest having a maximum of 10 vegetables in your stir-fry, otherwise the tastes become too confused. Serve in a bowl over brown rice.

David's Classic Stir-Fry

1 tbsp non-hydrogenated coconut oil or sunflower oil

1 small-medium onion, thinly sliced

1 medium clove garlic, crushed then minced

½ tsp minced fresh ginger

1 tbsp tamari soy sauce

½ cup vegetable stock or filtered water

1 medium carrot, julienned

1 broccoli stalk (½–1 cup peeled and julienned)

6 shiitake, cremini, or white button mushrooms, sliced thin

½ medium bell pepper, cut into thin strips

1 cup snow peas, tails and strings removed, if necessary

1 cup mung bean sprouts

1 green (spring) onion, finely sliced

sea salt and freshly ground black pepper, to taste

You've got to prep all your vegetables before you start to cook.

1 | Heat the oil in a large wok on medium-high. Toss in the onions. Cook for 2 minutes. Stir in the garlic and ginger, cook for a few seconds. Add the tamari, stock, and carrots. Toss everything and cover and allow to cook for 3 minutes. (Whenever the stir-fry is cooking covered, remove the lid once a minute or so and toss it so nothing sticks.)

2 | Add the broccoli, mushrooms, and pepper. Toss everything again and cover and let cook for another 2–3 minutes. Throw in the snow peas, toss, and cover again. Cook for 4 minutes.

3 | Add the sprouts and green onion and stir, cooking for about 1 more minute (uncovered). Add salt and pepper to taste. Serve over steamed brown rice.

Makes 2 servings.

GF

Onions

Nutritional virtues *If you eat onions regularly, you can reduce your risk of developing colon cancer and lower your cholesterol levels. Onions are rich in chromium, which will help your cells respond to insulin. They are good sources of vitamin C and many flavonoids.*

Varieties *There are two types of onions: spring/summer, and storage onions. Spring/summer onions have a mild or sweet taste. They include the Maui sweet onion (in season April through June), the Vidalia (in season May through June), and the Walla Walla (in season July and August). The most common varieties are storage onions, which are grown in colder weather climates. Once harvested, they are hung or spread out to dry so their skins become crisp. (I once worked on a farm in Québec where all I did was sit on a milk crate in a sea of onions in the loft of the barn and trim off their roots and tops while they lay around drying.) They tend to have a stronger flavor. These varieties include the white, yellow, and red onions.*

Buy it *Find onions that are clean and firm and have crisp, dry outer skins. Don't buy them if they are sprouting or look moldy. It pays to buy organic onions as the conventionally grown ones are often irradiated to keep them from sprouting. Sweet onions are best in season—spring till fall.*

Eat it/Make it *Chill the onions for an hour or so before cutting to lessen the tears you'll shed. Sweet onions are lovely chopped thinly and added raw to salads. Sautéed onions add nutrients and flavor to soups and sauces. Roasting onions makes them sweet and tasty.*

Keep it *Store your onions at room temperature in a well ventilated area, away from bright light. Once cut open, your sweet onions can be stored in a container in the fridge.*

Maple Syrup

Nutritional virtues Maple syrup has antioxidant properties, and since it is an excellent source of manganese and a good source of zinc it supports both heart and prostate health.

Varieties In the US it is usually graded according to the specifications of the USDA. Grade A syrup comes in light, medium, and dark amber. The taste gets stronger the darker the color. Grade B is usually used for cooking and baking.

Buy it Pure maple syrup is more expensive than blended syrups, but to my mind worth the money.

Eat it Enjoy maple syrup all year round, as once it has been made it will keep. It is local for those of us living where there are the maple trees from which it is made. That includes the Canadian provinces of New Brunswick, Nova Scotia, Québec, and Ontario, as well as Vermont and New York in the US.

Eat it/Make it If you want to make your own, of course you'll need to have maple trees to tap. When the sap begins to run in the early spring, pierce the tree and collect the liquid that runs out. Boil it until most of the water has evaporated, leaving the sweet sticky maple syrup. It takes 40 quarts/liters of sap to make 1 quart/liter of maple syrup. It's best to do the boiling outside as it can leave your walls a bit sticky. It's a great but arduous adventure to usher in the spring.

Keep it Cans and bottles can be stored unopened on the shelf, but once opened should be stored in the fridge. If mold develops on top, throw it out.

100% PURE MAPLE SYRUP

Cakes, Pies, & Crumbles

basket of fresh sour cherries

☀ Maple Layer Cake

2⅔ cups light spelt flour

2 tsp baking soda

½ tsp baking powder

½ tsp sea salt

1¼ cups maple syrup

1 cup applesauce (p. 98 or unsweetened store-bought)

⅔ cup softened non-hydrogenated coconut or sunflower oil

3 tbsp ground flax seeds (from 2 tbsp whole) + ½ cup filtered water, mixed

1 tsp pure vanilla extract

2 tbsp cider vinegar

½–1 cup whole and chopped pecans or walnuts (optional garnish)

Maple Buttahcreem Icing:

⅔ cup non-hydrogenated coconut oil or non-dairy, non-GM margarine

2¾ cups powdered sugar (organic and fair trade preferred)

⅓ cup maple syrup

1 tsp pure vanilla extract

It's no secret that maple syrup is a major staple in my kitchen— While it's often asked to take a back seat in other recipes, here cake itself is free of refined sugar—if you're avoiding the stuff The cakes are firm enough that you don't have to worry abou them (which makes this a great cake for beginning bakers).

1 | Preheat oven to 350°F (180°C). Prepare two 8 round cake pans with a light coating of oil. Line the unbleached parchment paper to easily remove cak

2 | Whisk together the flour, baking soda and po bowl. Add the maple syrup, applesauce, oil, flax m and stir just until all of the flour is absorbed. Quicl it's evenly distributed.

3 | Portion batter evenly between the two cake 25–35 minutes, until the tops are domed and a t comes out clean. Allow to cool in the pans for 10 to a rack. Cool completely before frosting.

Maple Buttahcreem Icing:

1 | Beat the oil (or marg) in a medium bowl wi strong arm and your favorite utensil for such ac cup at a time. Add the syrup and vanilla, and b texture is achieved (careful not to over mix or t out and the creamy texture will be lost). Sprea Garnish with the nuts.

Makes about 12 servings.

SF, NF

☀ Rawsberry Cheesecake

Crust:

1 cup raw pecans or walnuts

1 cup raw almonds

¼ tsp sea salt

¼ cup packed pitted and chopped dates

"Cheese" Layer:

2 cups raw cashews, soaked overnight (or at least 4 hours)

¼–⅓ cup agave nectar, to taste

2 tbsp–¼ cup filtered water

about 2 tbsp fresh lemon juice

1 tsp pure vanilla extract

½ cup non-hydrogenated coconut oil, melted

Fruit Layer:

2 cups raspberries

3 tbsp agave nectar

You can say "rawsberry" with a British accent, or you can just roll your eyes at my dorky choice of recipe title. I love the rich decadence of this cheesecake paired with the tart and fresh taste of the berries. Get soft, fresh honey or Medjool dates for the crust if you can, but if your dates are dry, allow them to soak with 1–2 tbsp warm water for at least 10 minutes. Make this more of a Lemon-Rawsberry Cheesecake by adding the juice of a whole lemon to the "cheese" layer and a proportionally smaller amount of water. You know me; I'm here to give you options when I can!

Crust:

Combine the nuts and salt in a food processor or blender and process until the nuts are all crumb-like. Throw in the dates and process the mixture further just until there are no chunks left and the mixture holds together when you pinch it. (If this cohesiveness isn't happening for you, add a touch of filtered water, just 1 tbsp at a time, until it happens.) Press the crust mixture firmly into a 7 x 11 x 2.5-in (18 x 28 x 6-cm) baking pan (preferred) or an 8 or 9 in (20 or 23-cm) springform pan. Flatten and smooth it with the underside of an offset spatula (or something similar). Set aside.

"Cheese" Layer:

Drain and rinse the cashews. In the clean work bowl of a food processor, add the cashews and pulse to break them up into tiny pieces. Add the agave, water, lemon juice, and vanilla and blend again until the mixture is completely smooth. Stop the machine and scrape bits down off the sides with a silicone spatula at least 2 or 3 times. As the machine continues to run, add the coconut oil in a steady stream, then stop the machine immediately so that the coconut oil doesn't get tempted to separate out again. Pour this creamy mixture in an even layer on top of the crust. Place this in the freezer to firm up just a bit, about 30 minutes.

Fruit Layer:

Rinse the work bowl out, and throw in the berries and agave. Give this a quick whirl until uniformly smooth and pour it on top of the creamy layer. Let this set in the fridge for at least 4 hours or 1–2 hours in the freezer, then 2–3 hours in the fridge. Serve cold, but not frozen.

Makes 15 square-shaped servings (from the 7 x 11-in/18 x 28-cm pan) or at least 12 slices from a round pan. Will keep in the fridge for about 2 days, or in the freezer for up to a month.

GF, SF, NF, R

Strawberry Shortcake (page 212)

Pear Ginger Amaranth Crumble (page 230)

Blueberry Lavender Ice Creem (page 242)

✵ Plum Upside-Down Cake

Late summer plums are such a beautiful color—here's one way to show them off.

There's something festive-yet-homey about an upside-down fruit cake. It doesn't require the same amount of fanfare as a carefully frosted layer cake, but your guests will still appreciate all your efforts.

Fruit layer:

1 | Preheat oven to 350°F (180°C).

2 | Prepare a 9-in (23-cm) round (or a 7 x 11 x 2.5-in/18 x 28 x 6-cm) baking pan with a light coating of oil. Place the plum slices in an even layer on the bottom of the pan (get creative). Beat together the oil (or marg) and sugar—a handheld mixer works well for this—until the sugar dissolves (Sucanat won't dissolve completely). Pour this mixture over the fruit.

Cake layer:

1 | Combine the oil (or marg) and Sucanat (or sugar) with an electric mixer (I use a handheld one) in a large bowl. Add the applesauce, buttahmilk, and vanilla and mix again.

2 | Whisk together the flour, cornmeal, baking powder, spices, and salt in a medium bowl.

3 | Fold the dry ingredients into the creamy mixture, just until all the flour has been absorbed. Pour the batter over the fruit in the pan, evening it out with the spatula.

4 | Bake for 35–40 minutes, until it's bubbling at the sides, the top is no longer sticky, and a toothpick inserted into the center comes out clean.

5 | Allow to cool in the pan for an hour. Run a knife around the edge of the pan and then invert the cake onto a serving platter.

Makes 8 servings.

SF, NF

Fruit layer:

5 or 6 red or purple plums (about 1 lb/454 g), pitted and sliced—wide slices: 6–8 slices per fruit

⅓ cup non-hydrogenated coconut oil or non-dairy, non-GM margarine, melted

⅓ cup Sucanat or organic brown sugar

Cake layer:

½ cup softened non-hydrogenated coconut oil or non-dairy, non-GM margarine, plus more for the pan

½ cup Sucanat or organic brown sugar

½ cup applesauce (p. 98 or unsweetened store-bought)

⅓ cup buttahmilk (2 tsp apple cider vinegar + non-dairy milk)

2 tsp pure vanilla extract

1½ cups spelt flour

¼ cup cornmeal

2 tsp baking powder

½ tsp cinnamon or cardamom

½ tsp sea salt

Velvet Cupcakes

2 cups light spelt flour

1 cup organic sugar

3 tbsp unsweetened cocoa powder (preferably *not* Dutch process)

1 tsp baking powder

1 tsp baking soda

¼ tsp sea salt

1 large or 2 small-medium beets, chopped and steamed (for about 10 minutes)

1 cup buttahmilk (1 tbsp apple cider vinegar + non-dairy milk)

1 tsp pure vanilla extract

½ cup non-hydrogenated coconut or sunflower oil

Cooked Vanilla Frosting
¼ cup coconut flour (take ⅓ cup shredded coconut and grind to a fine powder in a clean coffee grinder)

¾ cup non-dairy milk

1¼ cups powdered sugar

¾ cup non-dairy, non-GM margarine

1 tsp pure vanilla extract

Red velvet cakes (and cupcakes) are most popular in the American south. Many recipes call for lots of bottled red food coloring, which can come from crushed bugs or from something synthetic, toxic, non-vegan, and non-health supporting! I like the idea of highlighting one of the most gorgeous-colored foods that exists in nature—the beet—instead. (Truth be told, the batter is stunning, but they don't come out of the oven all that red. Still, they're worth it.)

1 | Preheat oven to 350°F (180°C). Prepare a 12-cup muffin tray with liners or a light coating of oil and set aside.

2 | Whisk together the flour, sugar, cocoa, baking powder and soda, and salt in a large bowl. Place the beets, buttahmilk, and vanilla in a food processor or blender and combine. While the machine is running, drizzle in the oil in a slow, steady stream. Stop the machine once the beets are completely puréed. Mix together with the dry ingredients just until all the flour has been absorbed.

3 | Portion evenly into the prepared muffin cups. Bake for 25 minutes, until the tops are domed and a toothpick inserted in the center comes out clean.

4 | Allow to cool completely before frosting.

Cooked Vanilla Frosting
Boiled frosting is considered the traditional frosting for Red Velvet Cakes. A version of this recipe was passed on to me by a Twitter follower who is also the co-host of the radio show Animal Voices Vancouver, Christa Trueman. It's like no other frosting I've had before (it's not as sweet as some others) and worth a try.

1 | Whisk the flour and milk together in a small saucepan on low-medium heat until *very* thick. Chill thoroughly.

2 | Cream the sugar and margarine together, then add the vanilla. Beat in the thick flour mix 1 tbsp at a time, until it has the consistency of very thick whipped cream (it reminds me a bit of marshmallow fluff). Chill it before frosting your cake.

3 | Smear the frosting on the tops of the cooled cupcakes and serve.

Makes 12 cupcakes. Store in the fridge for up to 3 days. (The frosting, if stored separately in an airtight container, will keep for up to 2 weeks in the fridge.)
SF, NF

Pumpkin Cheesecake

Recently I wanted something different for Thanksgiving dessert. I just couldn't bring myself to put overly processed soy cream cheese in a cake (or in anything else, for that matter), so this rich and creamy almond mixture happily stepped in to take its place.

Crust:

1 | Preheat oven to 350°F (180°C).

2 | Combine cake or cracker crumbs, sugar, ginger, oil, and water in a large bowl. Press into the bottom a 9-in (23-cm) springform pan (or equivalent). Bake for 10 minutes, until dry (no longer glossy-looking). Remove from the oven and set aside to cool.

"Cheese" Layer:

1 | Add the peeled almonds to a food processor or blender and pulse to break them up into tiny pieces. Add the syrup, spices, and salt, and blend again until the mixture is extremely smooth. Stop the machine and scrape bits down off the sides with a silicone spatula at least 2 or 3 times. As the processor continues to run, slowly add the baked pumpkin.

2 | Pour this creamy mixture in an even layer on top of the crust. Slide into the freezer to firm up just a bit, about 30 minutes.

Spice Drizzle:

2 tbsp liquid non-hydrogenated coconut oil

2 tsp liquid sweetener (maple syrup, barley malt, brown rice syrup, date syrup, organic blackstrap molasses, or agave nectar)

1 tsp cinnamon

⅛ tsp cloves

⅛ tsp sea salt

12 pecan or walnut halves, as garnish

1 | Combine all the Drizzle ingredients together in a measuring cup or small bowl and drizzle it over the creamy layer. Garnish with the nuts.

2 | Put the cake in the fridge to set for at least 4 hours, or 1–2 hours in the freezer, then 2–3 hours in the fridge. Serve cold, but not frozen.

Makes 12 slices. Keep in the fridge for about 2 days, or in the freezer for up to a month.

SF, NF

Crust:

1½ cups crumbled oat cakes or ginger cookies (or graham-cracker crumbs if wheat-tolerant)

2 tbsp organic sugar

1 tsp grated ginger or ½ tsp ground ginger (omit if ginger cookies were used)

3 tbsp non-hydrogenated coconut or sunflower oil

2 tbsp filtered water

"Cheese" Layer:

2 cups almonds, soaked in filtered water for 4–8 hours then blanched (they should now slip out of their skins easily, but if they don't, give them a quick dip—say one minute—in just-boiled water)

½ cup maple syrup or agave nectar, or to taste

1 tsp cinnamon

1 tsp freshly grated ginger (or ½ tsp ground ginger)

½ tsp nutmeg

¼ tsp cloves

¼ tsp sea salt

1½ cups cooked pumpkin (or butternut squash)

Butternut Chipotle Chocolate Cake

3 cups spelt flour

1¾ cups Sucanat or organic/fair trade sugar

¾ cup Dutch-process cocoa powder (fair trade)

2 tsp cinnamon

1 tsp chipotle pepper powder

¼–½ tsp ground cloves

2 tsp baking soda

1 tsp sea salt

2 cups grated, peeled butternut squash

1¾ cups non-dairy milk

¾ cup non-hydrogenated coconut or sunflower oil

1 tbsp pure vanilla extract

3 tbsp apple cider vinegar

I made up this cake for my friend Richard for the release of Arcade Fire's second album, Neon Bible. Delivering it to the busy backstage area at the large Montreal church where they were playing sold-out shows, I wasn't sure the cake would make it home with him, but it seems it did—with rather positive reviews, if I remember right. (If you've really been digging into this book, you'll notice this is a winterized, somewhat Mexicanized version of the Zucchini Chocolate Spice Cake, p. 214.)

1 | Preheat oven to 375°F (190°C). Prepare a Bundt pan or a couple of 9-in (23-cm) cake pans with a light coating of oil. (If your Bundt pan has ridges, be sure it's oiled all over to ensure an easy release of the cake.)

2 | Whisk together the flour, Sucanat, cocoa powder, spices, baking soda, and salt in a large bowl. Stir in the squash until well coated with dry ingredients.

3 | Add the milk, oil, and vanilla extract, and mix with a silicone spatula just until all the flour has been absorbed. Once smooth, add the vinegar and stir quickly—you'll see pale swirls as it reacts with the baking soda. Stir just until the vinegar is evenly distributed throughout the batter.

4 | Quickly pour the batter into the cake pan(s) and bake for about 35 (for 2 cakes) to 50 minutes (Bundt), until a toothpick inserted into the center comes out clean.

5 | Remove cake(s) from your oven and allow to cool in the pans before removing and icing them.

Chipotle Chocolate Ganache

3-oz (85-g) squares semi-sweet chocolate

2-oz (57-g) squares unsweetened chocolate

1 tsp chipotle pepper powder

¼–½ cup filtered water or coconut milk for thinning, warmed to room temperature (cold liquid will make the chocolate seize up)

Chipotle Chocolate Ganache

1 | Finely chop the chocolate. Fill the bottom pot of a double-boiler with hot water and place it on the stove on medium heat. Place the chopped chocolate and the chipotle powder in the top pot of the boiler, and keep a watchful eye on it while it melts, stirring as needed; this is a tricky procedure, because chocolate can seize up. Once there are no lumps, add water (or non-dairy milk) to reach desired drizzling consistency. Cold liquid will mess with the temperamental chocolate.

2 | Turn off the heat and immediately drizzle the ganache somewhat evenly over the cake. Allow to set before slicing and serving.

Makes 12 or more servings.

SF, NF

❋ Ginger Rhubarb Galettes

I am an apprehensive pie baker. I think this comes from my childhood, which was full of pies with fantastic crusts baked by my mum. (Of course, she used white flour, butter, and maybe even an egg.) I can wrap my head around a galette (a rustic-looking free-form pie), though. Rhubarb is impossible to resist when it's readily available. In summer, you may also use the fruit filling from Blackberry Peach Cobbler (p. 229) with this dough.

Fruit filling:

Toss all the filling ingredients into a 3-qt/L saucepan, stirring with a silicone spatula so that the sugar and cornstarch are evenly distributed. Cook, covered, on medium to medium-low heat (check to see that there's no sticking at the bottom and reduce heat as necessary) for about 10 minutes, stirring every few minutes, until the rhubarb begins to soften and the juices thicken up noticeably. Remove from heat and set aside to cool.

Galette dough:

1 | You can make the crust in a food processor (or a large bowl). Pulse (whisk) the flour and salt together. Add the cold coconut oil and pulse (or cut with a pastry cutter or 2 knives) until there are just some pea-sized pieces of oil visible. Add all the syrup and then add the water 1 tbsp at a time. Pulse some more (or stir with a spoon or spatula), just until the dough forms a ball; you don't want it too sticky, but it should no longer be crumbly. Form the dough into a flat disk, wrap in plastic wrap, and place in the fridge to cool for 15 minutes.

2 | Preheat oven to 400°F (205°C). Prepare 3 or 4 baking sheets by lining them with unbleached parchment paper (or don't line them; I'm sure, with all the oil in the crust that'd be fine, too).

3 | Take the now-cool dough out of the fridge, peel off the plastic wrap, and slice it into 8 even pieces. Roll each one quickly (you don't want them to lose their cool or your crust will be less flaky!) into balls. Place a ball on one half of the piece of plastic wrap, fold over the other half (or rip off another piece to place on top), and roll out evenly with a pin to about 7 in (18 cm) across (make sure it's an even thickness, though the circle doesn't have to be perfectly formed). Peel off the top plastic, flop the circle down gently on a baking sheet, and peel off the rest of the plastic.

Fruit filling:

4 cups chopped rhubarb (½-in/ 1-cm cubes)

2 cups peeled and sliced apples

¾ cup organic brown sugar or Sucanat

2 tbsp non-GM cornstarch

1 tbsp finely grated ginger

Galette dough:

2⅔ cups spelt flour

½ tsp sea salt

1 cup cold non-hydrogenated coconut oil

2 tbsp maple syrup (or other liquid sweetener)

up to ⅓ cup cold filtered water

4 | Portion ½ cup filling in the middle of each circle of dough and fold up the edges as best you can to keep the filling from oozing out. Repeat until all the dough and filling has been used (you should get 8 galettes).

5 | Slide the trays into the oven and bake on the highest rack(s) for about 30 minutes, just until the folded-up crust begins to brown and the underside of the crust turns golden.

6 | Enjoy warm or at room temperature, maybe with some Cashew Creem (p. 131) or organic non-dairy ice creem (pp. 239–244).

Makes 8 individual galettes.

SF, NF

✱ Sweet Cherry Pie with Lattice-Top

To make someone a cherry pie using fresh cherries, you either gotta really love them or have a cherry pitter. Or both. Creating a lattice top isn't always a walk in the park, either, so if you think it might just put you over the edge, feel free to skip it and do a solid top (with some pretty slits cut in it), or try something else creative that's not as finicky.

Crust:

1 | Add the flour and salt to a food processor and pulse a couple times to combine. In a bowl, roughly chop up the coconut oil if it's in one lump; don't take your time on this, as the oil shouldn't heat up too much. Add the chopped oil to the flour mixture and process until it becomes the texture of coarse sand. Turn this mixture into a large bowl, pour in the sweetener and water (starting with the smaller amount), and then fold it in with a silicone spatula. The dough should stick together but not be sticky, so add water only as needed to get that consistency.

2 | Divide the dough into 2 equal pieces, then form each into a 5-in (13-cm) disk, wrap each in plastic wrap, and place in the fridge for 1 hour.

3 | Roll one of the disks of dough between 2 pieces of unbleached parchment paper or plastic wrap to form an 11 x 15-in (28 x 38-cm) rectangle, about ⅛-in (⅓-cm) thick. Place this on a large baking sheet, and peel off the top sheet of parchment (or plastic). Trim the sides of the dough with a paring knife or a pizza cutter (or a fluted pastry wheel if you want to get fancy) to make all the edges straight, then cut the rectangle lengthwise into 8 even strips, about 1¼-in (3-cm) wide and 15-in (38-cm) long. Slide into the freezer and allow the strips to firm up for about 20 minutes.

4 | Preheat oven to 500°F (260°C), adjusting the rack to the lowest position.

5 | Roll the other disk of dough between 2 pieces of unbleached parchment paper or plastic wrap to form a 12-in (31-cm) circle, about ⅛-in (⅓-cm) thick.

6 | Transfer the dough to a 9-in (23-cm) pie plate by peeling off the top piece of parchment, flipping the dough onto the plate, gently pressing the dough into place, and then peeling off the second piece of parchment. Resist futzing with the dough that hangs raggedly over the sides. Put the dough-lined pie plate into the fridge while you make the filling.

Crust:

3 cups whole spelt flour

1 tsp sea salt

1 cup cold non-hydrogenated coconut oil

2 tbsp liquid sweetener

⅓–½ cup cold filtered water

Filling:

5½ cups pitted cherries (from about 2 lbs/1 kg cherries)

¼–½ cup liquid sweetener or more if you're using sour cherries

½ tsp pure almond or vanilla extract

¼–½ tsp ground cardamom or cinnamon

¼ cup non GM-cornstarch or tapioca flour

For great tips on making and baking pies, be sure to see my first book, Get It Ripe: A Fresh Take on Vegan Cooking and Living.

Filling:

Place the cherries, sweetener, extract, and spice into a large bowl. Sift in the cornstarch, and mix gently to combine. Set aside.

To assemble:

1 | Timing is important here, so make sure everything is in order. The strips of dough should have become firm enough in the freezer, but not rock hard; they should be malleable enough for some gentle weaving.

2 | Remove the dough-lined pie plate from the fridge and pour in the cherry mixture. Remove the strips of dough from the freezer and place 4 pieces lengthwise across the pie, evenly spaced. Weave the remaining 4 pieces with the first four, 1 at a time (over, under, over, under). Work gently but as efficiently as you can so the crust doesn't warm up to room temperature. Adjust the lattice as needed (as well as you can; I know it's tricky).

3 | Trim any overhanging dough from the edge of the pie plate, using your non-dominant hand to secure as needed. (Later, you can press together and roll out the pieces you cut off to make a little tart.) Press the latticed dough to the bottom dough all the way around the edge of the pie using the tines of a fork.

4 | Lower the oven temperature to 425°F (220°C). Take a moment to breathe, if this whole thing made you tense, then place the pie on a baking sheet and bake for 25 minutes. Rotate the pie, reduce the heat to 375°F (190°C), and bake for another 25–30 minutes, until the crust is a deep golden brown and the juices are bubbling. Allow the pie to cool at room temperature for at least 2 hours before serving. (For the cleanest cut, chill for 1–2 hours in the fridge, slice, and re-warm to serve.)

Makes about 8–12 servings. Any leftovers will keep in a sealed container in the fridge for up to 5 days (I like to reheat it before eating).
GF, SF, NF

Note: *If you think you will be pressed for time on the day you want to serve the pie, the dough for the crust can be prepared up to 2 days in advance. Just be sure to remove it from the fridge and allow it to warm up just enough to be malleable before attempting to roll it out.*

Live Lime Tarts

None of the ingredients in this recipe are local to me, but if you live in southern California, Mexico, or somewhere else warm where avocados and citrus grow, enjoy the gorgeous abundance of what's near you! (And know that I'm jealous, because for me these are far-away treats.) Be sure to zest your lime before you slice it open for juicing.

This raw dessert is adapted from a recipe by my friend and colleague Julie Daniluk from her debut book Meals that Heal Inflammation.

Pie Crust:

1 | Combine the nuts and 1 cup of coconut in a food processor and pulse to a coarse meal. Add the dates and salt and pulse again until you get a uniform mixture that begins to stick together.

2 | Transfer this mixture into a 9- or 10-in (23- or 25-cm) pie plate, or portion evenly into a dozen muffin cups. Using your fingers or the back of a spoon (or both) press the mixture to make a very compact crust. Slide it into your freezer for 15 minutes to set.

Filling:

1 | Rinse out the bowl of the food processor so it's ready to use again. Put the avocado flesh, agave nectar, lime zest, and juice in a food processor and process until smooth. Remove the pie plate or muffin tray from the freezer and pour this creamy filling into it, smoothing it out as desired, and sprinkling with some shredded coconut if you like.

2 | Return to the freezer to set for at least 15 minutes. You may defrost them for 10 minutes before serving. To remove the tarts from the muffin tray, simply run a paring knife around the edge, and they should release with ease.

Makes 1 pie (about 8–12 servings) or 12 little tarts plus about ½ cup leftover lime mousse. Store any leftovers in the freezer.

GF, SF, NF, R

Pie Crust:

1 cup raw walnuts and/or cashews

1 cup shredded coconut (plus a little extra for garnish)

½ cup packed pitted dates (they need to be soft like fresh honey dates or Medjool dates)

¼ tsp sea salt

Filling:

3 medium-large avocados (not over-ripe)

½ cup raw agave nectar

1 tsp finely grated organic lime zest (from 1 lime)

3 tbsp lime juice (from 1 or 2 limes)

🍁 Classic Apple Pie

Pie Crust:

3 cups whole spelt flour (or 2½ cups light spelt and ½ cup oat bran)

1 tsp sea salt

1 tsp cinnamon (optional)

1 cup cold non-hydrogenated coconut oil, chopped in small pieces (sunflower oil will do in a pinch)

2 tbsp maple syrup (optional)

2–4 tbsp cold non-dairy milk or ice water

Filling:

7 large apples (about 3½ lbs/ 1½ kg), peeled, cored, and sliced into ⅙-in (½-cm) pieces

zest of 1 organic lemon

1 tbsp fresh lemon juice

⅔ cup organic sugar

3 tbsp chopped candied ginger (optional)

¼–½ tsp cinnamon

¼ tsp nutmeg

⅛ tsp allspice

¼ tsp sea salt

1–2 tbsp non-dairy milk

Everyone's got to have a recipe for apple pie—it's a classic! It's best to use tart and juicy apples like Cortland, Fuji, Golden Delicious, Granny Smith, Jonagold, McIntosh, Northern Spy, Pippin, and Rome Beauty. In this pie you might like to use two different varieties.

Pie Crust:

1 | Pulse flour, salt, and cinnamon (if using) in a food processor. Add oil and pulse until the mixture looks like coarse cornmeal. Pour in the maple syrup (if desired) and milk or water as needed and process until the mixture forms a ball of dough. Divide into 2 even pieces. Wrap in plastic and place in the fridge for just an hour (if it stays in the fridge for any longer, you'll have to let it warm up until it's workable again before rolling).

2 | Roll out one piece onto a clean, floured surface (or maybe between 2 pieces of unbleached parchment paper) and gently fit into a 9-in (23-cm) pie plate. Trim the edges and prick the bottom and sides a few times with a fork. Roll out the second piece between 2 pieces of parchment, and set aside until after the pie has been filled. Keep both pieces of dough in the fridge until they're needed.

Filling:

1 | Preheat oven to 425°F (220°C).

2 | Toss all the ingredients for the filling together in a large bowl. Place the mixture, including the juices, into the prepared pie shell, arranging so it's slightly domed in the middle. Peel the parchment off the second piece of pie dough and gently lay it on top of the pie (over the filling).

3 | Trim the dough to about ½ in (1 cm) beyond the lip of the pie plate and press the 2 layers of dough together around the edges with the tines of a fork to seal. Cut about 4 slits in the top dough for ventilation (you can get creative with this). Brush the top with a bit of non-dairy milk and sprinkle with a bit of sugar if you like.

4 | Bake for 25 minutes, until the top crust is golden, then turn heat down to 375°F (190°C), rotate the pie, and bake for about 30 minutes more, until the juices start to bubble and the crust is a deep golden brown.

5 | Remove from the oven and let cool for about 4 hours on a wire rack before serving, maybe with Frangipane Creem (p. 245).

Makes 1 9-in (23-cm) pie, about 8 servings.

SF, NF

Sweet Potato Pie

It's kinda like pumpkin pie, only different.

1 | Bring a large pot of water to a boil and add sweet potatoes. Cook for 10–15 minutes, until tender. Remove from heat and drain. Set aside.

2 | Preheat oven to 350°F (180°C). Combine flour, oats, sugar, cinnamon, and salt in a food processor, and pulse a few times until just mixed. Add the oil and pulse just until mixture resembles coarse cornmeal. Add the cold water and pulse just until mixture barely holds together (adding the additional water if needed). Roll out and lay into a 10-in (25-cm) pie plate.

3 | Blend the tofu, sugar, oil, spices, and salt in the food processor. Add the potatoes and blend until smooth.

4 | Pour the filling into crust and smooth it out. You can drizzle up to a tbsp of molasses in a fancy pattern over the top. Bake for 30 minutes. Allow to set for at least 1 hour before serving.

Makes 12 servings.

NF

Crust:

1½ cups light spelt flour

½ cup rolled oats (quick oats are okay)

¼ cup organic brown sugar or Sucanat

1 tsp cinnamon

¼ tsp sea salt

½ cup non-hydrogenated coconut oil

2 tbsp (+ up to 1 tbsp more) cold water

Filling:

7 cups (approx) peeled, diced sweet potatoes—Garnet preferred (about 2 lbs/1 kg)

1 cup mashed silken non-GM tofu

¾ cup Sucanat or organic brown sugar

⅓ cup sunflower oil

1½ tsp cinnamon

1 tbsp fresh ginger finely grated or 1 tsp ground)

¾ tsp nutmeg

1 tsp sea salt

✵ StRAWberry Crumble

Crumble Top:
1 cup fresh buckwheat sprouts (see sprouting directions, p. 101)

1 cup almonds, pecans, or walnuts, soaked overnight (or for at least 4 hours) then drained, rinsed, and chopped

½ cup unsweetened shredded coconut

¼ cup agave nectar

½ tsp cardamom or ¼ tsp cinnamon

¼ tsp sea salt

Fruit Bottom:
2 cups sliced strawberries (about 1 qt/L)

2 cups whole strawberries (about 1 pint/473 mL)

3 tbsp agave nectar

1 tbsp fresh lemon juice

When I put a bunch of ingredients together on my kitchen counter one afternoon, I don't think this is what I originally planned to make, but I'm glad I did. It's such a nourishing sweet treat that you could enjoy it for breakfast or a snack.

Crumble Top:

1 | Toss all the crumble top ingredients together in a medium bowl. Spread on a Teflex sheet and dehydrate in a food dryer at 115°F (46°C) for about 8 hours, or on a dry baking sheet in the oven at 170°F (77°C) with the door propped open with something heatproof for about 4 hours, until mostly crisp (but not completely dry—unless you plan on making it well in advance, in which case, do dry it out).

Fruit Bottom:

1 | Distribute the sliced strawberries evenly among 6 custard bowls (or ramekins). Blend the whole strawberries, agave, and lemon juice together in a food processor or blender just until there are no big chunks of berry left (but not yet completely liquid). Pour this mixture over the sliced berries.

2 | Evenly distribute the crumble on top of the fruit. Serve immediately.

Makes 6 servings.

GF, SF, NF, R

✿ Blackberry Peach Cobbler

I don't know if I'd ever had a cobbler before making this one, but I figured if they were anything like a crumble, I was game! In mid-August, colorful baskets of berries and peaches appear on farmers' market tables, and I couldn't be happier. Serve this with non-dairy ice creem (would Ginger Peach Ice Creem on p. 240 be peach overkill?) and enjoy! In the spring, you may also use the fruit filling from Ginger Rhubarb Galettes (p. 221) with this biscuit top.

Fruit Filling:

1 | Preheat oven to 375°F (190°C).

2 | Whisk the sugar, starch, spice, and salt together in a large bowl. Gently fold in the fruit with a silicone spatula. Scrape this fruit mixture into a 9-in (23-cm) pie plate and slide into the oven to bake for about 25 minutes, until it is bubbling at the edges.

Biscuit Top:

1 | While the fruit filling is in the oven, whisk together the flour, sugar, cornmeal, baking powder and soda, and salt in a large bowl. Pour the buttahmilk, oil, and vanilla into a smaller bowl, and mix the wet ingredients into the dry just 1 minute before the filling is ready to come out of the oven. Stir just until all the flour has been absorbed.

2 | Take the pie plate out of the oven and increase the heat to 425°F (220°C). Divide the biscuit dough into 8 equal pieces and plop them on top of the hot fruit, evenly spaced about ½ in (1 cm) from one another (so they're not touching). Sprinkle the dough tops with a pinch or two of sugar, and bake for 15–18 minutes longer, until the biscuits are golden on top and cooked right through. Allow to cool for about 20 minutes before serving.

Makes 6–8 servings.

SF, NF

Fruit Filling:

⅓ cup organic sugar

2 tbsp non-GM cornstarch or arrowroot powder

¼–½ tsp ground cinnamon or cardamom

⅛ tsp sea salt

5 cups sliced peaches (from about 5–6 medium fruits)

1 cup blackberries

Biscuit Top:

1 cup oat or spelt flour

¼ cup organic sugar, plus more for sprinkling

2 tbsp non-GM cornmeal

2 tsp baking powder

¼ tsp baking soda

¼ tsp sea salt

⅓ cup buttahmilk (⅓ cup non-dairy milk + 1 tsp apple cider vinegar)

¼ cup sunflower or softened non-hydrogenated coconut oil

½ tsp pure vanilla extract

2 tbsp organic sugar

❦ Pear Ginger Amaranth Crumble

Fruit bottom:

5 largish pears, peeled, cored, and sliced

2 tbsp amaranth

2 tbsp whole grain flour (like oat flour)

1 tbsp freshly grated ginger

Crumble top:

⅔ cup rolled oats

½ cup whole grain flour (such as oat flour)

½ cup Sucanat or organic fair trade sugar

1 tbsp amaranth

1 tsp freshly grated ginger or ½ tsp ground ginger

½ tsp sea salt (use only ¼ tsp if you used margarine)

⅓ cup non-hydrogenated coconut oil or non-dairy, non-GM margarine

I'm more of a crumble person than a pie person myself, as long as the crumble top is the right balance of flour and rolled grains. Always looking to include nutritious amaranth in a recipe, I find the grains add a nice texture here. And the pear and ginger—need it be said that they complement each other so nicely?

Fruit bottom:

1 | Gently toss the pears with the amaranth, flour, and ginger in a 2–2½ qt/L baking dish, using a silicone spatula.

Crumble top:

1 | Preheat oven to 350° F (180°C).

2 | For the crumble top, whisk the oats, flour, sugar, amaranth, ginger, and salt in a medium bowl, then cut in the oil or marg. It should be kind of clumpy.

3 | Spread crumble over prepared fruit and bake for about 40 minutes, until fruit is soft (poke a knife in to see). If the top is paler than you'd like, turn the oven to broil and brown, but only for about 3 minutes—and keep a watchful eye on it because it can quickly burn. Serve warm, maybe with a drizzle of coconut milk.

Makes about 6 servings.

GF (option), SF, NF

Cookies, Ice Creems, & other Sweet Treats

Elias in the apple tree
(while Freya waits below)

❀ Crunchy Granola Cookies

2 cups rolled oats

½ cup sunflower seeds

1½ cup oat or spelt flour

½ cup raisins

¼ cup flax and/or sesame seeds

1 tsp baking soda

1 tsp cinnamon

½ tsp sea salt

½ cup sunflower oil

1 cup maple syrup (or other liquid sweetener)

These are so seedy and oaty, you could eat them for breakfast!

1 | Preheat oven to 300°F (150°C). Spread the oats and sunflower seeds over a baking sheet and bake for 30 minutes, turning halfway through the baking time. Set aside to cool.

2 | Increase the heat to 350°F (180°C). Prepare 2 baking sheets with unbleached parchment paper or a light coating of oil, and set aside.

3 | Whisk the flour, raisins, seeds, soda, cinnamon, and salt in a large bowl. Add the toasted oat mixture, oil, and maple syrup, and mix with a silicone spatula just until all the flour has been absorbed. Drop tablespoons of dough, evenly spaced, onto the baking sheets, pressing down slightly on each ball to flatten (just a bit!).

4 | Bake for 15–17 minutes, until they're golden and no longer shiny (the way wet dough is), and then let cool on the sheets for at least 10 minutes before transferring to a cooling rack.

Makes 30 cookies.

SF, NF

❀ ✿ Peppermint Crisps

These are my friend Heather's favorite cookies of all time. It's something about the strong yet not overpowering mintiness and the crunch they have 10 minutes after they've come out of the oven.

1 | Preheat oven to 325°F (165°C). Prepare 2 baking sheets with unbleached parchment paper or a light coating of oil.

2 | Whisk together the flour, sugar, mint, baking powder, and salt in a large bowl. Add the oil, applesauce, 2 tbsp of the water, vanilla, and peppermint essential oil and mix just until all the flour has been absorbed. Add the final tbsp of water if needed to reach smooth dough consistency.

3 | Roll into walnut-sized balls and place them on the baking sheet. Press each ball gently with the bottom of a sugared glass (like a floured glass, but with sugar) to flatten, to about ¼-in/⅔-cm thickness. Alternately, you could roll out the dough with a rolling pin to ¼-in thickness, then use cookie cutters and sprinkle with sugar.)

4 | Bake for 13 minutes, just until they don't look shiny and the bottoms are golden.

5 | Let cool completely on the baking sheet before storing in an airtight container.

Makes about 30 cookies.

SF, NF

3 cups spelt flour

⅔ cup organic, fair trade sugar, plus more for sprinkling

2 tbsp minced fresh peppermint leaves (or 1 tbsp crushed dry leaves)

½ tsp baking powder

¼ tsp sea salt

⅔ cup non-hydrogenated coconut oil or sunflower oil

3 tbsp applesauce (page 98 or unsweetened store-bought)

2–3 tbsp filtered water (as needed)

½ tsp pure vanilla extract

8 drops peppermint essential oil

Pecan Ginger Cookies

2½ cups spelt flour

1 tbsp ground ginger

1 tsp baking soda

½ tsp sea salt

½ cup non-hydrogenated coconut or sunflower oil

⅔ cup maple syrup or agave nectar

¼ cup barley malt (or brown rice syrup)

3 tbsp applesauce (p. 98 or unsweetened store-bought) or puréed peach (½ a medium fresh or frozen and thawed peach, blended or well-mashed)

1–1¼ cups chopped dried peaches or dried cranberries (optional)

1 cup chopped pecans (or cashews, almonds, and/or macadamia nuts)

2 tbsp minced fresh ginger

Say you like ginger in baked goods, but you're not a big fan of molasses (a common pairing in cookies), or you're just looking for something different. Look no further. Barley malt offers a more complex flavor than sugar, but isn't so molasses-intense.

1 | Preheat oven to 350°F (180°C). Prepare two baking sheets with unbleached parchment paper or a light coating of oil.

2 | Whisk together the flour, ginger, baking soda, and salt in a large bowl. Add the oil, liquid sweeteners, fruit purée, dried fruit, nuts, and fresh ginger and stir with a silicone spatula just until all the flour has been absorbed.

3 | Drop heaping tablespoons of dough onto the baking sheets, and flatten to about ½-in/1-cm thickness with your palm.

4 | Bake for 14–16 minutes, until they are lightly browned on the bottom.

Makes up to 30 cookies.

SF, NF

Old-Fashioned Oatmeal Raisin Cookies

All my testers who tried this recipe were really excited about these humble cookies. Lisa wrote, "Are you kidding? These are pure nostalgic comfort in cookie form. The cinnamon and maple syrup provide a great complexity of sweet flavor to play off the oatmeal's heartiness." That's just what I was going for, of course!

1 | Preheat oven to 350°F (180°C).

2 | Whisk together the flour, oats, baking soda and powder, and salt in a large bowl. Toss in the raisins, nuts, and cinnamon.

3 | Mix the coconut oil, maple syrup, and vanilla thoroughly in another bowl. (If you have an electric mixer and the energy to clean it off afterwards, I suggest you use it.) Add the wet ingredients to the dry and mix just until all the flour has been absorbed.

4 | Drop heaping tablespoons of dough onto an unoiled baking sheet and bake for 13 minutes, until golden.

5 | Eat 'em warm, or let cool completely on a rack before storing in an airtight container.

Makes about 3 dozen cookies.

NF, SF

2½ cups spelt flour (can use ½ cup oat flour)

2 cups rolled oats

1 tsp baking soda

½ tsp baking powder

½ tsp sea salt

1½ cups organic raisins

½ cup coarsely chopped walnuts (optional)

½ tsp cinnamon

1 scant cup softened non-hydrogenated coconut or sunflower oil

1 cup maple syrup

1 tsp pure vanilla extract

Chai Pumpkin Seed Cookies

2½ cups spelt flour

⅔ cup Sucanat or organic/fair trade sugar

2 tsp ground cinnamon

1 tsp ground cardamom

1 tsp ground fennel or anise seeds (optional)

1 tsp freshly grated ginger or ½ tsp ground

¼ tsp ground cloves

freshly ground black pepper

½ tsp sea salt

½ tsp baking soda

½ cup pumpkin seeds, whole or roughly chopped

⅔ cup softened non-hydrogenated coconut or sunflower oil

3 tbsp liquid sweetener

1 tsp pure vanilla extract

Although they have numerous health benefits, I've added pumpkin seeds to this tasty, spicy cookie because I like their beautiful green color.

1 | Preheat oven to 350°F (180°C).

2 | Whisk together the flour, Sucanat (or sugar), spices, and salt in a large bowl. Sift in the baking soda, toss in the pumpkin seeds, and whisk again. Pour in the oil, sweetener, and vanilla, and mix just until all the flour has been absorbed.

3 | Roll dough into walnut-sized balls and place them on a lightly oiled baking sheet. Press each ball gently to flatten, to about ½-in/1-cm thickness.

4 | Bake for 13 minutes. Allow to rest on the cookie sheet for a few minutes. Eat 'em warm or transfer to a rack to cool completely before storing in an air-tight container.

Makes about 20 cookies.

SF, NF

◼ Constellation Cookies

The little yellow amaranth seeds look like stars in a dark chocolate galaxy. Amaranth is a beautiful plant that grows happily in Africa, Asia, and South America, but it will grow in my bioregion (southern Canada), too!

1 | Preheat oven to 350°F (180°C). Prepare a baking sheet with unbleached parchment paper or a light coating of oil.

2 | Whisk together the flour, cocoa, amaranth, baking soda, and salt in a large bowl. Cream together the oil and sugar in another bowl, preferably with an electric mixer, for about 1 minute. Beat in the applesauce and vanilla.

3 | Add creamy mixture to the dry ingredients, and mix just until all the flour is incorporated. Add the chocolate and mix to evenly disperse throughout the dough.

4 | Roll dough into walnut-sized balls and place them on the baking sheets. Press each ball gently to flatten, to about ½-in/1-cm thickness. Bake for about 15 minutes, just until crusty on top but still soft.

5 | Eat 'em warm or let cool completely on the baking sheet before storing in an airtight container.

Makes about 30 cookies.

SF, NF

2½ cups light spelt flour

½ cup Dutch-process cocoa powder (fair trade)

2 tbsp amaranth

1 tsp baking soda

½ tsp sea salt

1 scant cup softened non-hydrogenated coconut oil or sunflower oil

1¼ cups organic/fair trade sugar

½ cup applesauce (p. 98 or unsweetened store-bought)

1 tsp pure vanilla extract

1¼ cups bittersweet chocolate chunks or chips

Apricot Lemon Cornmeal Biscotti

4½ cups light spelt flour

1½ cups organic/fair trade sugar

1 cup non-GM cornmeal

1 tbsp baking powder

½ tsp sea salt

1 cup chopped dried unsulfured apricots

2 tbsp finely grated lemon zest (from 2 organic lemons)

1 cup sunflower oil

½ cup applesauce (p. 98 or unsweetened store-bought)

½ cup lemon juice (from about 2 lemons)

1 tbsp pure vanilla extract

Corn grows in so many parts of the world; it's quite likely you can source some nearby cornmeal if you're willing to ask around. Lemons, unfortunately, grow in fewer places, so if you live in that kind of climate, feel free to gloat as you dip this delicious "twice-baked" treat in your next non-dairy chai latte.

1 | Whisk together the flour, sugar, cornmeal, baking powder, and salt in a large bowl. Mix in the apricots and zest just until coated with flour. Add the oil, applesauce, lemon juice, and vanilla, and mix just until all the flour is absorbed. Form dough into a large ball, cover, and refrigerate for 1 hour.

2 | Preheat oven to 300° F (150°C). Prepare a baking sheet with unbleached parchment paper. Divide the chilled dough into 2, place on the parchment, and form 2 13 x 3-in (33 x 7-cm) loaves. Bake for 30 minutes.

3 | Remove from the oven and let cool for 5 minutes. Cut each loaf diagonally into ½-in (1-cm)-thick slices with a serrated knife. Return to the oven and bake, cut side up, at 275°F (135°C) for 20 minutes, then flip and bake on the other side for another 10 minutes.

4 | Transfer to a rack and let cool completely before storing in an airtight container.

Makes about 32–40 biscotti.

SF, NF

✷ Cherry Chocolate Ice Creem

Rich and chocolaty, with bursts of gorgeous July cherries. This dessert is all raw (depending on your sweetener), and you won't miss the soy (or dairy) from commercial frozen desserts one bit. You'll want a cherry pitter; it's well worth it for prepping the cherries.

1 | Drain and rinse the cashews and place them in a blender or food processor. Add 1 cup of the filtered water, sweetener, and vanilla, and process for at least 1 minute, until very smooth. Sift in the cocoa (or sift the cocoa and then add it in), and process again. While the machine is running, pour in the final ⅓ cup water.

2 | Process until a uniform mixture is achieved, then pour it into an ice cream maker, along with the finely chopped cherries. Process as per your ice cream maker's directions (this will likely involve freezing the mixture for about 30 minutes before pouring it into the ice cream maker).

3 | Fold in the halved cherries just before the creamy concoction goes in the freezer. Freeze until firm, about 3–6 hours.

Makes 5 cups.

GF, SF, NF, R

2 cups cashews, soaked in filtered water (about 1½ cups) overnight or for 4–8 hours

1⅓ cups filtered water

⅔–¾ cup agave nectar or maple syrup

2 tsp pure vanilla extract

½ cup Dutch-process cocoa powder (fair trade)

2 cups pitted cherries—1 cup finely chopped, 1 cup halved

Cherries

Nutritional virtues *A good source of iron, cherries also offer some calcium and vitamins A and C.*

Varieties *Sweet, dark red Bing cherries are the most widely known. The lighter Lamberts and golden-yellow Rainiers are fragile and often more expensive.*

Get it *Locally available from early summer through July. Look for richly colored, firm, and glossy fruit.*

Eat it/Make it *Sweet cherries can be eaten raw and added to salads. Sour cherries are used in cooking and offer a more complex flavor in pies and preserves (although you'll have to use more sweetener than if you used naturally sweet cherries).*

Keep it *Cherries will keep for several days in a cool area of the fridge.*

Ginger Peach Ice Creem

2 cups cashews, soaked in filtered water (about 1½ cups) for 4–8 hours (or overnight)

1 cup filtered water

⅔ cup agave nectar or maple syrup

1½ tbsp grated fresh ginger

2 tsp pure vanilla extract

2½ cups peeled and diced organic peaches (about 2 lbs/907 kg or 6 medium fruits)

⅓ cup candied ginger, finely chopped (optional)

What says summer the way that peaches do? And ice creem on a hot day—what's better than that? If you're not a ginger fan, or a bit of an ice cream purist, feel free to omit the ginger. But if you are, be sure to add the candied pieces too.

1 | Drain and rinse the cashews and place them in a blender or food processor. Add the fresh water, sweetener, ginger, and vanilla, and process for at least 1 minute, until very smooth. Add 1½ cups of the peaches, and process again for 1–2 minutes, until a uniform mixture is achieved.

2 | Process as per your ice cream maker's directions (this will likely involve freezing the mixture for about 30 minutes before pouring it into the ice cream maker).

3 | Fold in the remaining peaches just before the creamy concoction goes in the freezer. Freeze until firm, about 3–6 hours. Sprinkle with candied ginger before serving.

Makes 5 cups.

GF, SF, NF, R

Peaches

Nutritional virtues *Peaches are high in vitamins A and C and also contain calcium.*

Varieties *Peaches are either clingstone (whose flesh sticks to the pit) or freestone (whose flesh releases easily). There are yellow- or white-fleshed varieties; and there's even a less common-shaped one called a doughnut peach. Lighter colored varieties tend to ripen earlier.*

Get it *Ripe locally in summer, usually July and August. They get mealy at the end of their season. Peaches should be soft enough that they yield to gentle pressure when touched; if you buy them rock hard, they rarely ripen well. Buy organic or "low spray." Even if they have the virtue of being local, conventionally grown peaches are at the top of the Environmental Working Group's "Dirty Dozen" list (foodnews.org/walletguide.php), meaning they're sprayed with a whole lot of pesticides, so make sure to get fruit that's organic, or at least low-spray.*

Eat it/Make it *There is nothing better than biting into a ripe, juicy peach. However, peaches are delicious cooked in pies and crumbles with other fruits or berries. They can also be dried or canned or frozen. I freeze slices for the winter months to use in smoothies or in baked goods.*

Keep it *Let peaches ripen at room temperature and then store them in the fridge where they will keep a week or more.*

✦ Blueberry Lavender Ice Creem

2¼ cups wild blueberries (fresh or frozen)

1½ cups cold filtered water or—for a richer dessert but with less of a color punch—1½ cups coconut milk

⅔ cup agave nectar or maple syrup

2–3 tbsp fresh lavender flowers (or 2 tbsp dried)

1½ cups or 1 13.5-oz (400-mL) can coconut milk (in addition to above, if using)

2 tbsp liquid non-hydrogenated coconut oil

What you've got here is a gorgeous color and a sophisticated taste!

1 | Combine 1 cup of the blueberries, water, sweetener, and lavender in a blender or food processor, and process for 1 minute, until very smooth. While the machine is running, pour in the coconut milk and coconut oil in a steady stream.

2 | Process as per your ice cream maker's directions (this will likely involve freezing the mixture for about 30 minutes before pouring it into the ice cream maker). Freeze until firm, about 3–6 hours.

Makes about 5½ cups.

GF, SF, NF, R (option)

✸ Mint Chocolate Ice Creem

Mint is pretty easy to find in the summer months. For this recipe, I recommend Swiss mint, orange mint, or chocolate mint, but it's really up to you (and what options are available). Use the spirulina for the teeniest nutritional boost, but more so to color the dessert a lovely shade of shamrock.

1 | Combine the coconut milk, sweetener, vanilla, and peppermint oil in a blender or food processor, and process. While the machine is running, pour in the water in a steady stream, then do the same with the coconut oil. Add the spirulina, and process for at least 1 minute, until very smooth.

2 | Process as per your ice cream maker's directions (this will likely involve freezing the mixture for about 30 minutes before pouring it into the ice cream maker). When the minty mixture is in its last few seconds in the ice cream maker, drizzle in the Chocolate Ribbon (but don't let it mix for more than 10 seconds, or the whole concoction will turn a muddy color). Freeze until firm, about 3–6 hours. Serve cold.

Makes 5 cups.

GF, SF, NF, R

Chocolate Ribbon:

Combine ingredients in a small bowl or food processor until smooth. Will keep in the fridge for about a week, or in the freezer for up to a month.

Makes ½ cup.

GF, SF, NF, R

1½ cups or 1 13.5-oz (400-mL) can coconut milk (not light)

⅔ cup liquid sweetener)

1 tsp pure vanilla extract

10 drops pure peppermint essential oil

1¾ cups filtered water

2 tbsp liquid non-hydrogenated coconut oil

½ tsp spirulina powder (optional)

¼ cup chiffonade fresh mint leaves (optional garnish)

1 recipe Chocolate Ribbon (below)

Chocolate Ribbon:

½ cup cocoa powder (fair trade preferred)

½ cup liquid sweetener

1 tbsp softened non-hydrogenated coconut oil

Apple Spice Ice Creem

2 cups cashews, soaked in filtered water (about 1½ cups) for 4–8 hours (or overnight)

1 cup filtered water

⅔ cup maple syrup or agave nectar

1 tbsp freshly grated or 1 tsp powdered ginger

1–1½ tsp cinnamon

½ tsp nutmeg or cardamom

¼ tsp cloves

1 tsp pure vanilla extract

2½ cups peeled and diced apples (about 1½ lbs/680 g or 5 medium fruits)

As the weather cools off in autumn, the ice creem cravings don't always subside. This is a nice way to enjoy local apples (I have a tree in my own backyard and try to get the fruit before the wasps do!). You can also use apple juice in place of the cup of water for an even deeper apple flavor. The spices help make this treat a little more warming.

Drain and rinse the cashews and place them in a blender or food processor. Add the fresh water, sweetener, spices, and vanilla, and process for at least 1 minute, until very smooth. Add 1½ cups of the apples, and process once more for 1–2 minutes, until a uniform mixture is achieved (you may need to help your machine out by stopping it and pressing the apple chunks down toward the blades), then process as per your ice cream maker's directions (this will likely involve freezing the mixture for about 30 minutes before pouring it into the ice cream maker). Fold the remaining apples into the churning machine just before the creamy concoction goes in the freezer. Freeze until firm, about 3–6 hours.

Makes about 5 cups.

GF, SF, NF, R

Chocolate-Dipped Strawberries

4-oz (115-g) squares bittersweet or semi-sweet chocolate

about 12 large strawberries, rinsed and dried *completely*

These make a classic Valentine's Day dessert, though there are environmental impacts of using fruit that's out of season and has to travel a long way. You might want to make these part of a romantic summer picnic instead. Splurge on organic strawberries and spend less time worrying about pesticides and more time enjoying the sensually delicious experience!

1 | Prepare a baking sheet lined with unbleached parchment paper. Fill the bottom of a double boiler with water and heat until simmering. Add the chocolate and melt it (make sure that the top of the double boiler is not touching the water below).

2 | Remove from heat just as it's completely melted, and stir until smooth. Dip dry strawberries in the chocolate and place on the baking sheet to harden. You can refrigerate strawberries to hasten hardening.

Serves 2–4.

NF, SF

❖ Near Devastation Parfaits

In my first few weeks of working at Aux Vivres Restaurant in Montreal, I decided to take my classic chocolate cake recipe and make mini-loaves. They smelled incredible as they baked in their little pans, but as I tried to release them once they'd cooled, they crumbled to bits; even though I had oiled the pans, they were just too delicate to be baked in that way. As an alternative, we decided to use the broken and still delicious pieces of cake in parfaits—layered with pudding and chopped fruit, they made a fantastic treat!

1 | Layer the ingredients in each glass in 6 medium-sized wine glasses as follows:

> 2 tbsp cake pieces
>
> 1 tbsp Berry Coulis
>
> 2 tbsp fruit
>
> 1 tsp sweetener
>
> 2 cups Sweet Cashew (p. 213) or Frangipane Creem

2 | Repeat layers in this order 2 more times, or until you reach the top of the glass (or run out of ingredients). Garnish with candied pecans or mint leaves (if desired) and serve within the hour. (Leftovers may get soggy.)

Makes 6 servings.

GF, SF, NF, R   possibly—depending on what you're working with!

Frangipane Creem:

Drain soaking water off the almonds and rinse. (If you can get the skins off them, feel free to do so!) Combine ingredients (starting with the smaller amount of water) in a blender or food processor and process for about 2 minutes, until smooth. Add extra water if mix is too thick. Refrigerate until ready to serve.

Makes about 2 cups. Keeps in the fridge for up to 5 days, or in the freezer for up to a month.

GF, SF, NF, R

2 cups crumbled cake, sweet loaf, muffins, or cookies (or your favorite granola)

1 cup Berry Coulis (recipe following) or use jam in a pinch (but then omit the liquid sweetener below)

2 cups chopped fresh fruit (berries; pitted and halved cherries peaches, apricots, or plums, sliced; apples or pears, sliced and sautéed)

⅓ cup liquid sweetener (agave nectar or maple syrup)

2 cups Sweet Cashew Creem (p. 213, if using cake) or Frangipane Creem or pudding (if you have a recipe you love)

¼ cup candied pecans (recipe following), chopped nuts, or 12 fresh mint leaves (optional garnish)

Frangipane Creem:

2 cups almonds, soaked in water to cover for at least 4 hours or overnight

½ to 1 cup filtered water (as needed)

¼–⅓ cup liquid sweetener

2 tsp pure vanilla extract

¼–½ tsp pure almond extract (optional)

Berry Coulis:

2 cups berries (blueberries, raspberries, blackberries, or chopped strawberries)

2 tbsp liquid sweetener

Candied Pecans:

½ cup pecan halves

3 tbsp maple syrup or barley malt

¼ tsp cinnamon (optional)

⅛ tsp sea salt

1 tbsp non-hydrogenated coconut, sunflower, or olive oil

Berry Coulis:

Blend or mash the berries and the sweetener in a medium bowl, blender, or food processor until relatively smooth. Refrigerate until ready to serve.

Makes 1 cup. Keeps in the fridge for up to 5 days, or in the freezer for up to a month.

GF, SF, NF, R

Candied Pecans:

This recipe can easily be doubled or tripled, just be sure to use a larger skillet.

1 | Toss pecans in a small skillet and toast on medium heat for up to 5 minutes, stirring once or twice to toast evenly. Shake them out of the pan and set aside.

2 | Combine the syrup, cinnamon, and salt in a small bowl. Stir and set aside.

3 | Heat the oil in the same skillet, still on medium heat. Add the pecans and the syrup mixture, and stir constantly for about 4 minutes, until all the pecans are coated and the syrup thickens a bit.

4 | Scrape onto a plate lined with a piece of parchment and let cool (and harden) before chopping the pecans into smaller pieces, if desired. Use to garnish parfait, ice creem, mousse, pudding, or pie—whatever your little heart desires!

Makes ½ cup.

GF (option), SF, NF

Port-Poached Pears

Port is a fortified wine traditionally from Portugal; in Europe, a bottle of the stuff can only be labeled "Port" if it's from there. Port-style wines are made in many other parts of the world, though, so see what you can find that comes from closer to where you live. Enjoy this dessert in the fall when local pears are still available, but the weather is crisp enough that the warming spices are really appreciated. Serve with a drizzle of coconut milk, a dollop of Frangipane Creem (p. 245), or Apple Spice Ice Creem (p. 244).

1 | Carefully core the pears though their bottom ends using a paring knife or a long pointed vegetable peeler.

2 | Heat the port, sweetener, and spices in a medium pan on medium heat for about 2 minutes. Add the pears and orange zest (if using) and bring to a boil. Reduce heat, cover, and simmer until tender, turning every 5–7 minutes, about 25–30 minutes in all.

3 | Gently remove the pears and place them in a serving dish (or individual dishes). Increase the heat under the pot of simmering liquid and bring to a boil for 10–15 minutes, until thickened and reduced by about a half. Pour the reduction over the pears and serve hot or cold.

Makes 4 servings.

GF, SF, NF

4 medium pears (Bosc preferred), peeled

1½ cups port + ½ cup filtered water, or 2 cups red wine (organic and local preferred)

1–2 tbsp liquid sweetener (maple syrup, agave nectar), or to taste

1 stick cinnamon, 4 whole cloves, or 1–2 star anise

zest from ½ an organic orange (optional)

☼ 🍁 ❄ Apple Berry Squares

Crust:

3 cups rolled oats

3 cups whole spelt flour

½ cup Sucanat or organic/fair trade sugar

1 tsp cinnamon

½ tsp sea salt

½ tsp baking powder

½ tsp baking soda

zest of 1 organic lemon or orange

1 cup non-hydrogenated coconut oil or sunflower oil

⅓ cup filtered water

Filling:

4 cups peeled, cored, and sliced apples

1 cup fresh or frozen berries (not thawed)

¼ cup Sucanat or organic sugar (or ⅓ cup if unsweetened cranberries are used)

2 tbsp whole grain flour

1 tbsp fresh lemon juice

¼ tsp sea salt

These are thick and dense as a bar should be. They're not too sweet, and have a number of different flavors that happily complement one another.

Crust:

1 | Preheat oven to 350°F (180°C).

2 | Combine the oats, flour, sweetener, cinnamon, salt, baking powder, and baking soda in a large bowl. Add the lemon zest, oil, and ¼ cup of water and mix into an even meal. If you find the crust is too dry, add the rest of the water, or 1 or 2 tbsp of oil.

Filling:

1 | Combine the apple slices, berries, sweetener, flour, lemon juice, and salt in a medium bowl and toss together.

2 | Press half of the crust mixture into the bottom of a 9 x 13-in (23 x 33-cm) baking dish. Evenly spread the apple mixture over top, then sprinkle with the rest of the crust mixture. Bake for 30–45 minutes, until the apples are soft and the top is lightly browned. Allow to set for 30 minutes before cutting into bars.

Make 15 bars.

SF, NF

Baked Apples with Nuts and Spice

A cozy, spicy dessert for colder weather that makes your kitchen smell like heaven as it bakes. Serve with Sweet Cashew Creem (p. 213), Frangipane Creem (p. 245), or non-dairy yogurt.

1 | Preheat oven to 400°F (205°C). Prepare a baking pan (large enough to fit the apples upright) with a light coating of oil.

2 | Take each apple and cut a shallow ring around its circumference (to prevent them from exploding when they bake). Gently push an apricot to the bottom of the cored hole of each apple (creating a bathtub-plug-type effect).

3 | Mix the nuts, currants, sweetener, oats, spices, and salt together in a medium bowl with a fork. Drizzle in the oil and mix in to get a crumbly texture. Portion the mixture evenly among the apples, stuffing it into the holes (being careful not to dislodge the apricot).

4 | Bake for 30–40 minutes, until the apples are tender. Serve warm.

Makes 6 servings.

GF (option), SF, NF

6 medium apples (like Cortland, Gala, Granny Smith), cored

6 dried unsulfured apricots

⅓ cup chopped almonds, pecans, or walnuts

¼ cup currants or raisins

¼ cup liquid sweetener

⅓ cup rolled oats (quick oats are okay, or gluten-free flour)

1 tsp freshly grated ginger

1 tsp cinnamon

¼ tsp nutmeg

¼ tsp sea salt

1–2 tbsp liquid non-hydrogenated coconut oil, sunflower oil, or non-dairy, non-GM margarine, plus more for the pan

Polenta Spice Pudding

4 cups non-dairy milk (I like almond milk for this)

½ cup finely ground cornmeal (you can blast coarser cornmeal a few times in a coffee grinder)

2 tbsp non-hydrogenated coconut oil, plus more for the dishes

½ cup packed organic brown sugar or maple syrup (either wet or dry sweetener is okay)

¼ cup organic unsulfured blackstrap molasses

1 tsp cinnamon

1 tsp finely grated fresh or ½ tsp ground ginger

⅛ tsp ground cloves

¼ tsp sea salt

½ cup soft silken non-GM tofu, puréed (optional)

1 tbsp fresh lemon juice

This pudding is spicy, warming comfort food. You can leave the tofu out, but you'll get a slightly less firm and less creamy result. Serve with a drizzle of coconut milk or a dollop of non-dairy ice creem (like Apple Spice, p. 244), if you like.

1 | Preheat oven to 325°F (165°C). Prepare 6 ovenproof custard cups or a 2-qt/L casserole dish with a light coating of oil.

2 | Whisk together the milk and cornmeal in a saucepan on medium-high heat until smooth. Bring to a low boil, reduce the heat, and simmer, stirring often, for about 10 minutes, until somewhat thickened. Remove from heat and stir in the oil, brown sugar, molasses, spices, salt, tofu, and lemon juice.

3 | Pour the pudding into prepared custard cups or casserole dish. Place the filled cups or dish in a rimmed baking pan that has about an inch of very hot water in it. Bake until the pudding is fairly firm around the edges but still slightly soft in the middle. (Baking time varies, depending upon the size and shape of the dishes used.) Begin to check the pudding after 40 minutes, but even if using the casserole dish, do not bake for longer than 1 hour and 15 minutes. (Overbaking will result in a rubbery texture.) Serve warm.

Makes 6 servings.

GF, SF (option), NF

PART III:
Appendices

Herbs
25¢
a
Sprig!
picked
today!

dinner with just-picked garden greens.

Seasonal Menu Suggestions

Balancing flavors, textures, colors, and nutritional needs (from all of the vegan food groups) is not a simple task. I say this as a nutritionist with menu-planning training who humbly worked on the following for longer than I care to admit, so that you don't have to. You can be sure you and the family and friends you feed will be satisfied!

SOPHISTICATED SPRING SUPPER

Fresh green salad with toasted nuts or seeds and Creamy Ramp Dressing (p. 136)
    or Maple Apple Cider Vinaigrette (p. 136)

White Bean and Lovage Soup (p. 154)

Mushroom Asparagus Risotto (p. 189)

Ginger Rhubarb Galettes (p. 221)

SPRING FLING DINNER PARTY

Superhero Spinach Dip (p. 126) with Sunny Flaxtastic Crackers (p. 134)

Savory Stuffed Mushroom Caps (p. 128)

Asparagus and Spring Onion Quiche (p. 188)

Wild Rice with Wild Leeks (p. 174)

Roasted Fiddleheads with Garlic (p. 172)

Strawberry Shortcake (p. 212) or Maple Layer Cake (p. 210)

SPRINGY PACKED LUNCH (FOR A ROAD TRIP, OR JUST TO TAKE TO WORK OR SCHOOL)

Springtime Tabouleh (p. 140)

Classic Veg Pâté (p. 127) in a lettuce leaf or collard wrap

Crunchy Granola Cookies (p. 232) or Strawberry Rhubarb Muffins (p. 110)

SUMMERY BACKYARD OR BALCONY MEAL

Pretty in Pink Lemonade (p. 90)

Tomato-Basil Amuse-Bouches (p. 131)

Fresh green salad with Berry Vinaigrette (p. 137)

Raw Mexican Stuffed Bell Peppers (p. 191)

Plum Upside-Down Cake (p. 217) with Blueberry Lavender Ice Creem (p. 242)

HOT SUMMER IN THE RAW

Hippie Herb Garden Tea (p. 87) or Watermelon Juice (p. 81)

Sunny Flaxtastic Crackers (p. 134) with Parsley Pesto (p. 146)

Favorite Summer Gazpacho (p. 155)

Pad Thai in the Raw (p. 199)

Rawsberry Cheesecake (p. 216)

SUMMER NIGHT DINNER

Strawberry Daiquiris (p. 89)

Herb Garden Hummus (p. 130) with crackers or chopped veggies

Baked Mexican Stuffed Bell Peppers (p. 193)

Tomato Chard Bake (p. 175)

Blackberry Peach Cobbler (p. 213) or Sweet Cherry Pie with Lattice-Top (p. 223)
    with Ginger Peach Ice Creem (p. 240)

FALL LUNCHEON

Love Soup (p. 162)

Build a Sandwich (lay out lots of ingredients and let guests build their own!)
    (p. 205)

Apple Berry Squares (p. 250) with Apple Spice Ice Creem (p. 244)

FALL BIRTHDAY FEAST

Creemy Kale Soup (p. 160)

Sesame Arame Broccoli Salad (p. 142)

Dinner Party Pad Thai (p. 200)

Pumpkin Cheesecake (p. 219)

CASUAL FALL DINNER

Chipotle Black Bean Soup (*a winter recipe that works great for fall, too!*) (p. 166)

Fennel and Pink Pearl Barley Salad (p. 143)

Pear Ginger Amaranth Crumble (p. 230) with Sweet Cashew Creem (p. 213)

FANCY FOR FALL

Pear Parsnip Soup (p. 159)

White Wine-Braised Fennel Bulbs (p. 179)

Roasted Romanesco (p. 178) with Rosemary Mushroom Gravy (p. 150)

Zucchini Boats (p. 201)

Sweet Potato Pie (p. 227) and/or Port-Poached Pears (p. 247) with Sweet Cashew
    Creem (p. 213)

WINTER ROAST BUFFET

Polish Neighborhood (Cabbage Potato) Soup (p. 164) with Herb Garden Biscuits
(*using dried herbs*) (p. 119)

Heart Beets (p. 182)

Squash Au Gratin (p. 180)

Balsamic-Roasted Brussels Sprouts (p. 181)

The Best Darn Lentils (p. 183)

Butternut Chipotle Chocolate Cake (p. 220)

Hot Toddies (p. 92)

NEW YEAR'S DAY BRUNCH

Good Mood Winter Tea (p. 88)

Herbed Carrot Soup (p. 161)

Grandma Palmer's Baked Beans (p. 105)

Oatmeal Soda Bread with Walnuts (p. 124)

Roots and Shoots Salad (p. 144)

Baked Apples with Nuts and Spice (p. 251) and Sweet Cashew Creem (p. 213)

WINTER WARMUP SUPPER

Curried Golden Split Pea Soup (p. 167)

Roasted Spiced Cauliflower (*a fall vegetable you may be able to get in winter, in
some parts of the country!*) (p. 178)

Turmeric Tofu Triangles (p. 184)

Coconut Curry with Seasonal Veg (p. 204) over frozen spinach or brown rice

Polenta Spice Pudding (p. 250) with Sweet Cashew Creem (p. 213)

Resources

This is by no means an exhaustive list of resources. I'm really only scratching a small patch of topsoil here with titles on my bookshelf, things I've read or watched, and sites that I've browsed. I can't promise that all these resources are vegan-sensitive, but you're bound to get something out of any of them. I would like to see more resources and organizations that deliberately get more people of color, working-class people, and people with disabilities involved in alternative food systems.

Read

Entertaining (with more of a narrative):

Haeg, Fritz. *Edible Estates: Attack on the Front Lawn.* New York: Metropolis Books, 2008.

Kingsolver, Barbara, Steven L. Hopp, and Camille Kingsolver. *Animal Vegetable Miracle: A Year of Food Life.* New York: HarperCollins, 2007.

Smith, Alisa and J.B. MacKinnon. *Plenty: Eating Locally on the 100-Mile Diet.* New York: Three Rivers Press, 2007. (Also published 2007 by Random House Canada as *The 100-Mile Diet: A Year of Local Eating.*)

To learn:

Food and Agriculture Organization of the United Nations. *Livestock's Long Shadow: Environmental Issues and Options.* Online at: *www.fao.org/docrep/010/a0701e/a0701e00.HTM*

Logan, William Bryant. *Dirt: The Ecstatic Skin of the Earth.* New York: Riverhead Books, 1995.

Patel, Raj. *Stuffed and Starved: The Hidden Battle for the World's Food System.* Brooklyn: Melride House, 2008.

———. *The Value of Nothing: How to Reshape Market Society and Redefine Democracy.* New York: Picador, 2010.

Pollan, Michael. *In Defense of Food: An Eater's Manifesto.* New York: Penguin Press, 2008.

———. *The Botany of Desire: A Plant's Eye View of the World.* New York: Random House, 2001.

Roberts, Wayne. *The No-Nonsense Guide to World Food.* Toronto: Between the Lines, 2008.

Shiva, Vandana, ed. *Manifestos on the Future of Food and Seed.* Cambridge, MA: South End Press, 2007.

Tasch, Woody. *Inquiries Into the Nature of Slow Money's Investing as if Food,*

Farms, and Fertility Mattered. White River Junction, VT: Chelsea Green Publishing, 2008

DIY Guides:

Flores, H.C. *Food Not Lawns: How to Turn Your Yard into a Garden and Your Neighborhood into a Community.* White River Junction, VT: Chelsea Green Pub., 2006.

Sandor, Ellix Katz. *Wild Fermentation: The Flavor, Nutrition, and Craft of Live-Culture Foods.* White River Junction, VT: Chelsea Green Pub., 2003.

Kellogg, Scott and Stacy Pettigrew. *Toolbox for Sustainable City Living: A Do-It-Ourselves Guide.* Cambridge, MA: South End Press, 2008.

Madigan, Carleen. *The Backyard Homestead: Produce All The Food You Need on Just a Quarter Acre!* North Adams, MA: Storey Pub., 2009.

Riley, Britta and Rebecca Bray. *Window Farms: Hydroponic Edible Gardens for Urban Windows.* Online at: *windowfarms.org*

Watch

Benenson, Bill and Gene Rosow. *Dirt!: The Movie.* DVD. Santa Monica, CA: Common Ground Media, 2009. *dirtthemovie.org*

Fox, Louis. *The Meatrix.* DVD. Berkeley, CA: Free Range Studios, 2003. *themeatrix.com*

———. *Grocery Store Wars: The Organic Rebellion.* DVD. Berkeley, CA: Free Range Studios, 2006. *storewars.org/noflash/*

Garcia, Deborah Koons. *The Future of Food.* DVD. Mill Valley, CA: Lily Films, 2004. *thefutureoffood.com*

Kenner, Robert. *Food, Inc.* DVD. New York: Magnolia Pictures, 2009. *foodincmovie.com*

Mann, Ron. *Go Further.* DVD. Toronto: Mongrel Media, 2003. *mongrelmedia. com/dvd/info.cgi?id=1119*

Browse (By Country of Origin)

Canadian Organic Growers (Canada) *cog.ca*

TransFair Canada (Canada) *transfair.ca*

Local Food Directory (Canada, BC) *localfooddirectory.ca*

Lifecycles (Canada, BC, Victoria) *lifecyclesproject.ca*

Santropol Roulant (Canada, Montreal) *santropolroulant.org*

The Rooftop Gardens Project (Canada, Montreal) *rooftopgardens.ca*

Farmers' Markets Ontario (Canada, Ontario) *farmersmarketsontario.com*
Ontario Natural Food Co-op (Canada, Ontario) *onfc.ca*
FoodShare (Canada, Toronto) *foodshare.net*
Not Far from the Tree (Canada, Toronto) *notfarfromthetree.org*
Toronto Food Policy Council (Canada, Toronto) *toronto.ca/health/tfpc_index.htm*

Biodynamic Agricultural Association (UK) *biodynamic.org.uk*
Soil Association (UK) *www.soilassociation.org*

The Center for Food Safety (USA) *truefoodnow.org*
Cornucopia Institute (USA) *cornucopia.org*
Family Farm Defenders (USA) *familyfarmdefenders.org*
Food First (USA) *foodfirst.org*
Food Routes (USA) *foodroutes.org*
Local Harvest (USA) *localharvest.org*
Mighty Foods (USA) *mightyfoods.com*
The National Sustainable Agriculture Coalition (USA) *sustainableagriculture.net*
Organic Consumers Association (USA) *organicconsumers.org*
Sustainable Agriculture Research and Education (USA) *sare.org*
Tree People (USA, Los Angeles) *www.treepeople.org*
Forage Oakland (USA, Oakland) *forageoakland.blogspot.com*

International Federation of Agriculture Movements (International) *ifoam.org*
La Via Campesina Peasant Movement (International) *viacampesina.org/en*

Get involved
- Join your local food co-op. Try an Internet search on "cooperative grocer(s)" or "food co-op" and the name of your city or town.
- If you want to really get your hands in the dirt (and do a bit of traveling), research organizations such as: World Wide Opportunities on Organic Farms (International): *wwoof.org* or Organic Volunteers (International): *growfood.org*
- Join your local vegetarian or vegan association. Try an Internet search on "vegetarian" and/or "vegan" and the name of your city or town.
- Check out your local chapter of Slow Food (International): *slowfood.com*

jae steele is a registered holistic nutritionist and runs the vegan blog "Domestic Affair." She has authored various self-published cookzines including *Vegan Freegan* and *Ripe*. Formerly from Montreal, she now lives in Toronto. Her first book, *Get It Ripe*, was published in 2008 and is now in its second printing.